JADUNAMA

JADUNAMA

Javed Akhtar's Journey

ARVIND MANDLOI

Translated By Rakhshanda Jalil

AMARYLLIS

AMARYLLIS

First published in 2022
This updated and reformatted edition first published in 2025

Amaryllis, an imprint of Manjul Publishing House
Editorial and Sales Office:
Manjul Publishing House Pvt. Ltd.,
C-16, Sector 3,
Gautam Buddha Nagar,
Noida – 201 301, U.P., India
Tel: +91 120 455 7655/455 7755
Email: sales@manjulindia.com
www.manjulindia.com

Registered office:
• 2nd Floor, Usha Preet Complex, 42 Malviya Nagar,
Bhopal 462 003 – India

ISBN: 978-93-5543-997-0

English translation by Rakhshanda Jalil
Book Design by: Anuj Malhotra | fantomas.in
Cover Design by: Misha Oberoi

Printed and bound in India by Replika Press Pvt. Ltd.

For Ms Shabana Azmi

– Arvind Mandloi

There are three levels in a conversation—people, incidents and ideas. The lowest level of conversation is about people. When we rise to the rung above this, we talk of incidents whose circumference is a little wider than merely talking about people. But the most important conversation is the one about ideas because ideas are universal and far removed from Time and Circumstance.

– Javed Akhtar

People often tell me that Javed and I should have had an arranged marriage because our families were so similar, so was our value system in which an interest in art and literature as well as the importance of humanism, friendship, women's emancipation and the Ganga-Jamuni *tehzeeb* of Hindustan came to us as legacy.

– Shabana Azmi

CONTENTS

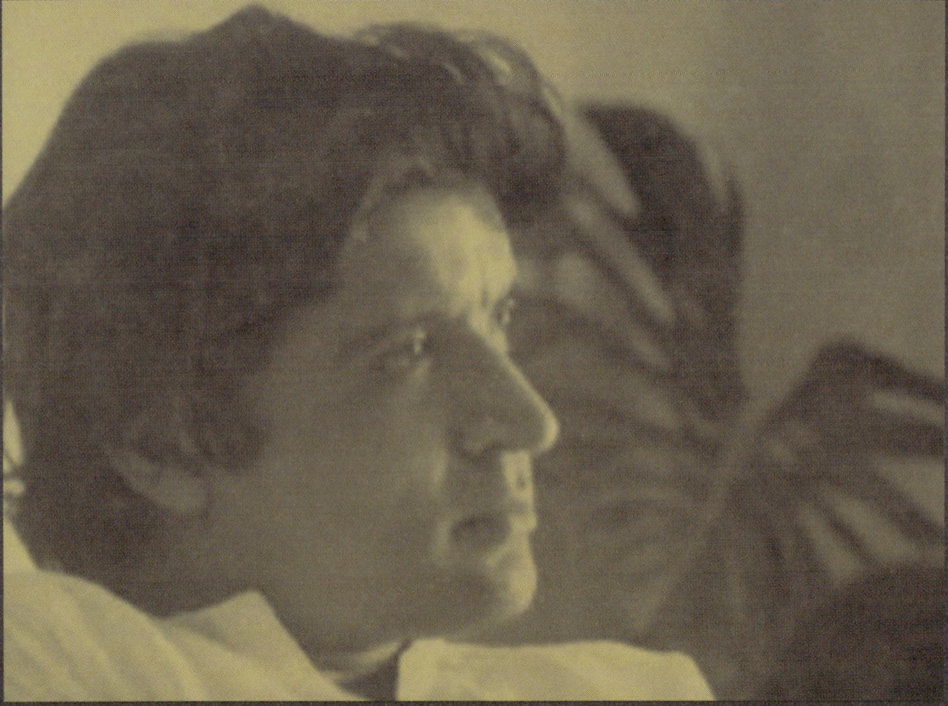

Why this book is in your hands

Arvind Mandloi

When you get a glimpse of Javed Akhtar's life and are able to peek into his past, you might find an echo of my story, too

Let me begin this introduction by first formally introducing myself; reading this might help you understand why this book is in your hands. A few centuries ago, my ancestors, having travelled from place to place, found themselves at Amjhera village near Dhar in present-day Madhya Pradesh, and decided to settle down there. Apart from its religious significance, this village is also known because its ruler, Rana Bakhtawar Singh, participated in the First War of Independence in 1857 and mounted an attack on the military cantonment, the Residency Kothi, at Indore. It was here that he was captured as a prisoner of war and hanged from a tree in full public display. Along with the raja, my ancestor, Shri Salukrao Mandloi, was also hanged. After the suppression of the revolt, Amjhera came under the rule of the Gwalior maharaja. In these changed circumstances, the *jagirdari* of Amjhera along with that of seven other neighbouring villages was granted to him.

This *jagir* remained intact after Independence till the Zamindari Abolition Act of 1950 came into effect. My grandfather was one of the beneficiaries of the compensation that came in the wake of the act. But with the passage of time, the small bonanza slipped through his fingers like sand. In the end, there was just an empty hand. My grandfather became a teacher in a government school. You can well imagine how he would have raised his eight children on a meagre salary. He could barely afford to give even a basic education to his children. My father was the eldest among his siblings; and that was all I got from him by way of legacy. From a very young age, I learnt to face the bitter realities of life and I experienced, at first hand, its roughness and coarseness. My earliest memories are of a time when nights brought neither dreams nor sleep. The reason being that starvation had decided that instead of making a daily round, it would just set up camp in our home. My childhood was spent in the lap of acute hunger and poverty.

When everything else is missing in life, what place can education have in it? For as long as I could stay in school without paying a fee, I managed to get by. The reason I wish to write all this here is so that you are under no illusion that this book is a rare literary offering on my part. When you get a glimpse of Javed Akhtar's life and are able to peek into his past, you might find an echo of my story, too. And it is also, perhaps, one of the major reasons why you have this book in your hands. This commonality between our stories has created a bond between us.

The echo of words has always given me strength and courage. In religious traditions, word and sound have been considered a manifestation of Brahma, the Creator who has no form, who is completely without blemish, or shape. Words and sound are a form of positive energy that propel your life towards improvement and betterment and also give you the courage to soldier on in the face of conflicts. Like thousands of other people, my first meeting with Javed sahab was definitely through *Tarkash*. I don't recall when I read it, that is to say how many years after its release, but what I do remember most vividly after reading it is feeling as though his story was my story. Javed sahab's story left a deep impression on my heart, one that is intact to this day.

Propelled by the winds of humanism, [Javed sahab] is like that ship sailing in the sea that has cast its anchor in the many ports of Time.

Javed sahab's life is not the story of a river flowing through a plain; instead, it is the tale of the waterfall that cascades down from a great height, forms a pool as it flows down from the mountain, becomes the point of origin for a gushing stream and, then, as it flows towards the sea, gathers into itself many tributaries and rivulets. The story you will read in the pages of this book is the story of a man who has held Time in his hand, created a mould, melted himself in the fire of struggle and strife and poured himself in that mould to create a hallmark of success. It is said that a child's future can be detected from infancy. Wherever you find a mention of Javed sahab in the letters written by his mother, Safiya Akhtar, you will notice that she had already foreseen Javed sahab's future. The epic tale of Javed sahab's life has steadfastly refused to follow a timeworn narrative, nor does it like to journey through trodden paths. Propelled by the winds of humanism, he is like that ship sailing in the sea that has cast its anchor in the many ports of Time. See the days of his infancy, then his childhood and youth, then look at the time he entered the film industry, look at his poetry, look at how he became a lyricist, and you will find that the ship cast anchor at different ports at different points in time, but at no point has he declared that the journey is complete. This ship is still in sail.

The successful duo of Salim–Javed made their work classic and iconic and proved that scripts and dialogues can also be the surety of a successful film. It was only Javed Akhtar who could have penned all those memorable dialogues that have since become part of our daily idiom. From the time they were first written to this day, all those iconic dialogues can be recited from memory by at least three generations. And by using them in their daily conversations, people continue to derive pleasure from them.

Some people have the great good fortune of being born with incredible talents; others obtain them through dint of hard work. Javed sahab was born with a phenomenal memory. In fact, so prodigious is his memory that the famous writer Rahi Masoom Raza has written that he has seen only two people who possess such a combination of an incredible memory and the ability to remember thousands of *sher*s on a range of subjects. One was Ali Sardar Jafri and the other is Javed Akhtar.

During Javed sahab's stay in Bhopal, he endured many hardships and all sorts of bitterness that life could possibly throw his way. But even in this state of hunger and homelessness, he had announced that he would live life on his own terms. The incredible thing is that he managed to find friends and create happy memories even during this stage of his life which would have felled a lesser man. During those days of struggle and penury, he was an atheist and he remains one even today. His speech on the trappings of religiosity given during his college days in Bhopal, raised questions on the existence of God. After a long and fruitful journey, while speaking at the India Today Conclave, we can see the clear imprint of that maiden speech. It is difficult to find instances of such constancy in one's beliefs. He carries

Javed Akhtar with Amitabh Bachchan and Salim Khan

To choose his own yardstick and then prove himself worthy of it is a unique aspect of Javed sahab's personality

with him the fragrance of the city of Bhopal wherever he goes. In the midst of wounds caused by the thorns of time, he has managed to find flowers of beauty, and he has the rare ability to constantly smell their fragrance. His usage of typical Bhopali words in his daily conversations demonstrates that Bhopal has remained with him throughout his travels. His two published collections of poetry, *Tarkash* and *Lava*, help us understand his life, but both books are free of any pretensions of being sentimental and judgemental or of offering to be a guidebook of any sort.

I have experience at first hand the emotional and human side of his personality, and witnessed it too. For nearly forty to forty-five years, Ramu, his domestic assistant who was also his driver, manager and cashier, was treated like a member of the family. When he retired, his care was taken up as one would for one's brother or father. Ramu wanted to spend the last few years of his life in his village; moreover, he was also a little unwell. His son came to take him home. For some reason, I happened to be with Javed sahab at the time. With a choked throat, he had said, 'This may be my last meeting with him.' And then Javed sahab and Shabana ji had to go away somewhere. I was waiting in the drawing room for them to return. Shabana ji entered the drawing room and told me that Javed sahab was crying uncontrollably in his room. Later, when I saw him, I found that his tears had abated but his eyes were red. I said, 'Javed sahab, what is this?' He answered, 'Blood has seeped into my eyes.' To be able to cry at life and smile with equal ease is a skill that comes after immense toil and some are never able to master this skill. Who knows what unseen power has given him this talent!

Once we were going to someone's house for lunch in Bhopal. Javed sahab's former wife, Honey Irani, called on his cell phone and suddenly the network dropped from his phone. When he called Honey ji from my phone, she said, 'Jadu, I need the number of such-and-such eye doctor. My eyes are troubling me a lot.' Javed sahab said, 'I will send the number to you, but what is the point of going to an eye doctor? You have already used your eyes to see whatever you had to see!' Seldom does one see people having and maintaining such a relationship of camaraderie, that too without the slightest trace of bitterness, with a woman who was once your wife and beloved. As soon as he disconnected the phone, I asked him precisely this: how was it possible to have such a relationship? And he said that if one were to continue doing good towards somebody without bitterness and prejudice, then one day it is certainly possible.

The friendship that exists between Javed sahab and Shabana ji predates their marriage. It is evident that even marriage could not diminish or destroy their friendship. Javed sahab's feminism is not limited to mere words or speeches or the female characters in his films; he has, in fact, given an equal status to all the women who have entered his personal domain. Javed sahab was a frequent visitor at the home of Krishan Chandar, the famous Urdu fiction writer, and during his days of struggle he spent most of his evenings there. Krishan Chandar's wife, Salma Siddiqui, introduced Javed sahab to Sultana ji, who was a paying guest in their home. That relationship is still strong. Whenever Javed sahab introduces Sultana ji to someone, he never fails to mention that she is like a younger brother in his life and he himself is her elder sister! Just think: how many people would you have met who have given such a place to a woman? Not only does he acknowledge that women are emotionally stronger, but he also has no hesitation in accepting this publicly.

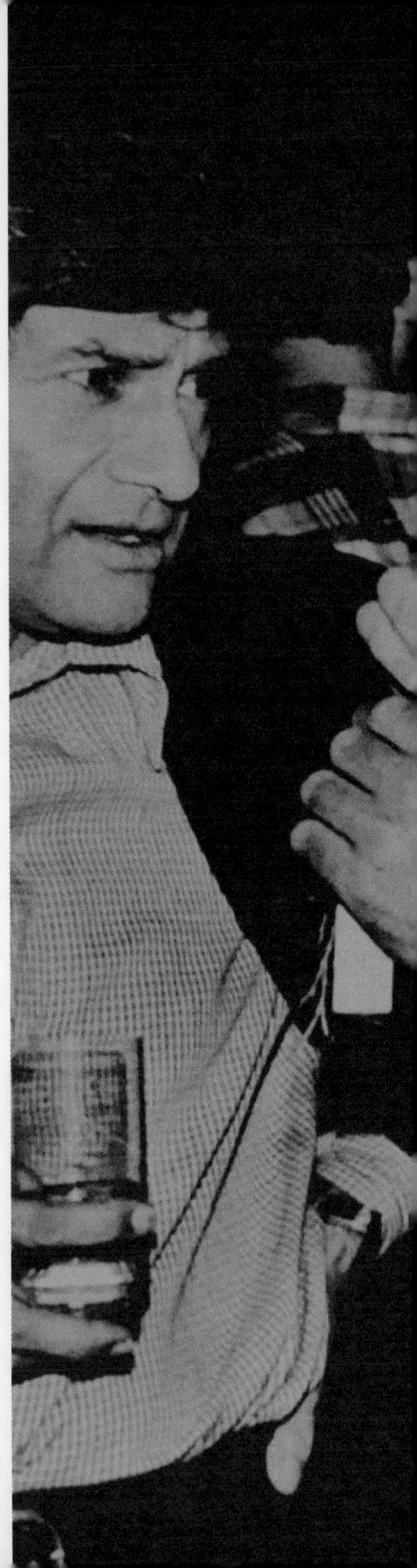

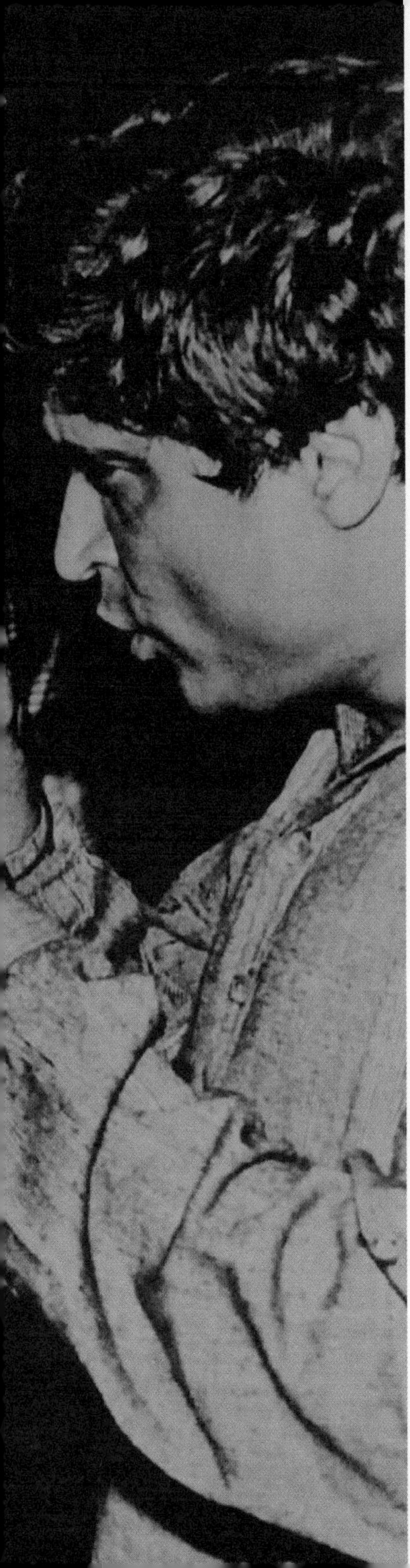

During his worst days of struggle and starvation, Javed sahab maintained his self-respect. An example of having a clear opinion about people and remaining steadfast in it was offered by his friend from those days, the poet Suryabhanu Gupt, whose interview appears in the pages ahead. As Gupt narrates, despite being hungry, Javed sahab refused to eat from someone else's account because the person in whose name Gupt ji was eating was someone that Javed sahab did not have a high opinion of. Gupt ji narrates how he repeatedly said that while I am eating in the account of that person I will repay him, I will not eat for free. Javed sahab, however, still chose to remain hungry but steadfast in his opinion.

He met and parted ways with Salim Khan, his collaborator from his film script writing days. The writing imprinted on the wall of Time by this duo leaves people amazed. But the mystery remains as to why the two of them broke up. Javed sahab has never given any reasons, either in public or in private, for the break-up. He has always maintained that the success could not have been possible without Salim sahab. Professional partnerships are formed in all professions, and they break up too. And after the break-up, due to the bitterness that creeps into the former partnership, it begins to give off a strange, rancid sort of

Javed Akhtar with Dev Anand

stench. But entirely in keeping with his own character, Javed sahab has never allowed his relationship with his former partner to become the subject of gossip and speculation.

To a well-known poet, he offered the opportunities to write film songs by saying that he can write better for those situations. To help discreetly and fade from the scene is part of his nature. At such times, he is known to say, 'They were very talented people; they would have been successful even if I had not helped them.' I know many people who find themselves at a similar height of success and I also know for a fact that their telling and retelling of how they have helped others is part of their repertoire of conversations. Sometimes, the telling of these incidents crosses all boundaries of decency. Therefore, Javed sahab's silence and discretion in such matters shows yet another facet of his personality.

To choose his own yardstick and then prove himself worthy of it is a unique aspect of Javed sahab's personality. During his days of penury and unemployment, he would hold Meena Kumari's *Filmfare* trophy in his hand and then decide what he would say and all the people he would thank when he would be awarded this trophy. To have such faith in one's own self is so typical of Javed sahab. His rock-solid belief and his stubborn determination are the reason why, finally, the Copyright (Amendment) Act, 2012 came into being, providing composers and lyricists with powerful new rights.

When one delves deep into Javed sahab's life story, one sometimes wonders how his timing was always perfect in all that he has done. It wasn't just Rahi Masoom Raza who was impressed by his prodigal memory; it was also his maternal grandfather. When Javed sahab was still a child, his grandfather gave him the Holy Quran and told him that if he recites one verse correctly from it, he would reward him with a 50-paisa coin. The very next day, Javed sahab recited a verse before his grandfather. When his grandfather was instructing him to memorise another verse for the next day, his grandmother interrupted and said, 'Look, had this child's parents been here would they have educated him like this? Certainly not!' His uneducated grandmother had seen with the eye of experience that this child was not memorising the verses for the sake of religious duty or obedience to elders. When I heard Javed sahab narrate this incident two or three different times in different contexts, I understood how his timing was always perfect for everything that he has done in life.

When I turn my gaze towards incidents from my own life, I find that Javed sahab's life is a part of mine. And so, this book is my way of expressing my gratitude to my shareholder. As one's personality grows, one rises above daily realities and everyday troubles. One begins to distance oneself from all such small strife as one grows in stature. To be surrounded by a certain kind of person and to only stay in touch with them, that is what one normally sees with 'big' names. And if, perchance, they sometimes look down upon earthly reality, those who come to meet them immediately sense it. Despite being such a famous personality, Javed sahab has kept himself aloof from this trait of 'big' people. Even today, he remains in touch with the common man; he feels their pain. Not for a moment do you feel that you are interacting with a great person when you meet him. Despite all that life throws his way, he is intent on leading his life his own way. Be it his personal life or professional, he has always stood up for humanism. He has always spoken out in favour of the truth. Certainly, tomorrow when history is written along with all his other works, Javed sahab will be remembered for his unwavering beliefs and his consistent espousal of humanism.

One ends up repeating words when one is writing about such a successful, intelligent and famous personality since so much has already been written about him. Friendship is one of those bonds where nothing else matters: not religion or caste or creed or gender. The seeds of affection are sown from its very inception. This book is the outcome of a pure and unadulterated love for Javed sahab. His personality has affected several hidden corners of my life and personality and brought about changes in me. And not just Javed sahab, but Shabana ji too has given me her time, affection and care. One can say that they have both taught me that there is a world beyond the stars. This book is merely the first instalment of my attempt to say 'Thank You!' Shabana ji has considered this dream of compiling and publishing this book not mine but hers. And now when this dream has come true and this book is in your hands, my eyes often become moist when I think of her contribution. This book is just like a film where different people have worked in different departments; their names have been recorded, with my heartfelt gratitude, in the last page of this book.

As I have said earlier, Javed sahab's life is like a ship in full sail. I have tried to gauge the depth of scores of incidents from his life in this book. Not only do I consider this attempt my great good fortune, but I also look upon it as my responsibility. Now this book, every single page of it, is in your hands like a sonar (an instrument to measure the depth of the seas). What are the colours in these depths and what is the intensity of these colours, that is for you to experience!

My name is Jadu

Usually, the nickname comes from the real name, but the exact opposite happened in my case. The word Javed means 'eternal', Akhtar means 'star'. Eternal star!

I was born on 17 January 1945 in Kamla Hospital in Gwalior. My father and his friends went to the hospital from the office of the Communist Party and as he was sitting in the hospital looking at me and talking about me, someone said: 'Do you know that when a child is born in a Muslim home, the azan is sounded in his ear?' My father's friends said: 'But our belief is different; what should we do?' My father happened to be holding *The Communist Manifesto* in his hand; he said, 'All right then, let us sound this in his ear.' Someone reminded my father that when he had married my mother, Safiya, he had written a *nazm*. A line of that nazm was: '*Lamha lamha kisi jadu ka fasana hoga* (Every moment will be the story of a certain magic)'. So, why not name the boy Jadu? And I was named Jadu. For a long time, I was called just Jadu. But when it was time to put me in kindergarten, people felt that Jadu was not a serious name. But by then my name was Jadu and so they had to search for a name that was sort of similar. And this is how they arrived at the name Javed. Usually, the nickname comes from the real name, but the exact opposite happened in my case. The word *javed* means 'eternal', *akhtar* means 'star'. Eternal star!

◂ *Javed Akhtar in his study*

The 1857 War of Independence and Fazl-e-Haq

Fazl-e-Haq had a multi-faceted personality. Some of his books are to be found in the library of Chicago University...He was considered an authority on religion

My parents belonged to Uttar Pradesh. My father's family was from Khairabad which is 80 miles away from Lucknow, and my mother's family was from Rudauli which, too, is approximately 80 or 100 miles from Lucknow. People from my father's side of the family were intellectuals and litteratéurs. My great-grandfather's father, whose name was Fazl-e-Haq, lived in the days of Ghalib and was a close friend of the great poet. Fazl-e-Haq was a scholar of logic, philosophy, religion and literature. He had even edited Ghalib's *diwan* or selected works. Ghalib was far ahead of his time. During those days, there was no tradition of poets editing their works, but Ghalib asked my great-grandfather's father to edit his poetry because he greatly admired Fazl-e-Haq's intellect.

Fazl-e-Haq had a multi-faceted personality. Some of his books are to be found in the library of Chicago University. They are also part of the curriculum for higher studies in Egypt. He was considered an authority on religion. He took part in the First War of Independence in 1857, for which he was arrested and sent to Andaman (*Kaala Pani*, as it was then known) where he eventually died. He had a daughter named Hirma who was a poet in the 19th century. Hirma's husband was also a poet. They had two sons, Bismil and Muztar; both were poets. Muztar was younger, and he was my grandfather.

Javed Akhtar with his sister Uneza at the Khairabad railway station

A government notice to demolish the house of Javed Akhtar's great-grandfather Fazl-e-Haq Khairabadi, who had taken part in the Revolt of 1857 against the British. Such orders were issued by way of further punishment for those who were sent away to the Andaman jail. A certain patriotic Thakur Raja sahab took permission to cart away the rubble from Fazl-e-Haq's demolished house and had it safely sheltered on his estate.

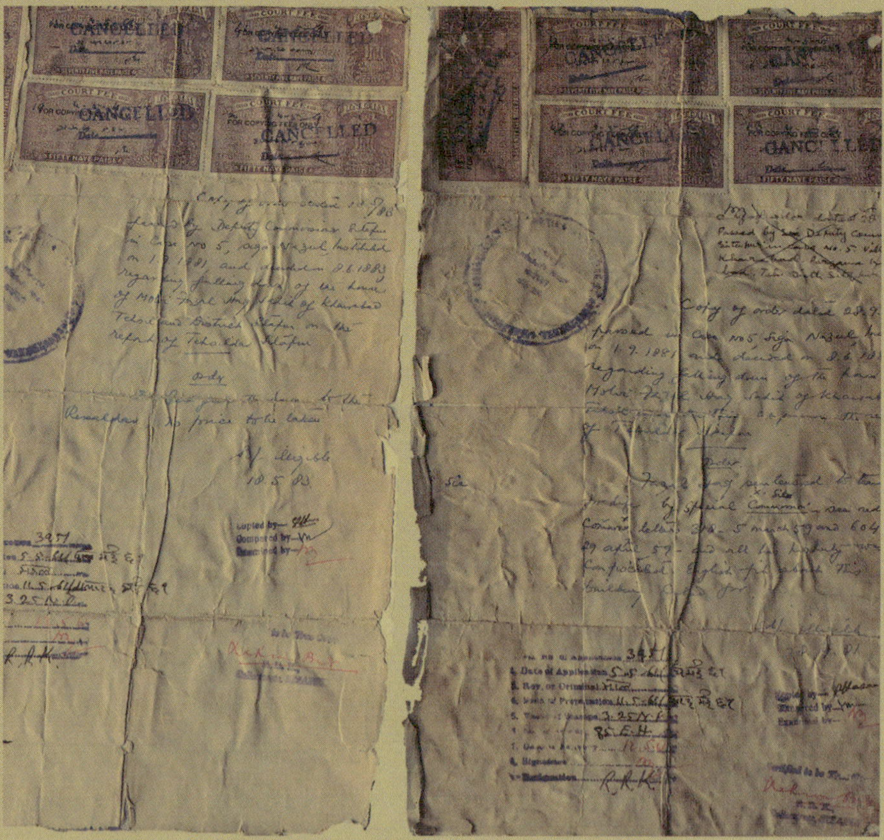

The tomb of the great Sufi scholar, poet and freedom fighter Maulana Fazl-e-Haq Khairabadi (1797–1861), Andaman

Muztar Khairabadi (1869–1927)

Grandfather Muztar Khairabadi...

A great deal of my grandfather's poetry is still very well known. He wrote all kinds of poetry; not just the ghazal, but also *qasida*, *kajri*, *holi*, *thumri* and *geet* in Hindi. One of his *kajris*, '*Chha rahi kaali ghata, jiyara mora ghabraye hai*', was sung by Begum Akhtar. He was a sessions judge in the Gwalior state where my father was born. Poetry was all around my father and that is why he began to write poetry from the age of fourteen.

Na kisi ki aankh ka noor hoon
Na kisi ke dil ka qarar hoon
Jo kisi ke kaam na aa saka
Main woh ik musht-e-ghubar hoon

...and his *Khirman*

The care and attention bestowed by Javed Akhtar and the hard work and dedication of his friends and well-wishers have given Khirman *its rightful place as a rare document*

Several years after my father's death, when the family began to feel that the house they were staying in was too small and it was time to change it, a bundle of letters, papers, copies and books were found tucked away under a bed. When I was given these papers, I, too, put them away. After many years, one day I suddenly remembered this bundle and opened it. My gaze fell upon scores of ghazals by Muztar Khairabadi. It was many years later that *Khirman* came into existence.

The care and attention bestowed by Javed Akhtar and the hardwork and dedication of his friends and well-wishers have given *Khirman* its rightful place as a rare document. The famous ghazal, '*Na kisi ki aankh ka noor hoon*', has been proven to be Muztar's with the help of some very substantial evidence given in the book.

◂ *At the release of* Khirman, *Javed Akhtar with the vice president of India Hamid Ansari and the Urdu scholar Gopichand Narang, New Delhi (2015)*

▾ Khirman, *the collected works of Muztar Khairabadi, published by Javed Akhtar in 2015*

Childhood, cricket and the dream of getting rich

LUCKNOW

When people write about themselves, they usually begin by talking about the city they belong to. Which city shall I call my own?... The crime of being born was committed in Gwalior, but it was in Lucknow that I found my senses, lost my senses for the first time in Aligarh, then became a little sensible in Bhopal, but it was in Mumbai that I finally came to my senses. So let me create a small flashback of my life. In this way, your job, which is to read it, and my job, to write it, will become easier.

The city of Lucknow... Characters: My nana and nani (maternal grandparents), other family members and I... I am eight years old. My father is in Mumbai, my mother in the grave. All day long I play cricket with my younger brother in the courtyard of our house. A scary-looking master sahab comes to give me tuitions in the evening. He is given ₹15 per month (I remember this very clearly because every day I was told so). A half-anna is given to me every morning as pocket money and a one-anna coin every evening. So there is no shortage of money. I buy brightly coloured toffees from the grocer Ramji Lal's shop in the morning and, in the evening, I squander my anna on the chaat stall set up by Bhagwati on the footpath across the road. Life is good. The schools have opened. I am admitted in the sixth standard in Lucknow's famous school, the Colvin Taluqdars' College. Earlier, only the sons of taluqdars could study here; now the less well-born like me can also study here. It is still a very expensive school... My fee is 17 rupees per month (I remember this very clearly because every day... anyhow, let it go). Many children in my class wear a watch. They are all from rich families. They have such nice sweaters. One of them even has a fountain pen. During recess, these children buy chocolate worth 50 paise from the school canteen (I no longer like Bhagwati's chaat). Yesterday, Rakesh was telling everyone in the class that his father has said that he will send him to England to study further. Yesterday, my grandfather was saying... You wretched boy!

◂ *Javed Akhtar, eleven years old, Lucknow*

If you were to pass the matric examination at least you will get a job in a post office putting stamps on letters. At this tender age, when boys dream of becoming an engine driver, I have decided that I will grow up to become a rich man....

'In his childhood, he used to play rowdy games with me, but then he could also charm everyone. He was very naughty. The two of us used to climb the guava tree and pluck guavas. He would never sleep during the day. He would come home and fling his satchel aside. He barely studied. He used to sit down with us and tell stories. He would always say that when I make a movie, it will be with a lot of fight sequences. And you, Chhutkaniya, must go and see it. He never looked sad. He was always acting alone. Years later, when he came, he sent for me. He met me and cried a lot.'

Chhutkaniya's parents used to cook in Javed Akhtar's grandfather's house. There were two sisters: Chhutkaniya and Badkaniya. Both have been close witness to Javed Akhtar's childhood.

Chhutkaniya

Colvin Taluqdars' College, Lucknow

Javed (right) with his mother Safiya Akhtar and younger brother Salman (1950)

'Your Jadu is enough for me'

'Your Jadu is enough for me...'

Some letters written by my mother Safiya Akhtar to my father Jan Nisar Akhtar:

23 February 1946, Aligarh
Anyhow, your Jadu is enough for me. He has become so mischievous and unruly that he is no longer in my control. The only time we have peace is when he is sleeping. Yesterday, he upturned a full bottle of Swan ink on the floor; painted his entire body with the ink and licked it heartily too! Right now he is sleeping so innocently and looking like an angel.

15 May 1947, Lucknow
Jadu's antics cannot be described; they can only be seen. He is always happy, and talks nonstop. If one were to ask him, who is your grandfather, the answer is: 'Stalin.' And the name of your chacha *(paternal uncle)? 'Chacha Dalib' (he lisps Dalib for Ghalib). He talks about his Chacha Ghalib all the time. In fact, he goes around dancing, holding a portrait of Ghalib.*

14 September 1951, Bhopal
Jadu and Owais remember every single thing about you, and keep repeating them happily. Owais was delighted to hear the news about the motorcar and Jadu's vanity took such a blow that he immediately began to cry. He has started stringing words together into poetry. Two nights ago, Owais was making a din on the bed and refusing to sleep. I was sitting on the settee and, in desperation, called out, 'So jaao mere pyare'. *And Jadu sahab was lying on the bed. From there he called out,* 'Kya thtat hain tumharey'. *If Jadu were to get entangled in poetry, of which there is a very real likelihood, then be warned that for the next seven generations no one will thrive in our family and only the Red Revolution can save us from calamity.*

My parents' married life lasted only nine years, and of this they mostly lived separately. All the letters that my mother wrote to my father, he had them published in the form of a book. This turned out to become a very famous book and from 1954–55 till now, every year one or two editions of this book are reprinted. My mother was a wonderful letter writer; she would write letters nearly every day.

◂ *Mother Safiya Akhtar*

JAN NISAR AKHTAR

My relationship with poetry is from birth

My relationship with poetry has existed since birth and I've always had an interest in it

In our family, normally no one bequeaths any money, property, factory, lands, fields or orchards and groves to their children; but we do give something else: a different sort of ability to think, a different kind of knowledge, one that has no price. I remember that my father had once said to me that it is very easy to write in a difficult language, but it is very difficult to write in a simple language. You can only write in a simple language when you are absolutely clear in your thoughts about what you wish to say. If your language is clear, then what you are saying is immediately clear. So your thoughts have to be clear in the first place. I see this in Jan Nisar's poetry. There are very few difficult words in his poetry. Clearly, this man has no problem with his vocabulary; in fact, his vocabulary is vast. Yet 90 per cent of his poetry is written in absolutely simple and clear words which I think is a very good thing. Jan Nisar's poetry is the poetry of a lambent flame.

Despite his communism, despite all his progressive thoughts, the old passions that were steeped in him never quite left him. It is often said that when a love is unsuccessful it becomes immortal, whereas if there is a 'happy ending', there can be no poetry. But Akhtar sahab has written an entire book called *Ghar-Angan* (*The Home and the Courtyard*) in which all the poetry is about life after marriage and it is very beautiful poetry. Yet I feel that the woman who emerges from it is a traditional Indian woman, which means that the woman of his fantasy is a traditional Indian woman.

My father died on 18 August 1976 (nine days before his death, he gave me an autographed copy of his book in which he had written: 'You will remember me a lot when I am no longer here.') And he was right. Till this point, I had seen myself as a rebellious and angry son. So who am I now? I looked at myself and all around me with new eyes. Is this all I wanted from life? As yet others don't know about it, but all those things that gave me joy now seem false and artificial. Now I am more interested in those things that, if one were to use a worldly expression, have no benefit. My relationship with poetry has existed since birth and I've always had an interest in it. Ever since my youth I have known that if I want, I can write poetry, but I have not done so yet. This too, is a sign of my anger and rebelliousness. I write poetry for the first time in 1976, and with that one sher, I make peace with my legacy, and with my father.

◂ *Javed Akhtar's father Jan Nisar Akhtar (1914–1976)*

With their father Jan Nisar Akhtar, Javed and Salman, Lucknow (1957)

GUFTAGU

In conversation with Javed Akhtar

Arvind Mandloi

I felt my mother's absence in my childhood and youth very acutely

Your mother passed away at a very early stage of your life. Was there ever a moment when you felt: My mother should have been here right now?

Now that is an interesting question. My mother was thirty-five or thirty-six years old when she passed away. Both my children are older than her. So how shall I think of a mother who is younger than both my children? How do I think of her? How much do I think of her? At first, I didn't have the courage to think of her or to look back because that wound was fresh and deep, but I have travelled so far that when I turn to look back, I realise how much I have missed my mother in my life. Earlier, I never acknowledged it, not even to myself because if I were to acknowledge it, how could I ever be happy? How could I have lived? But I know that I felt my mother's absence very acutely in my childhood and youth. But then, if you remove Scene No. 36 then it is possible that Scene No. 64, which is

Safiya Siraj (Akhtar) and Jan Nisar Akhtar. Safiya, a well-known writer, was the sister of the famous poet Majaz, Lucknow (1943).

the highlight of the story, might also be deleted. Now who is to know if my mother had been alive, what would I have been? I might have been teaching in some university or I might have been a journalist, I don't know what I would have been. Or it is possible that I would have been exactly this. So, my dear, we all have joys and sorrows in life.

There is much speculation about your relationship with your father, that you were a rebellious son, and that you never behaved with him as a son should with his father. Have you, at any point, felt that I should have shared such-and-such thing with my father, or that I should have involved him more in my life? Or at this stage in your life, now that you are a grandfather, do you ever feel that perhaps you may have been remiss in creating this image of a rebellious son?

No, whatever happened had to happen. See, the thing about the rebellious son is that my mother had died when I was eight. I was raised in other people's homes, even though the others were my own. First my grandfather, then my aunt; I lived in their homes. Then when I came to Bhopal, for one year I stayed in the home of my step-mother. I lived with her family. She used to live in Mumbai with my father. Later, I started living separately, with my friends. When I went to Mumbai, I stayed with my father for three–four days. Then I moved away because I found no place for myself in that house.

As far as success is concerned, I began to get work from 1970. *Zanjeer* was released in 1973 and that is when I truly earned fame. From 1970, I had begun to eat two square meals a day. My father died in 1976. At best, he saw three years of my success; otherwise, he mostly saw my days of failure. For the most part, I was the vagabond, homeless, vagrant son. Anyhow, let bygones be bygones. But in those three years, my relationship with my father improved somewhat.

It is not possible that a father and son who have lived separately should become a normal father and son in one day. But it has been my experience that no matter what happens, whether the sky crashes against the earth, the sun and the moon break into smithereens, no matter what happens, love doesn't quite leave certain relationships. There is no reason for this. After all, why do you love someone? But it is there. Perhaps the relationship between a father and a son is like that. So the love and respect I had for him always remained in some part of my heart, and it is still there.

Majaz and the beauty of being a vagabond

Majaz, or Majaz Lakhnawi, has been called the Shelley and Keats of Urdu poetry.

The moment his name is taken, the very first poem that comes to mind is 'Awara':

Shahr ki raat aur main naa-shaad-o naa-kaara phirun
Jagmagati jaagti sarhkon pe awaara phirun

(The city night and I am wandering joyless and useless
On the brightly lit awake roads I roam like a vagrant)

The vagabond who leaves the unknown and familiar paths, who sets off alone, in whose fate lie loneliness, sadness and cold nights, and the burden of sleep too. But while searching and seeking, if he were to find his destination, then all this vagrancy becomes a beautiful thing. When this wandering takes you somewhere then that place becomes special. And all those people who have always trodden on the straight and narrow path look at you with amazement and respect.

Majaz with his nephews and nieces: Behind him are Salman Akhtar (left) and Javed Akhtar (right). Beside him are Asma Irfan, Unfi Farzana, and Rukhsana. Irfan Salim and Sumbul Warsi are sitting on the chair on the left, and standing behind the right chair is Salma Zaidi.

Freedom fighter Ansar Harvani

The freedom fighter Ansar Harvani was Javed Akhtar's maternal uncle. Being a Member of Parliament and a graduate of Aligarh Muslim University, he was also a law graduate. He was one of the founders and a general secretary of the All India Students Federation (1936–1939). He was elected Member of Parliament from the Fatehpur constituency in the second Lok Sabha elections (1957–62) and from Bisauli in Uttar Pradesh in the third Lok Sabha elections (1962–67). He was the chief reporter for the *National Herald* and special representative for the *Anand Bazar Patrika* and the *Bombay Chronicle*. Reading books on history and politics was his special passion and interest. His active role in the National Congress caused him to be expelled from the university. He edited several pamphlets, news-sheets, etc. He was active in the Quit India Movement and was imprisoned from 1942 to 1946. He was the president of the Lucknow Zila Congress and member of the All India Congress Committee. He was a member of the national committee of the All India Forward Bloc (1939–48) and president of the All India Youth League (1946–52).

◂ *Javed Akhtar's maternal uncle, Ansar Harvani*

▾ ***Standing from left to right:*** *Mahbub Alam, Taufiq-ur Rehman, Raisuddin, Iqbal Husain, Khalid Mukhtar, Naushad Ahmad, Satish Kumar Bajaj, Hamiduddin, Abdul Karim, Rasul Ali*
Seated on chairs: *Farhan Mujib (treasurer), Wizarat Husain (teacher-in-charge), Raj Kishan Razdan (group leader), Syed Muhammad Tonki (headmaster), Ahmad Fazil Jafri (assistant group leader), Javed Akhtar (cultural-in-charge)*
Seated on the floor: *Haji Ahmad, Adil Hayat, Shuja Baig Chughtai, Najmul Hasan, Munis-ur Rehman*

School textbooks could not hold my interest

ALIGARH

The city of Aligarh...

Characters: my *khala* (maternal aunt), other family members and I... My younger brother Salman has been kept in my nana's house in Lucknow whereas I have fallen to my khala's lot, her having come to Aligarh now. And it is only right after all. No single family can keep two orphan children. In front of my khala's house, as far as the eye can see, there is an empty open space. My school lies beyond it...I am in the ninth standard. I am fourteen years old. The winter in Aligarh is not to be taken lightly. The first class is at 7 a.m. I am going to school. A rapier-sharp icy cold wind is coming towards me. Even if I touch my face I can't tell if everything is in its place or whether the wind has chopped off my nose and ears. I barely manage to pass my exams as I am not that good at studies. Which is why while getting me admitted in this school that is called Minto Circle, my khalu had told the teacher, 'Remember that he is less interested in studies and more interested in film songs.' I have seen Dilip Kumar's *Udan Khatola* and Raj Kapoor's *Shri 420*. I remember many film songs by heart, but at home I am not allowed to listen to them, let alone sing them. And so, on my way back from school, I sing these songs loudly (excuse me, but while going to school in the morning, it is so cold that one can only sing classical ragas.)

My school is in the university area. Apart from a few boys from school, most of my friends are from the university. I like to sit in hotels like the older boys. Often, I run away from school. Complaints come from the school. On several occasions, I am beaten up at home but it makes no difference. It does not matter to me that school textbooks do not hold my interest. I love to read novels. I am scolded for it, but I still read them. I remember many a sher. Whenever there is a *baitbazi* (a bit like *antakshari* but featuring Urdu sher) in the university, I represent my school and win a lot of prizes. All the boys and girls in the university recognise me. I am pleased that boys recognise me, but it pleases me a lot more that girls know me.

S.T. High School, Minto Circle

The first and last love letter of my life

Javed, posing in the style of his favourite actor, Dev Anand

I am a little older. I am fifteen years old. I am writing a letter to a girl for the first time in my life. My friend Biloo is helping me. We prepare this letter together. The next day, I meet that girl in an empty badminton court. Gathering all my courage, I give her the letter. This is the first and last love letter of my life. (I have forgotten what was written in that letter, but I remember that girl even today.) I am leaving Aligarh after matric. My khala is crying copiously. My *khalu* is trying to quieten her by saying, 'You are crying as though he is going to a battlefield and not Bhopal' (at that time neither he nor I knew that I was indeed going to a 'battlefield').

Today life is good for me in every way, but I still remember that day from my childhood: 18 January 1953. The place is Lucknow, my nana's house. My distraught khala takes my younger brother Salman, who is six-and-a-half years old, and me by the hand and brings us to the big room in the house. There, many women are sitting on the floor. My mother, wrapped in a white shroud, is placed on the *takht*; her face is uncovered. My old nani, sitting at the head of the takht, is crying softly, slowly, as though she is exhausted. Two women are supporting her. My khala takes both of us children to that takht and says, 'See your mother for the last time.' It was just yesterday that I had turned eight. I am old enough. I know what death is. I look closely at my mother's face so that I remember it well. My khala is saying, 'Promise her that you will become something in life. Promise her that you will do something in life.' I am unable to say anything. I just keep looking at her till some woman pulls the shroud over my mother's face, covering it.

Ek khilona jogi se kho gaya tha bachpan me
dhoondta phira usko woh nagar nagar tanha

(An ascetic once lost a toy in his childhood
He looked for it all alone in city after city)

The years in Aligarh left a deep impression on Javed

Farhan Mujib

The way Javed uses Urdu, the way he talks, especially his sense of humour, I think the years he spent in Aligarh proved to be very important ones for him

It must have been the year 1957; I was in standard seven or eight. That is when he was admitted to our school. We were not in the same section though we were in the same class. I think we first met in the corridor and then we became friends.

Even then, Javed was different from the rest of us children. He seemed very mature. He had come from a bigger city and he had a certain aura about him that said: I know everything about life! He was great at playing with words, such as telling jokes and narrating humorous incidents. He had an extrovert personality. Also, he had immense self-confidence. Within four–five months, the entire school knew who he was. Then there was his name, Jadu, which was so different and unique. He knew about things we had not even heard of. Moreover, he had even met people whom we had merely heard about. He had friends who were much older than him. He was friends with the boys and girls from the university. Even today, Jadu can sit down and talk on any subject with anyone—be it a girl or boy, or young or old. Then there is this other

Javed Akhtar with Farhan Mujib and other friends

Javed Akhtar, fourteen years of age, Aligarh 1957

thing. Aligarh has a certain culture; it's called *khinchai*, as in pulling someone's leg. Javed was very good at it. At the time when Javed was studying here, the left-leaning individuals held great sway over Aligarh. Revolution, freedom, equality... all these were discussed at home all the time. It was all part of our daily conversations.

The way Javed uses Urdu, the way he talks, especially his sense of humour, I think the years he spent in Aligarh proved to be very important ones for him. There is a distinct sense of humour that is unique to Aligarh. You are not likely to meet anyone here who does not have a sense of humour. Javed used to consider Dev Anand his ideal. So, he too would turn up his collar, comb his hair into a puff and deliver dialogues in Dev Anand's distinctive style. Javed was very good at mimicry.

Javed never forgets anything; this is something that you will find in the character of Amitabh Bachchan. I am not talking about revenge here, but about things that might have caused pain. He will remember those things for a long time till either he himself is able to erase them or he gets the other person to admit: 'I quit.' You will find this trait in the characters enacted by Amitabh Bachchan.

I like Javed's poetry. I especially like some of his romantic poetry. There is a glimpse of the past in his poems. He is a very romantic person deep inside, and this 'cool' style that he adopts is only on the surface. There is an intensely emotional core hidden inside him. Sometimes, you see this emotional quality in his poetry which is very lovable. His ghazal '*Main aur meri awargi*' or his poem 'Banjara', which I like very much, carries the memory of leaving someone far behind.

His lyrics are incomparable. I consider him a very fine lyrics writer. Jadu has written some exceptional songs in the film *Silsila*. '*Ghar se nikalte hi*' too, is a lovely song. I think it is a pure Aligarhiya song because the boy's sentiments expressed in it are sentiments that he can never express to the girl.

When we were thirteen or fourteen years old and Jadu was here, any one could tell that he was a different sort of a boy, one who will mould his life differently, and that he will not grow up to become an engineer or a lawyer. Everyone could tell that he was different from the rest, one who would not follow the straight and narrow path. I met him next in 1963 when he visited Aligarh for a few days, and thereafter in 1973, and then in 1977 when we spent a month together in England. After that, we kept meeting regularly.

Javed would come to our home, sit in my room and we would talk about friends, sing songs and tell jokes. Sometimes we would just sit. Time would flow. My mother would ask him to stay for dinner. Sometimes, on hot summer afternoons, we would lie on the cool drawing room floor and talk for hours. Jadu was friends with my cousin too. We would all be together, talking, wrestling with each other, having fun! Javed liked the more impressionable songs. His favourite song then was '*Jeevan ke safar mein raahi*'. I was a bit simple and liked the more decent songs such as '*Nain se nain naahi milao*'. We would sit at home and sing songs. At that time, I had a high-pitched voice and Jadu's voice was lower, so I would sing in the girl's voice and Jadu in the man's. There was a song from the film *Eik Musafir Eik Haseena*: '*Main pyaar ka raahi hoon, teri zulf ke saaye mein kuchh deir thhahar jaoon*' sung by the man to which the girl replies: '*Tum ek musafir ho, kab chhorh ke chal dogey, ye soch ke ghabraoon*'. At one point, when the man says, '*Nazneen, tu nahi ja sakegi*', Javed would look at me and we would both burst out laughing. In my room, there was a glass-fronted bookshelf. My collection of Firozabadi glass animals was kept in it. Javed was fascinated by them. Years later he told me, 'Remember you had those glass peacocks in your house? How lovely they were! In fact, your entire room was lovely.' I have no such recollection. Javed has told me several times how well he remembers all the toys kept in that room. I don't know if I should mention this here, but the room that is mentioned in one of his poems is a room I have seen. It is a room I have spent a lot of time in. An artist always draws inspiration from here and there. That room is Shabana's. The room that is described in Javed's poem is Shabana's room in Janki Kutir, not my room in Aligarh.

Occasionally, Javed gives a rare, insightful glimpse of himself and the emotions that are buried deep inside him. I can recall a few such incidents. The film *Don* was under production. Its producer is my brother-in-law, and Javed, being a celebrity, was very important for the producer. He called Javed, me and my wife Fawzia for dinner. Those days Javed used to drink. Javed came. He drank. Then he asked me to sing. I sang Faiz's ghazal '*Kab tak dil ki khair manaiyen.*' Suddenly, Javed began to cry. I had never seen Javed cry till then. I realised that somewhere deep inside him, Javed was grievously hurt. That moment is forever imprinted in my memory.

That empty room in the college compound

BHOPAL

The city of Bhopal...

Characters: All those countless benefactors, many friends and I. On the way from Aligarh to Mumbai, my father has dropped me in Bhopal or you could say he has left me halfway. For some days, I stay in the home of my step-mother, but then that too is gone. I study in Saifia College and live on the kindness of my friends, so many friends that if I sit down to make their list, I will end up with a book as thick as a telephone directory. These days I am in the second year of BA. I live with my friend Ejaz. He pays the rent. I simply live with him. He studies and gives tuitions to get by. All our friends call him 'Master'. I have fought with Master over something. We are not talking to each other. Therefore, these days I am not asking him for money. I take whatever I need from his pant that is hanging from a peg on the wall in front of me. Sometimes he leaves a rupee or two by my bedside without saying a word.

I am in the final year of BA. This is my fourth year in this college. I have never paid the fees. The college administration has never asked for it either. This can only happen in Bhopal. In the college compound is an empty room which has been given to me free of charge. When my classes are over, I pick up two benches from any classroom and take them there. I join the benches, spread my bedding and it becomes my bed. Everything is fine except that there are a lot of bedbugs. The hotel in which I used to eat has shut down because it was always feeding freeloaders like me. A shoe shop has opened in its place. What shall I eat now? I am ill, alone and hungry. I have a high fever. But my hunger is even greater. Two boys from the college, whom I don't know too well, bring me food in a tiffin box. Neither is an especially close friend. Both are fools. But I am very clever. I will not let them know that when they leave, I will cry. I get well soon. The two boys become my close friends.

I have become very fond of taking part in debates. I have been winning the Bhopal Rotary Club debate for the past three years. I have won many trophies for inter-college debates. On behalf of Vikram University, I have also participated in the Delhi Youth Festival. There are two parties in college and both are asking me to speak on their behalf. I am only interested in speaking, not in the election. And so I give a speech for both sides.

MEMORIES OF BHOPAL, FRIENDS FROM BHOPAL

WAHAJUDDIN

'One day, Fatehullah brought Javed Akhtar to our room and told my elder brother that he would now be staying with us. A new life coursed through our room with Javed's arrival. Javed was never one to sit silently. He immediately became the rightful occupant of the space that had thus far been ours. I soon became friends with him. I was almost obsessed with watching films in those days. Javed was quite well informed about English films. He had a lot of friends who would be in our room. All day long, all sorts of jokes and humorous incidents would be narrated.'

EJAZ ANSARI

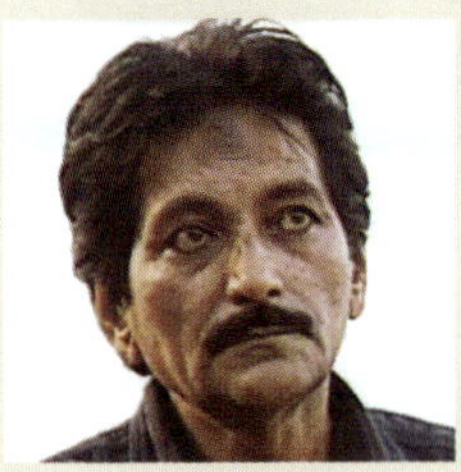

'Wherever Javed began to speak, he would make an instant impression. He was very intelligent. He never bought any books. He didn't need to because books came of their own accord to him and spoke to him. We used to stay together in Ibrahimpura. He was a caring, compassionate man. I loved him. Even today when he meets us, he asks about each one of us individually. And whenever he comes here, he calls all of us over. And we spend all our time together. Back in those days, he used to often say that when I come back here, I will come in a car.'

FATEHULLA

'We were together in all sorts of social activities. All our friends used to sit in front of the lakeside temple. Javed used to be a good mimic. I can't remember any debating competition in which Javed took part and did not win. He was the only one who was chosen from the Vikram University team for the youth festival. Today, when I see his success, I am not at all surprised. After all, as the saying goes, you can tell a lot about a baby from its earliest time in the cradle. And we had seen his talent and capabilities back then.'

EHSAN

'We were together in college. He was very interested in films. He was so used to rebelling against his surroundings. He would often recite film dialogues and poetry. We always thought that he would become somebody. He proved that it is not necessary that you should have all possible facilities if you want to become a big man, an important person. He was great at giving speeches. And he was always right when he said that the biggest thing is humanism.'

MANNAN

'We were together in college. He had come from Aligarh to Bhopal to study, whereas people would go to Aligarh to study. We used to say that perhaps he was way beyond the control of the people of Aligarh. There was a magnetic quality to his personality. We became friends very quickly. We were especially happy to have him in our midst because we had found a champion. We used to have a baitbazi competition in our college and normally we used to be defeated by the girls. But once Javed came, he had no equal in baitbazi. Often it would so happen that when someone from the opposing team was still reciting a sher, Javed would already produce a sher in reply. He was a master of mimicry. He would always say that he would join the film industry. The sort of poetry he is writing for films these days is a rare, difficult thing. That is his remarkable quality.'

Javed Akhtar sitting in the first row of this group photograph with his friend Mushtaq Singh (from left to right on the seventh and eighth chair)

The iron bangle of Mushtaq Singh

The room in the college is also gone. Now I stay with Mushtaq Singh. Mushtaq Singh has a job and he studies too. He is the head of the college Urdu Association. My Urdu is very good, but his is even better. I know countless sher by heart; he knows even more. I am away from my family; he has no family. See, he is better than me at everything. For the past year, he has been bearing the burden of keeping our friendship fed and dressed, that is, he feeds me and also gets my clothes stitched. He is a devout Sikh, but it is his responsibility to buy cigarettes for me.

Now I have begun to drink too sometimes. The two of us are sitting and drinking one night. He is telling me about the Partition and the riots of those days. He was very young then, but he remembers how two Muslim girls were pushed into a burning tar coal drum in Karol Bagh in Delhi and how a Muslim boy was... I interrupt him by saying, 'What do you want, Mushtaq Singh? For the past one hour, you have been telling me about all these incidents... Are you trying to turn me into a supporter of the Muslim League? The clap of cruelty was sounded with both hands. Now tell me an incident from the other side, too.' Mushtaq Singh laughs and says, 'All right, I will tell you, but shall I tell you what befell the world or what I experienced at first hand?' I reply, 'Tell me about what happened to you.' And he replies, 'I had eleven people in my family; ten of them were murdered in front of my eyes.'

I have been living in Mushtaq Singh's room for a year. I still don't understand one thing: 'Mushtaq Singh, why did those people leave you? Good people like you, no matter which caste or religion they might be born in, are always hung from the gallows. How did you escape?' He is in Glasgow these days. When the two of us were parting, I had taken his iron bangle to wear. I still have it on my wrist. Whenever I think of him, I feel he is in front of me, and he is saying:

Bahut nakamiyon par aap apni naaz karte hai
Abhi dekhi kahan hai aapne nakamiyan meri

(How proud you are of your failures
You have not yet seen my failures)

I would like to clarify certain important things at the very beginning. There is no secret in the fact that I am an atheist. My name is Javed Akhtar. I have no religious belief. I have no faith in spirituality either.

Heaven is hidden in the sweat of the labourer...

The first speech delivered at age sixteen, during a debating competition while still in school

Chairman sir and friends,

If religion could turn this world into a paradise, then why would Asia, the cradle of so many religions, have been such a hell for centuries? If religion can make this world a paradise, then why did it make a heaven far removed from this world? Surely the fact that religion created a heaven in the skies is the greatest proof that it cannot make a paradise in this world.

Any garden, where the flowers of unity, progress and peace have blossomed, has the right to be called a heaven. The hand of religion has brutally crushed every partly opened bud of peace. If the blood that has been shed in the name of religion were to be collected, then all the temples, mosques and churches of the world would surely drown in it. I am convinced that if Mahmud Ghaznavi did not have attractive words such as 'jihad' or 'idol-smashing', then perhaps his lust for wealth would not have destroyed a temple as beautiful as Somnath.

I am convinced that fourteen years ago, if religion had not gone to the head of Indians, making them mad with passion, then the waters of Ravi and Chenab would not reek of human blood. Those people who admit that Hitler was a tyrant and a murderer, I want to tell such people that an animal such as him had the blessings of the Pope. Those people who admit that the Nazi forces did their utmost to turn this word into a living hell, will today have to admit that this effort was made in the shade of the Holy Bible. Every religion says that the evil-doers and tyrants will be punished when the goblet of their sins has brimmed over. Mr Chairman sir, that is like a police constable saying he will keep watching a thief breaking a safe but he will only catch the thief after he has finished spending all the money he has stolen. Is handing over the key to your house to such a custodian not tantamount to having your house burgled?

And then, if one were to believe that religion can turn this world into heaven, the question arises: Which religion has the capability to bring about this noble deed? Is the person who says that the poor, the uncouth, the low caste, the animals are a low form of life worthy of being given this responsibility? Or those who say: Tell your women their voices should not go beyond the four walls of the house. That world would be

hell, not heaven, where half the population of the world would sob till it dies. That world would be hell, not heaven, where half the population of the world is treated worse than animals.

Will such a religion make this world a heaven that says pour molten lead into the ears of that untouchable who has, by mistake, heard the holy verses of the Vedas? Or the king in whose reign the kafir has only two options facing him: death or paying the *jaziya* tax? I ask you: Can such a society crafted by the hands of religion have the right to be called paradise when its doors are closed to kafirs, *malechhas* and untouchables?

I can say with complete confidence that religion can never create heaven on earth. And if it were to create something similar to paradise, then its boundaries will never be the same for all those who live on earth. In my eyes, at least, such a place has no right to call itself a paradise. Religion does not want, under any condition, a heaven on earth because the distance between earth and paradise is the only reason for the respect and greatness of heaven. People say that religion alone can make a heaven on earth whereas the truth is that religion is the only thing that has always stopped the world from turning into a heaven on earth. I remember, Socrates was handed the cup of poison by religion because he tried to teach the youth of his time to turn their world into a paradise. I remember, Jesus was hung on the cross by religion because he thought of turning every part of this world into paradise. I remember, Galileo was imprisoned because he attempted to give the people of the world

Letters sent to his address in Bhopal

The script of the speech written by Javed Akhtar for the debate competition, for which he was given the first prize

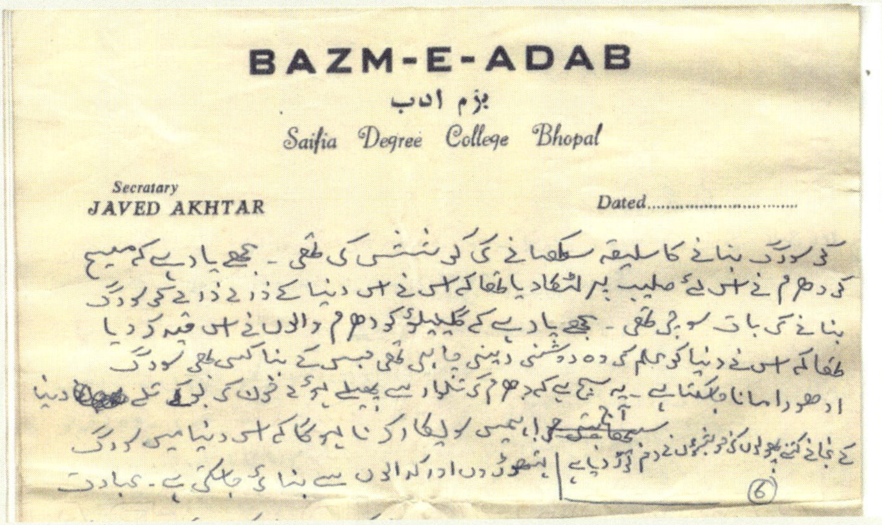
BAZM-E-ADAB

بزم ادب

Saifia Degree College Bhopal

Secratary
JAVED AKHTAR

Dated..............................

the light of knowledge without which any heaven can be considered incomplete. It is true that the fragrance of countless flowers has been smothered by the drops of blood splattered by the sword of religion. We will have to accept that heaven can be made from hammers and spades, not by worship and prostrations. We will have to accept that heaven is hidden in the sweat of the labourers, and not in the beads of the rosary and the *mala*.

We will have to admit that till the waves of religion rise in the Chenabs of the world, the Sohnis of this world will never be able to cross it. Till man loves the skies more than he loves the earth, the nymphs from heaven will not set foot on this earth. We will have to admit that it is not the books of religion but the hands of the untouchables, the kafirs and the malechhas that can turn this earth into heaven.

I am convinced that the forces that left Arabia for Syria and Spain had not gone there to create heaven. I am convinced that if religion had not gone to the head of Indians like a mad frenzy, then perhaps my country might not have been broken up into pieces, like a roti in the hands of two hungry people.

Who can refute the fact that the revolutions in Russia and France were an attempt to turn the dream of creating a heaven on earth into reality? The fact that the clergy were killed by the peasants and workers in both countries is proof that religion has become a wall in the process of creating a heaven on earth. Perhaps religion is fearful that if this world becomes a heaven, then the prices of its other-worldly religion might drop, tickets that its commanders sell with great zeal.

People say that religion can create a heaven on earth whereas the truth is that it is religion that has always stopped man from creating a heaven. It was proven thus: several years ago, when scientists had sent a dog named Laika in the spacecraft called Sputnik, resolutions were passed against the scientists in all the churches of Europe for perpetrating such an unspeakable cruelty on the dog. But where were these padres sleeping when thousands upon thousands of human beings were killed like dogs in the Hundred Years' War between Catholics and Protestants in this very Europe? After all, why were their feelings of compassion and humanity not wounded that day? Because under no circumstances does religion want the distance between heaven and earth to be reduced!

Man himself has tried to beckon heaven closer to him, but religion has turned itself into a sword and chopped off his hands. When man tried to raise his steps to move towards heaven, it was religion that wrapped itself around his feet like a chain.

Young students of Saifia College in Bhopal, taking selfies with perhaps the most celebrated alumnus of their college

Javed Akhtar sitting on the steps of the temple, beside the tank in Bhopal, where he used to spend many evenings with his friends

Javed Akhtar standing in front of Lyall Book Depot in Bhopal, from where he had bought his very first English novel: Inquilab, *by Khwaja Ahmad Abbas. Standing beside him is Vikas Rakheja, the owner of Lyall Book Depot*

Javed Akhtar standing in front of Bhopal Talkies, where Javed Akhtar had watched Nasir Husain's Jab Pyar Kisi Se Hota Hai *three times. Twelve years later, he co-scripted Nasir Husain's film* Yaadon ki Baaraat *(released in 1973).*

Part of Kamal Amrohi Studio, where Javed Akhtar used to sleep

For a year now, I have been living in Kamal Studio (which is now Natraj Studio). I sleep anywhere in the compound: sometimes in some verandah, sometimes under a tree, or on a bench or in a corridor. Several others, homeless and unemployed like me, live here like this.

The gate of Kohinoor Mills, Mumbai

As I pass by the gate of Kohinoor Mills, I think: Perhaps everything will change, but this gate will remain. One day, I shall go past this very gate in my car.

4 Oct 1964, Mumbai Central

It's been two years since I have been in Mumbai, but I have no roof over my head and no assurance of food

The city of Mumbai...

Characters: Film industry, friends, foes and I... I get off at the Mumbai Central Station on 4 October 1964. A verdict about my life is to be delivered in this courtroom. I have to leave my father's house six days after arriving in Mumbai. I have 27 paise in my pocket. I am happy that if one day I were to have 28 paise in my pocket, I would be in profit, and the world in loss.

It's been two years since I have been in Mumbai, but I have no roof over my head and no assurance of food, although I have written the dialogues for a small film at a salary of ₹100 a month. Sometimes I get work as an assistant somewhere. I get some small odd jobs somewhere, sometimes not even that. I have come to a producer's office in Dadar to ask for the money that is owed to me. He had asked me to write some comedy scenes for his film. The scenes will go under the name of the famous writer who is writing the film. The office is closed. I have to go back to Bandra which is quite far. I have just about enough money to either buy a bus ticket or eat something. But then I will have to go back on foot. I buy some parched gram and fill my pocket. Then I set off on my journey on foot. As I pass by the gate of Kohinoor Mills, I think, perhaps everything will change, but this gate will remain. One day, I shall go past this very gate in my car.

I have found work writing the dialogues of a film. I write some scenes and go to the director's house. He is sitting and eating pineapple for breakfast. He takes the scenes from me and reads them. Then he throws all the papers in my face. He throws me out of the film and says I can never, ever, become a writer. As I walk in the blistering sunlight, I wipe a tear from the corner of my eye and tell myself that one day I will show this director that I... Then, I don't know why, but the thought enters my mind: Does this director eat pineapple every day for breakfast?

◂ *Javed Akhtar in his early days in Mumbai*

Life, struggles and Jagdish

It must be two in the night. The monsoon in Mumbai, it looks like the sea is pouring down from the sky. I am sitting under the feeble light of a feeble bulb on the stairs in the portico of Khar station. Close beside me, three people are fast asleep, oblivious to the rain and the storm. In the far corner, a sopping wet dog is shivering with cold. It looks as though the rain will never ever let up. Torrential rain is coming down on the dark, empty streets for as far as the eye can see. The lights have long gone off in the silent buildings. People are sleeping in their homes. My father's house is also in this city. Mumbai is such a big city, and I am so small, so insignificant, as though I am nothing. No matter how much courage one has, sometimes one gets scared.

For a year now, I have been living in Kamal Studio (which is now Natraj Studio). I sleep anywhere in the compound: sometimes in some veranda, sometimes under a tree, or on a bench or in a corridor. Several others, homeless and unemployed like me, live here like this. Jagdish is one of them. I have become good friends with him. Every day, he comes up with a new strategy: how to find food, and where; who can get us a drink, and why. Jagdish has turned the act of how to stay alive in bad times into an art.

I have made the acquaintance of a man selling second-hand books on the footpath near Andheri station. And so I have no shortage of books. All night long, wherever there is a little light, I sit down and read. My friends tease me by saying that if I continue to read so much in such poor light, I will soon become blind... These days I have found the opportunity to sleep in a room. This room in the studio has tall cupboards lined against its four walls. Dozens of costumes from the film *Pakeezah* are kept in these cupboards. Meena Kumari is estranged from Kamal sahab; hence the shooting of *Pakeezah* is stalled these days. One day, I open one of the drawers in the cupboard; it is filled with old-fashioned shoes and slippers used in the film. Kept amongst them are Meena Kumari's three Filmfare awards. I dust them and keep them aside. This is the first time I have touched a film award. Every night I close the room from inside, I hold the trophy in my hands and stand in front of the mirror. I ask myself: When I get this trophy, how will I smile when I look at the people sitting in the hall that is resounding with applause, and how will I wave my hand at them? But before I can reach any decision, a notice is pasted on the board of the studio stating that all those people who do not work in the studio cannot stay in the compound.

◀ *Javed Akhtar during his days of struggle*

In the language of film people: 'Getting the right break'

When we are asked to leave Kamal Studio, Jagdish once again comes up with a new plan. Till we can make some other arrangement, we are going to live in the Mahakali Caves. (Mahakali is an area a little ahead of Andheri where there is dense habitation now and also the Kamalistan Studio. At that time, there was only a road, a jungle and several small hills where, centuries ago, Buddhist monks had carved out caves. The caves still exist, but in those days they were the haunt of *charas*- and *bhang*-consuming sadhus.) The mosquitoes in these caves are so big that they do not need to bite; even if they were to alight on your body, it is enough to wake you up. It took only one night to understand that no one could possibly sleep here unless one is high on charas. Somehow, I manage to spend three days. A friend in Bandra invites me to stay with him for a few days. I am going to Bandra. Jagdish tells me that in a few days he too will go somewhere (This was my last meeting with Jagdish. In the next few years, life took me places, but after eleven years, he died right here, in these caves, from drinking raw country liquor and consuming *charas*. The sadhus living in the caves and those from the nearby hutments collected donations for his last rites. And that was that. His other friends and I got the news of his death much later. I often wonder what is so special about me and what was wrong with Jagdish. It could well have been that three days after living in the caves, a friend of Jagdish's might have called him to Bandra and I might have stayed back in those caves. Sometimes, everything seems to be by chance. Why, then, do we pride ourselves, and on what?).

The friend with whom I have come to stay in one room in Bandra is a professional gambler. He and his two friends know how to fix cards. They teach me, too. For a few days, I get by on the basis of cards. Then these people leave Mumbai and I am back where I have been all this while. Who will pay the rent for this room next month? A famous and successful writer calls me and makes me an offer. If I were to write the dialogues for him (which would naturally carry his name, not mine), he would pay me ₹600 per month. I tell myself that these 600 rupees are equal to ₹6 crore for me at that time. I should do this job. Then I think: If I take up this job, I will never have the courage to leave it. I will keep doing it for the rest of my life. But then it occurs to me that I have to pay the next month's rent. I tell myself, I will see! After thinking about it for three days, I refuse the offer. Days, weeks, months, years pass. It's going to be five years since I have been in Mumbai. Roti is a moon; my circumstances are a cloud. Sometimes the moon is visible, sometimes it is hidden. These five years have been very heavy, but they have not been able to bow my head. I am not without hope. I am convinced that—something will happen, something will certainly happen. I was not born to die just like this. And finally, in November 1969, I get that work which, in the language of the film industry, can be called the 'right break'.

Littérateur Suryabhanu Gupt and Javed Akhtar

GUFTAGU

In conversation with Suryabhanu Gupt

Arvind Mandloi

I will prove to be the number one writer of this industry

Tell us, when did you first meet Javed sahab?

There's a suburb called Malad; I first met him there. There used to be a literary soirée there every month on a Sunday. I too used to go there. I must have been twenty or twenty-one years old. Many other poets used to come. Perhaps it was the year 1964 when Javed sahab also came to listen. Taj Bhopali sahab was with him. At the time, I used to only write nazms, not ghazals. People would listen to them and like them. What usually happened in these gatherings was that if people liked what a poet recited, only then would he be invited to recite in the second round. My turn usually came in the second round. Some poets didn't like that. But what could I do? Anyhow, Javed sahab kept coming for these soirées. So did Taj sahab. The latter used to live in the east; the programme used to take place in the west. He too was struggling, trying to find his feet. One day, sometime in the year 1965, I recited a nazm that Javed sahab liked very much. It was titled 'Suryast'. After the programme, he came to me and said, 'Have you written it yourself? Truly, have you written it?' I asked, 'Why? Why are you in doubt?' He said, 'No, seeing your health I am doubting it, because how can such a healthy person write such a nazm?' I answered, 'But I have written it!' He laughed and said, 'Can I get a copy of this?' I said, 'Yes, sure. I will give it to you in the next meeting.' And thus, this was our first meeting.

After some time, it so happened that I had to perforce come and stay at Kamal Studio. Kafeel Azar sahab was a poet who often came to the soirées. He said, 'Come over and stay at Kamal Studio with me, in my room; there will be no problem.' I did as he suggested. I found Javed sahab there as well. Now we met each other every day. One day he said to me, 'So, tell me Surybhanu sahab, what do you propose to do?' I said, 'I don't propose to live here; once peace is restored at home, I will go back.' Then I asked, 'And what will you do?' He said, 'I have to live and die here.' I said, 'There is no certainty here. You are a graduate; you can get a job anywhere.' He answered, 'Look here, I promise you that I will prove to be the number one writer of this industry.' This was at a time when he didn't know where his next meal was going to come from. One day, it so happened that he said to me, 'Suryabhanu, I have not eaten for two or three days. I don't have any money. So today, you get me something to eat.' I said, 'Yes, yes, of course. I am having my meals at the dhaba next door in Kafeel sahab's account.' To which he replied, 'In that case, I won't eat.' I replied, 'Arre you have been hungry for three days. I am going to return Kafeel sahab's money. I will go back from here and return all his money; I am not eating for free. You should eat; there is nothing wrong with it.' He said, 'No, yaar. Thank you very much.' I asked him repeatedly to eat, but he didn't agree. He kept saying, 'No.' Finally I asked, 'All right, then tell me what is the matter? Why won't you eat? What is the harm in eating? After all, I will repay him.' He replied, 'No yaar, I don't like that man.' And he didn't eat. A man who has been hungry for three days refuses to eat simply because the person paying for that food is someone he doesn't like. It was a huge thing for me to grasp. I said to myself: this man has a lot of character. Look at his values! Surely, he is from a good family.

After some time, I left that place. Eventually, I found a job. A man named Bihari gave out books on rent from a footpath in front of Moti Mahal in Andheri. That was Javed sahab's *adda*. He used to go there to get books. And I used to go there just like that, to indulge in some *addebazi*. Several other poets also came there. I would meet him there two or three times in a week. Sometimes, he would say, 'Come, let's go and have tea.' Tea used to be very inexpensive those days; it cost barely a rupee or two. Whenever I tried to make the payment, he would stop me. He would say, 'No, no, I have invited you; I will pay for the tea.' I would say, 'You give it, bhai. I have a job now; let me pay.' Javed sahab would say, 'No, no, the day I don't have any money, the day I am absolutely broke, you can pay then.' This too touched my heart. What sort of man was this? He was amazing! Even when he was dire straits, he would not let me pay. So, on days when he didn't have any money, he would say, 'Yaar, treat me to tea.' Or else he would always pay himself. And so the respect I had for him then, I still have in my heart. And he had the same respect for me. I have always received love from him, and the love I have for him, that has always been there. That man has truly struggled a great deal. No matter how many awards he gets from all over the world, they can never be enough. I have seldom seen such an honest man.

When did you meet him after his initial success? And how did this meeting come about?

I found his phone number from somewhere and so I spoke to him on the phone. Then one day, I went to his house. Afterwards, I had the opportunity to go there often because he used to hold a soirée every two or three months.

Dharamvir Bharti, Pushpa Bharti, Raj Bedi, Sharad Joshi, Padma Sachdev and her husband, Surendra Singh—all these people used to come here. For two or three hours, they would recite their poetry, talk and laugh, eat and drink, then go home. I used to meet him there and he would always leap up to greet me with the same honour, respect and love and embrace me. Even now when I meet him, he embraces me. There hasn't been any diminishing of the love I have always had for him in my heart. A lot of people are surprised. They look at me with amazement: Who is this man that Javed sahab is meeting with such warmth?

When did you come to know that Javed sahab has started writing poetry? That he is a poet now apart from being a scriptwriter?

Some of his poetry, and a brief introduction about him, were published in a page-and-a-half in the Hindi literary magazine, *Dharmyug*. When I read it for the first time, I was amazed, and also happy. When I met him I said, 'Yaar, when did you start writing poetry?' He said, 'Yaar, the thing is I knew I could write poetry anytime I wanted to.' So I asked, 'Why didn't you do it earlier?' He said, 'I wanted to secure a livelihood first.' His confidence was such that he knew he could write poetry whenever he wanted to. 'After all, I am the child of poets. Everyone in my family is a poet.'

Meeting Salim sahab and the decision to work together

I worked as a clapper boy for producer/director Kamal Amrohi at a monthly salary of ₹50. A short while later, I got a job with the director SM Sagar. I worked with him in 1966 on a film called *Sarhadi Lutera* in the capacity of an assistant director and clapper boy. He was making a stunt film with the actor Shaikh Mukhtar; Salim sahab had a romantic role in this film. SM Sagar was not able to find a dialogue writer; so I asked him if I could write a few scenes. And I wrote and showed him a few of the scenes. He liked the scenes and told me to write the dialogues. And so I became a dialogue writer apart from being the clapper boy. And that is when I met Salim sahab. Even then he could make up stories. We kept meeting each other even after SM Sagar's film was completed.

I was living in Andheri in 1963. Then I went to Bandra where I found a small place to live which happened to be close to Salim sahab's house. In the evenings, if I had nothing else to do, I would go over to his place. That is how our friendship deepened. We would sit together and create stories. At about this time, he sold the story of *Do Bhai to Brij* (Sadanah). The film featured Ashok Kumar, Jeetendra and Mala Sinha. The story of this film was Salim sahab's. The film didn't do too well, though it didn't really make any difference. I wrote the dialogues of a film called *Yaqeen*; that didn't do too well either. We didn't get any help at all from these films as a writer. And so the two of us were jobless.

And see the game destiny had planned for us. Once again, we met the director/producer SM Sagar. He knew that Salim sahab and I could write. He said, 'I have a story. I will give you some money to turn this story into a screenplay.' We agreed. Salim sahab and I decided that we would work on this film together. And that is how we wrote the screenplay for *Adhikar*. Ashok Kumar and Nanda acted in this film. Our names were not mentioned anywhere in the credits of the film.

◂ *Salim and Javed, discussing a script*

Our belief was that commercial cinema too can be sensible

Salim Khan

We met when we were both struggling. We had come from the same state: Madhya Pradesh; he from Bhopal, I from Indore. Javed used to live with some friend when he began to come to my house in Mumbai; perhaps he was a paying guest. I could see that he had talent, talent that should come to the fore. Though his ambition then was to become a director, I felt he would be a better writer. I was writing a script at that time. He began to help me. I then thought why should I take help; why shouldn't the two of us work as partners? And we began to work as partners. Our team was a natural one.

Actually, our first film was *Adhikar*, but we didn't get billing for it. The producer of this film had a story and he couldn't find anyone to write the screenplay. When he came to meet me, as fate would have it (and I very strongly believe in fate or destiny), Javed happened to be sitting with me. The producer even fixed a certain remuneration. As a matter of fact, Javed left the entire matter to me. I said we will share the money equally. After this, we joined Ramesh Sippy's story department. He was making *Andaz*. We worked in *Andaz*, for which we got billing. We were billed separately: as Salim Khan and Javed Akhtar. After this, for *Haathi Mere Saathi*, we were billed as Salim–Javed.

A lot of people thought we were similar people, but the truth is that we are totally different. For instance, I trust people whereas he is sceptical about them. He is very argumentative and logical. At a personal level, I can be convinced about any emotion. My life so far had been very different from his.

Here, I am only remembering the good days associated with him. We contributed to the making of some landmark films produced in our country, films that were good and successful. Our belief was that commercial cinema, too, can be sensible. And characters can be very close to life. Our first film that flopped was our tenth film together. We had given nine consecutive superhits.

Javed had the talent for writing lyrics and poems. He is a good lyrics writer. I like the song he wrote for the film *Saath Saath*. Sometimes, I play that song too. If you observe the tune and the lyrics, you will find that it is a complete song.

GUFTAGU

In conversation with Javed Akhtar

Arvind Mandloi

If you were to talk about the people who have contributed to my film career, I will take Salim sahab's name from number one to three

Who are the two or three people who have left the greatest impact on your life?

I will say, first of all my family. By family I mean my entire family: my parents, aunts and uncles, all of them have had an impact on my life, so the ideas that formed were a result of that upbringing and that atmosphere. They had the greatest influence on me. I had a friend named Khusro sahab; he was a jagirdar from Gwalior. I believe he had a great impact on my thinking, on my personality, my likes and dislikes. But if you were to talk about the contribution to my film career, I will take Salim sahab's name from number one to three. There can be no fourth person. And that is because I learnt a great deal from Salim sahab about life. And not just because we were partners for eleven years, we worked together in films for eleven years, wrote the scripts for eighteen or nineteen films together, but also because I learnt a great deal from him as a person. To have faith in oneself and to never give up courage in the worst of times; perhaps these were qualities I had from before because I had seen enough bad days. But I must applaud the courage Salim sahab has. The way we worked, the terms and conditions we set, the way our self-respect increased, the awards we won, the way we got people to recognise our name and our worth—all this is because of Salim sahab.

◂ *Javed Akhtar and Salim Khan on the occasion of the launch of the 3D version of* Sholay

The greatness of screenplay

Haathi Mere Saathi was the most successful film of 1971. It was included among Rajesh Khanna's successful films. It was produced by Chinappa Thewar and the story was also by Thewar. This film was the first partnership of Salim–Javed for which they were given due credit as screenplay writers. The film's subject and the treatment of its screenplay by Salim–Javed made *Haathi Mere Saathi* a huge hit with children. The film's heroine, Tanuja, remembers how her daughters held her (the character essayed by her) responsible for the death of Ramu the elephant, and for weeks they did not speak with her.

FILM *Haathi Mere Saathi*

DIRECTOR *MA Thirumugam*

1971

A change in the characterisation of women

S*eeta Aur Geeta* enjoyed an astonishing success at the box office. It was the highest grossing film for 1972. After this film, Hema Malini became the number one heroine of the film industry. *Seeta Aur Geeta* created yet another bit of history because it changed the way women characters were conceptualised and characterised in the film industry. There was no difficulty now for film producers and directors to present women in these new roles on the silver screen because it had become a fashion for women to perform action scenes. The film was made in other languages too, which included the Telugu film *Ganga Manga* (1973) and the Tamil film *Vani Rani* (1974).

FILM *Seeta Aur Geeta*

DIRECTOR *Ramesh Sippy*

1972

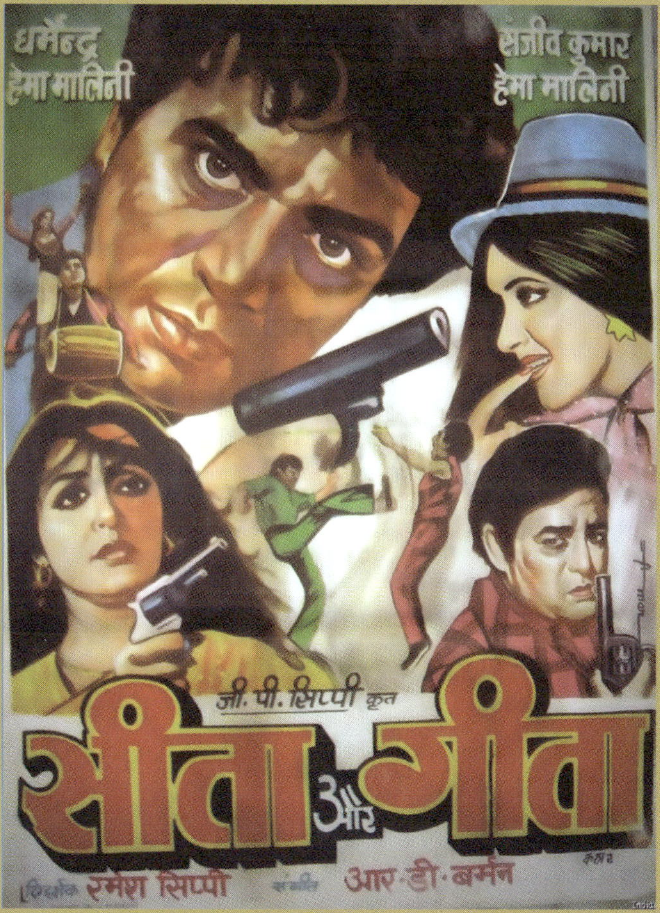

I met Honey Irani on the sets of *Seeta Aur Geeta*

Success is like Aladdin's lamp. Suddenly, I look around me and find that the world is a beautiful place and that people are kind and generous. I have found a great deal in a year, year and a half. And there is much that is waiting to come my way. I touch dirt and it turns to gold and I can see my first house, my first car. The days of my wishes coming true have arrived. But there is still a loneliness in my life. I meet Honey Irani on the set of *Seeta Aur Geeta*. She is an extremely cheerful girl with an open heart; she believes in calling a spade a spade. We are married four months after meeting each other. I have called several of my father's friends to my wedding, but not my father (some wounds cannot be healed by the jinn in Aladdin's lamp; only Time can do this job). Within two years, a daughter and a son are born to us, Zoya and Farhan.

The next six years bring twelve back-to-back superhit films, awards, praise, photographs and interviews in newspapers and magazines, money, parties, travel around the world, glittering days, glimmering nights—life is a technicolour dream, but like all dreams, this too breaks the first time our film is unsuccessful (later, other films will be flops and successes, but the happiness of success and the innocence of that happiness began to leach out). Gradually, a lot is changing inside me. Honey and I separate in 1983.

My marriage to Honey did indeed break, but even divorce could not destroy our friendship. And if there is no bitterness in our children over the separation of their parents, I deserve very little credit and Honey deserves much more praise. Today, Honey is a very successful film writer and a very dear friend of mine. Honey is one of the few people in this world for whom I have a great deal of respect in my heart.

◂ *Javed Akhtar, Honey Irani, Zoya and Farhan*

Javed Akhtar and Honey Irani on the sets of Seeta Aur Geeta

GUFTAGU

In conversation with Javed Akhtar and Honey Irani

Arvind Mandloi

Had I been a sensible person, one given to thinking coolly, one who could see things without letting bitterness creep in, perhaps this marriage might not have broken

Why did your first marriage not become a complete picture, what was the reason behind this?

It seems to me that we were both very young when we got married. Also, I had just begun to get good work. I had had a very topsy-turvy life so far with a great deal of bitterness. I had known many failures and my heart had been broken several times over. I don't think I was a very normal person. It took me some time to gradually remove all the enormous hurt, bitterness, the many storms and turbulence that had been brewing inside me. While on the one hand, all these things came in handy in my writing, they certainly created a lot of chaos in my personal life. When I turn back to look at this phase of my life, in all honesty I have to say, had I been a sensible person, one given to thinking coolly, one who could look at things without letting bitterness creep in, perhaps this marriage might not have broken. Honey was very young and inexperienced, and I was also not just young and inexperienced, but also quite mad, almost crazy. So naturally things went awry. But the good thing is that somewhere along the way, we both realised this, and respect and admiration for each other grew in our hearts, and today Honey and I are very good friends. I would give Honey more credit for this than myself because she never let any bitterness seep into our children. No matter how much decency and civility we may have displayed when we got separated, which indeed we did, undoubtedly there is some hurt, some bitterness in the act of separation. We were always mindful of the fact that any decision we would take regarding the children would be a joint one. It shouldn't be

Some people are meant to be very good friends; we make them husband or wife

that the father is saying one thing and the mother is saying something else. I would like to think we behaved very sensibly in this matter. But had we had the good sense before our divorce that we displayed afterwards, perhaps we would not have got divorced. But anyhow, this was meant to happen. After all these years, I can say with all earnestness that Honey is among the few truly good people that I have ever met.

Where and when did you first meet Javed sahab?

I think I met Javed sahab for the first time in 1971 or perhaps 1970. I was called to the office of Ramesh Sippy for the film *Seeta Aur Geeta*. That is where I met Javed sahab. He was there to narrate the story to me. I was told that Salim sahab was writing this film, so I thought Javed sahab must be his assistant. Salim sahab was not there at the time. Javed sahab said to me, 'I saw you in *Kati Patang* and I thought you can do this role quite well.' On the set I discovered that he is a writer, that the two work together and that he is not an assistant. But what I liked most about him was his knowledge and his sense of humour. Even today, I like such people. There was a great dignity about him. It was remarkable because we had worked with writers in our time who had no say in anything. In our time, writers were summoned, told to narrate their story and sent on their way. So, it was truly a pleasure to see the way Salim–Javed commanded dignity. And for this, I had a great deal of respect for him in my heart.

How did your romance begin?

Javed sahab used to come to the set every day and discuss the scene; this continued for some time. In fact, Ramesh Sippy even remarked, 'Bhai, you come to the set every day; what's the matter? Ordinarily, you seldom come, and that too, it's when we send for you. You come here every day to narrate the scene to her.... after all, I tell her about the scene and she comes fully prepared. I believe something is brewing between you two; the hair dresser had heard something.' Well, I liked him. Of course, I liked him. He told me he had seen me for the first time in the Gazebo restaurant and decided there and then: 'I have to meet this girl. And look at the coincidence, here we are!'

When the two of you decided to get married, I believe your mother said that the marriage would barely last a while.

She had said, 'He has nothing. He doesn't have a home. He doesn't have work. How will he support you? What will he do? This marriage won't last.' But I was eighteen years old and there wasn't much she could do. Then my mummy said, 'Okay, let her get married; she will come back. There's nothing to worry about.'

So how were those early days of struggle?

I wouldn't call it any great struggle because at that time, my elder sister, who was married to Kamran bhai, whose children are Farah and Sajid, supported us a great deal. Kamran bhai had a spare flat that he didn't use. He told us that we could stay there till we found a house of our own. So we moved into that house; it was a small one-bedroom flat, but it was enough for a newly married couple. We knew we had a budget within which we had to work. Javed sahab had told me that for at least the next two years we wouldn't have a servant. When the romance is new, everything is rosy. Javed was very helpful. Then his film *Zanjeer* became a huge hit, then *Seeta Aur Geeta*, and *Haathi Mere Saathi*. Things began to improve.

Javed sahab's own life had been a different kind of struggle. Not having a mother, not having the support of a father, not being able to get along with his stepmother and the vagabond life that he lived in the early years of his life.

So what was it that drew you away from Javed sahab?

For one thing, Javed sahab used to drink a great deal at that time. If he began drinking in the evening, he would drink right up till the morning. These things began to bother me. People would come to our home, sit till the morning, drinking and talking. That's how things began to go awry. When I objected, he would go out and drink; that would increase my tension. He was fond of driving. He had several accidents. All of these things combined to create stress. And he wouldn't listen. We used to have a lot of parties in our home, and I too used to enjoy them. But health-wise, risk-wise several things were wrong. Also, when you are climbing the ladder of success and you have reached the top, there are many people around you who egg you on and use you for their own ends. As a result, you lose your way and you are consumed by your ego. All this causes misunderstanding. I will not say that all of it was Javed sahab's fault. I must have been in the wrong as well. I was also young. So, taken together, all of these reasons combined to create a distance between us.

In a conversation, Javed sahab has said that had he displayed the same good sense before your divorce that you both displayed afterwards, perhaps your marriage would not have ended. What is the reason that the marriage did not last but the friendship has?

I can say with complete certainty that we were not compatible. I had nothing whatsoever in common with the sort of background he came from. That poetry, those poets, those people, those writers—I had never seen such people. And so, all of this was new for me, and I could not adjust to it. Perhaps I didn't have the maturity that was needed for it. I now feel we would have been better off as friends rather than as a married couple.

When marriages break, there is naturally some bitterness. How did you eventually deal with it?

All I know is that no matter what might have happened between us, for whatever reason, we never discussed it. What is past, is past. But I will admit that Javed is a very good man. At that time, I had a lot of anger, even hatred, or whatever. But in the midst of it all, I knew one thing: if tomorrow, God forbid, I have a problem, this man will be standing beside me. And I think he had the same belief: that tomorrow if something bad happens to me, Honey will be standing beside me. Some people are meant to be very good friends; we make them husband or wife and that's where the problems start. Had we stayed just friends, we would have been perfect.

When the two of you decided that the children would remain with you, what was Javed sahab's role in their upbringing? And how did the children make themselves mature enough to accept your decision?

First of all, when the two of us decided that we would separate, I told both the children that the way you people fight with your friends, it is the same with parents. The problem is between Papa and me; it has nothing whatsoever to do with the two of you. The other thing is that he gave us the house. Monthly payments would arrive. So we never really faced any problem. My sister, who was by now divorced from Kamran bhai, also came to live with me with her children, and there was great bonding between all of us.

You began script writing after your separation; was Javed sahab in any way the reason behind it?

Javed sahab did encourage me. When I got married, I used to write short stories, but I never showed them to anyone, not even to Javed because my handwriting was terrible, my spellings were bad, my grammar was wrong. I used to write secretly. One day, he came across my copybook. He said, 'Yaar, this is a good story. You write well; you should write more.' But the moment passed. After the divorce, I began writing again, but I was wondering who I could show it to. I was worried that people would think it must be one of Javed sahab's scripts left lying around that I was trying to sell. I mentioned it to Pam Chopra, who is Yash Chopra's wife. She is a very dear friend of mine. She heard me and said that I was writing very well. And that is how I began script writing.

You have known Javed sahab for a long time. What changes have you seen in him? Is there any deficiency or lack that had he repaired it, it would have been better and perhaps your marriage might not have ended?

The biggest change I find is that he stopped drinking. Once he stopped that, good things began to happen to him. That was the only negative thing about him. Drinking gave him a split personality, a sort of Jekyll and Hyde. Now that problem is gone, he is more at peace. And for this too, you must give him credit because it is not easy for an alcoholic to give up drinking. He decided on his own one day, 'I will not drink,' and from then on, he didn't! It's a remarkable thing. In any case, there is no point in talking about old things. I have no regrets. It is enough that the respect we have for each other should remain in our heart.

Javed Akhtar with Honey Irani

'Sher Khan ne shaadi nahi ki toh kya hua,
baaraatein bahut dekhi hai.'

PRAN IN THE ROLE OF SHER KHAN

FILM *Zanjeer*
DIRECTOR *Prakash Mehra*
1973

Our name on the film poster

The films *Andaz*, *Haathi Mere Saathi* and *Seeta Aur Geeta* were hits. Our fourth film was *Zanjeer* when we said, 'Bhai, our names should be on the poster too!' We were told: Look here, that's not how it works. No one puts the writers' names on the poster. This was the time when films were not released at the same time all over the country. Till the 70s, films were first released in the big cities, later in the smaller ones and later still, in the even smaller ones. So when Zanjeer was released in Mumbai, we took two jeeps on rent, seated three or four people in them, gave them ladders and paint and told them to go all over the city and wherever they saw the film's posters, they should write 'Written by Salim–Javed' on whatever space they could find on the poster. All night long those jeeps went around the city and it was written on every poster. Afterwards, the film industry decided: Okay, let us give them their name.

The character of the Angry Young Man was inspired by Birju from *Mother India*

The films that made an impact on me in my childhood included *Shri 420*, *Munim Ji*, *Do Bigha Zamin* and *Jagriti*. But the films that influenced me in my teenage years were *Pyasa* and *Mother India*. They left a deep impression on me. I liked *Mother India* very much. What I liked in *Mother India* was the rebel character of Birju who raises his voice against injustice. He stands up against the village moneylender who is sucking everyone dry. That is the reason why I really liked that rebel character. Years later, when I began to write films myself, that character of Birju whom I had liked, was the angry young man of his day, the one you could see in my films.

PRAKASH MEHRA P
"ZANJEER"
SC. NO.
MUHUR
20-6-72

Amitabh Bachchan in the opening shot of Zanjeer

Javed Akhtar with film actress Nargis, Nimmi and writer Salma Siddiqui

'Jadu Miyan' with his intelligent eyes

Pushpa Bharati

Perhaps it was the year 1975 or 1976 when another member was added to our clan. It so happened that one vital person in our extended family, Munir (whom everyone called Bilu), the son of Krishan Chander and Salma Siddiqui, was engaged to be married. One day, we had all gathered in Krishan ji's house in connection with making preparations for the wedding when a little while later, three young men came. They too joined our group. We were told that they were Bilu's friends. My attention was constantly drawn towards one of the three young men. Long, carelessly kept hair, casually worn clothes, he was slim-built. The other young men were sitting very decorously and listening respectfully to the others. But this youth with sharp, intelligent eyes, would interrupt and say something suddenly that would make everyone smile. Even his way of talking was very different from that of the others. Some of the greatest editors, writers, poets and novelists of the age were present in that gathering. Suddenly, the youth got up and went into one of the inner rooms. He came out holding a dholak and exclaimed, 'Bhai, it's our friend's wedding; there should be some music and singing!'

Three people dragged Bilu and they all sat down on the carpet and began to play the dholak. Many folk songs and ditties began to be sung to tease Bilu, and when the youth with those bright, gleaming eyes began to sing *'Sarota kahan bhool aayin pyari nanaduiyan'*, such nectar seemed to flow from his voice that all the famous people came and sat on the ground and began to sing along with him like practised musicians. They sang and danced till evening turned into midnight without anyone noticing it. In those few hours, all the people became his admirers. It was only later that we came to know that this gentleman was Javed Akhtar, the writer of a dozen hit films. We also came to know that he is the descendent of a family on which Mother Saraswati has bestowed her benevolence generation after generation.

Birds of the same feather flock together. It was only natural that he soon became a much-loved member of our clan, forever! And that too such a valued member that whenever the rest of us met, phones calls would immediately be made to ascertain his whereabouts. His boundless liveliness, his hilarious repartee, his sparkling banter would accompany our vivacious conversations and uproarious laughter. One of Javed's oft-repeated statements was repeated ad nauseam amongst us: 'This is the limit of too much!' One of us would say it and all the others would burst out laughing. After all, what was the limit of too much? And there were many such sentences that Javed loved to toss about. And not just sentences and anecdotes... once he truly went overboard. He had just returned from America and this time our clan's meeting was at his home. In America, he had seen a film that was banned. And he had seen it in a very surreptitious manner. The film was based on the atrocities of the Nazis. First, he kept telling us about incidents from the film and, when dinner was served, he went towards the kitchen saying that the special dish that had been prepared for the meal was not on the table.

Food was being served when suddenly the lights went out in the entire house. Candles were being located when, suddenly, some strange, scary noises were heard and we saw a black, ghostly figure standing before us. Its body was covered with black hair, there were long sharp nails on its fingers and it had large terrifying eyes, which were visible. Sometimes, its yellow teeth could also be seen when it emitted strange sounds. The cook, the bearer, the maid, everyone was called: 'Arre bhai, throw him out!'

We used to call Javed by his pet name, Jadu. Salma ji was so terrified that she crept under the dining table and began to mumble something softly. I was convinced she was reciting something like the Hanuman Chalisa. Everyone became quiet. An immense silence descended upon us. Suddenly, I shouted, 'Jaduuuu!' In the blink of an eye, a voice called out, 'Yes, Pushpa ji!' and Honey blurted out, 'Heck!' Mr Ghost's identity was revealed.

Mr Javed had gone to America during Halloween, a festival in which men, women, the young and the old... everyone dons comic or scary costumes and strolls about in malls and on roads. Our friend had bought this costume from there. After much ado, Salma ji was finally pulled out from under the table. She could scarcely believe that it was our 'Jadu miyan' and not a ghost.

Amitabh Bachchan with Javed Akhtar

We have been close friends and we have shared many moments together

Amitabh Bachchan

His conversations are not about things he has heard or the everyday or the commonplace worldly things; they are always about something unique and different

Javed sahab is the finest mind in the Indian film industry. He is a very creative writer. Without doubt, *Deewaar* has one of the best screenplays in Hindi commercial cinema, and this is not merely my opinion because I was a part of this film; everyone in the industry would agree. At the time, a journalist had asked me, 'You are doing so many films with Salim–Javed, but what if they fail?' I had said, 'If Salim–Javed fail, Amitabh Bachchan too, will fail.'

I believe that Javed sahab's creativity, his intelligence and thinking always fills one with passion. He reads a great deal. There have been many occasions when we have stayed away from professional matters and for hours and days, only talked about a range of issues. He can talk on just about any topic in the world. His conversations are not about things he has heard or the everyday or commonplace worldly things; they are always about something unique and different. He always presents them in such an inimitable manner that you will be surprised and you will say: Why didn't I think of it like this?

I don't think I have ever seen him angry. But I have been the recipient of several of his creations which are filled with anger and rage. He has shown anger in his writing. I have derived much pleasure in understanding that anger and his writing has made my work very easy. The anger that is present in the script is not my anger; it is his pain. I have only been a mere 'tool' for those emotions. Javed sahab has always been innovative and versatile in the work he has done for me, the actor. He has always tried to do something different.

We have been close friends and we have spent a lot of time together... both professionally and personally. Our fathers were poets. I didn't have the pleasure of meeting his father, but he met mine on many occasions. We have spent many evenings reciting and discussing poetry. Initially, he was a little hesitant about sharing his poetry; he was almost apprehensive. He spent many evenings with my father, and my father was among those people who encouraged him to publish his poetry. I think this is how he began writing songs and lyrics, and today the entire world knows what a fine writer he is.

We met on the sets of *Anand*

Years ago, when I was introduced to Amitabh Bachchan on the sets of *Anand*, I saw for the first time those deep and grave eyes that can penetrate right into you. And heard that voice which, who knows why, reminds me of the depths of the blue oceans. Of the height of the Himalayas. Of dense clouds. That day, a song was being picturised—'*Kahiin duur jab din dhal jaaye...*' And indeed, the day was ending. So was an age, an era. An epoch was coming to a completion. The dreams that crores of people had dreamt after Independence, the hopes that Indians had cherished, had been shattered. There was sorrow in the hearts of many, as well as resentment, anger, annoyance. And when this resentment, anger, annoyance became a character, then a great actor such as Amitabh Bachchan came before us as the Angry Young Man.

'Mere Paas Maa Hai'

SHASHI KAPOOR AS RAVI IN *DEEWAR*

FILM *Deewar*
DIRECTOR *Yash Chopra*
1975

Javed Akhtar with Amitabh Bachchan

GUFTAGU

In conversation with Javed Akhtar

I will say that Amitabh Bachchan's performance is superlative in three or four films; Mili *is one of those films*

You consider Amitabh Bachchan a great genius in cinema. Why is that?

Yes, that's true. I am a fan of several actors such as Dilip Kumar and Guru Dutt. The films that were made by Mahboob sahab, Bimal Rai, and the films that Raj Kapoor made in the early years of his career, such as *Awara* and *Shri 420*, are not ordinary films. *Pyasa*, *Sahib, Bibi Aur Gulam* and *Mother India* are not ordinary films. Dilip Kumar's performance in *Ganga Jamna* is not ordinary. The work he has done in *Madhumati* is extraordinary. Anyone who has any appreciation for acting should see *Madhumati*, should watch every scene, see the work that Dilip Kumar has done. I am a great fan of Dilip Kumar's. As far as Amitabh Bachchan is considered, he is a man of exceptional talent... exceptional! You can become Amitabh Bachchan with all this talent, but you also need many other things. You need discipline, which Amitabh Bachchan has. You need focus along with this talent which, again, Amitabh Bachchan has. Moreover, you also need the discretion that Amitabh Bachchan has. He is not known to ever speak ill of anyone. When you come to this huge a position, with its immense power, if you still manage to keep such control over your tongue, it is no ordinary feat. In fact, it is a difficult task, a very difficult task. In fact, it should be noted that during his peak period, he was working with every group, even with those groups that were at war with each other. He would work with everyone; he was neither foes with anyone nor friends. India's superstar used to reach at 7 a.m. sharp for shooting when even the unit had not shown up. And he would be waiting outside in his car for the doors to the studio floor to be opened so he could enter. Our last film together was *Main Azad Hoon*. It has been many years now, but at that time it seemed as though it was our first film together. He works like this when he has a film at hand, as though he has got a 'break' and he has to prove what he is capable of doing! This focus, this passion, this energy... few people have it! It is very rare.

Which is Amitabh Bachchan's best film, one that has been written by you? In which film has he given his best performance?

I can't say which is the best because he is always the best! Whatever he has done, has been perfect. If a film has not done too well, it is possibly due to a deficiency in the script. We have worked together in thirteen or fourteen films. Writers are finicky people, you see. 'Sahab, look at what I wrote and see how he has spoken it. This word is not even there!' I have never had this complaint with Amitabh Bachchan.

Once we had a discussion over the dialogue '*Aaj khush to bahut hogey tum*' ... as to where to begin the scene, what pitch to begin with, which note to end it on. We talked about the scene and in the end, it was proved that he was right. He said, 'I will speak it like this and show it to you.' And as it turned out, the way he was speaking that dialogue was the right way to do it. So, I never had this complaint with Amitabh Bachchan: 'Arre, this is what I meant and this is what you have said! Or this timing is wrong. He has changed the meaning of this sentence on his own.' No! Flawless! Never a mistake! Perfect! In fact, sometimes he has said it in such a way that he has enhanced the effect of what I have written.

Let me tell you something else. Forget my films. There are several of Amitabh Bachchan's films where he has done extremely incredible work and yet those films are seldom talked about, such as *Mili*. The story of *Mili* revolves around the character played by Jaya ji who is no ordinary actress. She has also done incredible work in the film. Dadamoni Ashok Kumar, too, has done great work in this film. But I will say that Amitabh Bachchan's performance is superlative in three or four films; *Mili* is one of those films. And no one talks about the film when they talk about Amitabh Bachchan. Such incredible work.... *Wah*, *wah*, *wah*, *wah*, *wah*, *wah*! It has been years since *Mili* was made and I still remember the scene where he takes out his handkerchief from his pocket and angrily throws it on the sofa. It was a strange gesture. To take out your handkerchief and throw it on the sofa ... that's not something you plan. No actor is going to plan that I am going to take out my handkerchief at this moment and throw it on the sofa. It is not possible. That man is living that moment and that is why this happens in that moment. It was great work... very great work!

Gabbar kept creating his own vocabulary

In my entire career, among the many characters I have enjoyed creating is the character of Gabbar Singh, the reason being that Gabbar was crafting his own vocabulary. I clearly remember that when I was writing *Sholay*, I used to get very excited at the thought that when I have finished writing these two scenes and the scene comes which has Gabbar in it, let me see what he says?

'Kitne aadmi the?'

AMJAD KHAN IN THE ROLE OF GABBAR IN *SHOLAY*

FILM *Sholay*
DIRECTOR *Ramesh Sippy*
1975

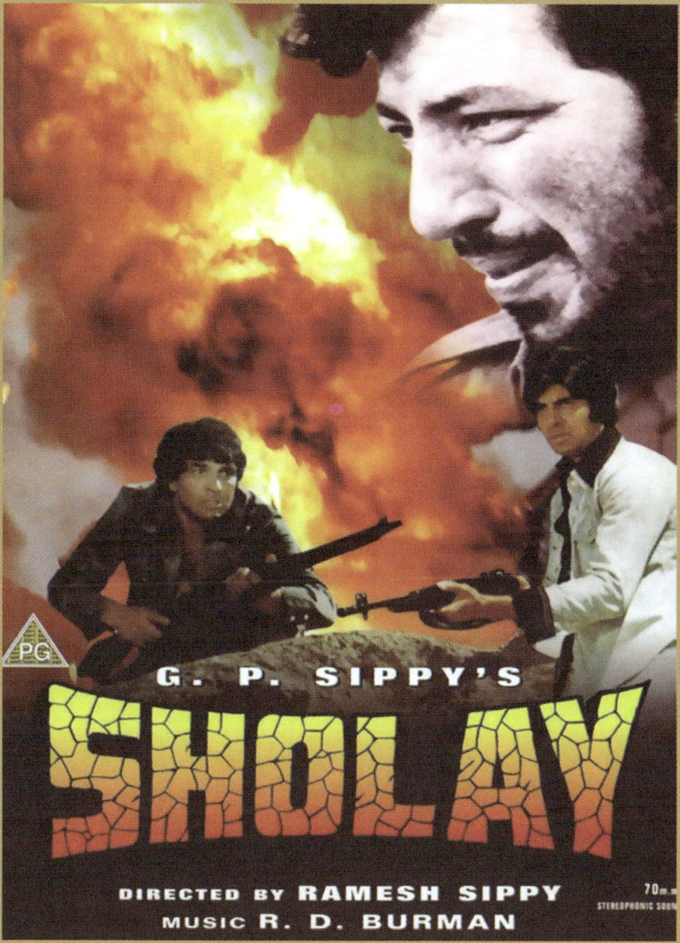

GUFTAGU

In conversation with Ramesh Sippy

Arvind Mandloi

We were about to start the writing department in December '69. Narendra Bedi, who used to work with us, told us that two boys were doing good work and he could call them if we wanted to meet them. Salim–Javed came to meet us. Javed sahab told us that they wanted to narrate a script to us. And he issued us a challenge of sorts: 'You won't be able to stop once I start narrating.' And indeed, once he began, it became a 'beginning to end' sort of telling. It is a different matter that the film was never made on the subject. Salim–Javed joined the department on a salary of ₹ 750 from January 1970. By then, *Andaz* was almost complete. We had made its script with Sachin Bhowmik and Gulzar sahab had been taken for the dialogues. Salim–Javed saw the rushes of *Andaz*. There was some contribution from them, too. Then we gave them the idea of making a film on the theme of *Ram Aur Shyam*, but with two girls. Javed sahab said that was indeed possible. And that is how, in fun and games, *Seeta Aur Geeta* also got made within a year. After this we started planning for *Sholay*.

Both made a great contribution as a team, but my sense is that Javed sahab had a greater role in working out the details of the dialogues. After our discussion on the story, characters, etc., sometimes Javed sahab used to come alone. He would ask, 'How is this? What do you think?' The subject of Gabbar came up, and I suggested some expressions. Javed sahab's individual contribution was immense. It is a little unfair for me to separate and view the work of Salim–Javed, but as I said earlier, the dialogue writing was certainly done by Javed sahab. But it isn't good to break things up after so many years. The contribution of each should be acknowledged. Javed sahab's single-handed contribution is unforgettable, in my life and in the lives of many other people too, including the life of Amitabh Bachchan. Javed sahab wrote everything—script, dialogues and lyrics—for my film *Sagar*.

Javed sahab's individual contribution was immense

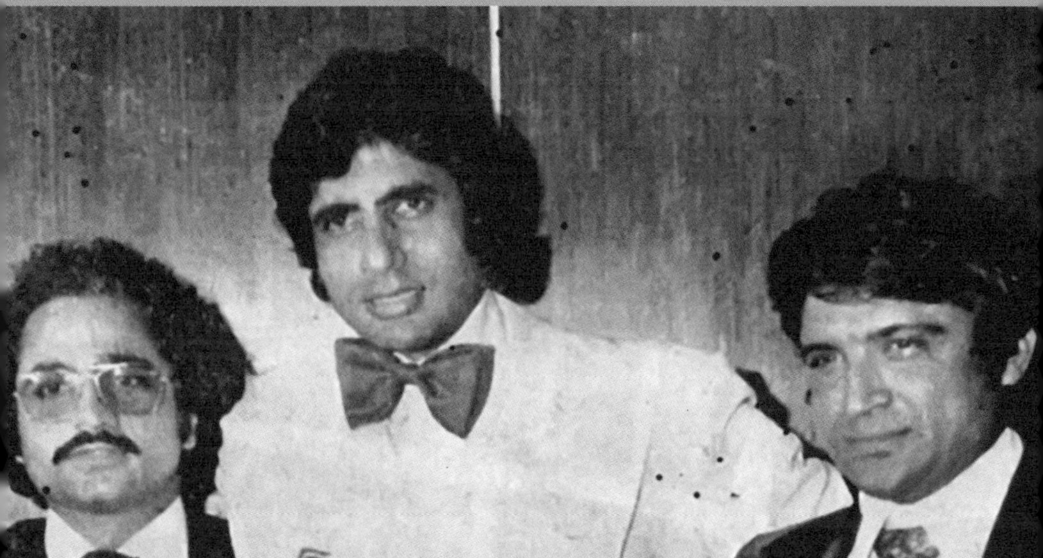

Javed Akhtar with Ramesh Sippy and Amitabh Bachchan

On the sets of Sholay*: Cameraman Dwarka Divecha, Dharmendra, director Ramesh Sippy, Sanjeev Kumar, Amitabh Bachchan and Amjad Khan*

There were two people who said, 'Give the role of Gabbar to me'

The film *Sholay* was definitely the magic of a team. Sometimes things fall into place perfectly. This was one of those films where a lot of things sat perfectly. For one, its screenplay was such that it had an enormous variety of characters. The basic story was Salim sahab's. It was one of his storylines which featured a retired army major whose hands had been blown away by a bomb, and there were two young men who had been expelled from the army due to indiscipline. But when the screenplay was developed, its scope kept expanding, especially the character of Gabbar. When the dialogue version of that character was narrated, two people said they wanted to play the role. One was Sanjeev Kumar and the other was Amitabh Bachchan. Ramesh Sippy's direction was flawless, of course, but the cameraman, Dwarka Divecha, whose name is seldom mentioned, had a huge contribution too.

Soorma Bhopali's character was inspired by Nihar Singh

There's an old anecdote... In California, there lived a mad sort of fellow who considered himself the king of the city, and the entire city helped him maintain this illusion. When he died, the people of the city took out his funeral as though he was indeed their king. One such *soorma* (braveheart) was Nihal Singh, and he enjoyed the same respect and honour in old Bhopal as one would accord a brave or valiant person, which he actually wasn't! Someone told him: 'Javed has based a character on you and is raking in money in Mumbai; you should file a case against him.' A lawyer was hired and the local Bhopal newspapers carried a photograph of Soorma Bhopali handing over legal documents to the lawyer. Obviously, all this was done in jest. While this was going on, the film *Deewaar* was released. Soorma Bhopali went to watch the film with his lawyer and other friends just to see if there was anything incriminating in this film too. There was no character based on Soorma Bhopali in this film, but he was hurt by Amitabh's dialogue: 'I have a bungalow, car, bank balance... what do you have?'. Piqued, he said, 'This is not Amitabh; this is Javed speaking to me.'

'Itna sannata kyun hai, bhai?'

AK HANGAL IN THE ROLE OF IMAM SAHAB

Sholay ran continuously for five years from 1975 to 1980

GP Sippy's film *Sholay* was released on 15 August 1975 in the 1500-seater Minerva Theatre in Mumbai's Grant Road. It ran continuously for the next five years from 1975 to 1980. Outside the theatre, on either side of the road, there would be long queues of people, and for two years the situation was such that unless you had made your bookings one week in advance, you could not get a ticket. Even today, *Sholay* is a splendid example of the success of commercial cinema in the Indian film industry. At the Plaza Theatre in Delhi, buses would ply to and from Punjab to bring viewers all the way, with 'Sholay Special' painted on them. In the year 2000, to mark the film's twenty-fifth anniversary, BBC India declared it to be the 'Film of the Millennium'.

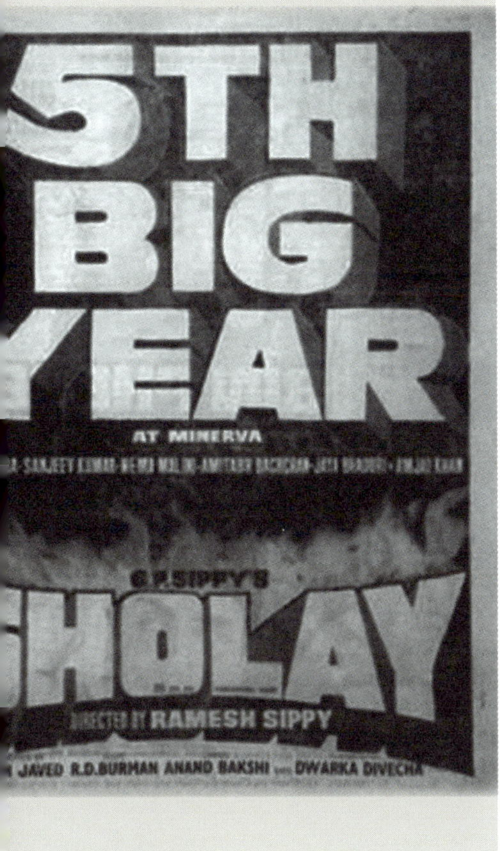
5TH
BIG
YEAR
AT MINERVA
G.P.SIPPY'S
SHOLAY
RAMESH SIPPY
JAVED R.D.BURMAN ANAND BAKSHI
DWARKA DIVECHA

MINERVA

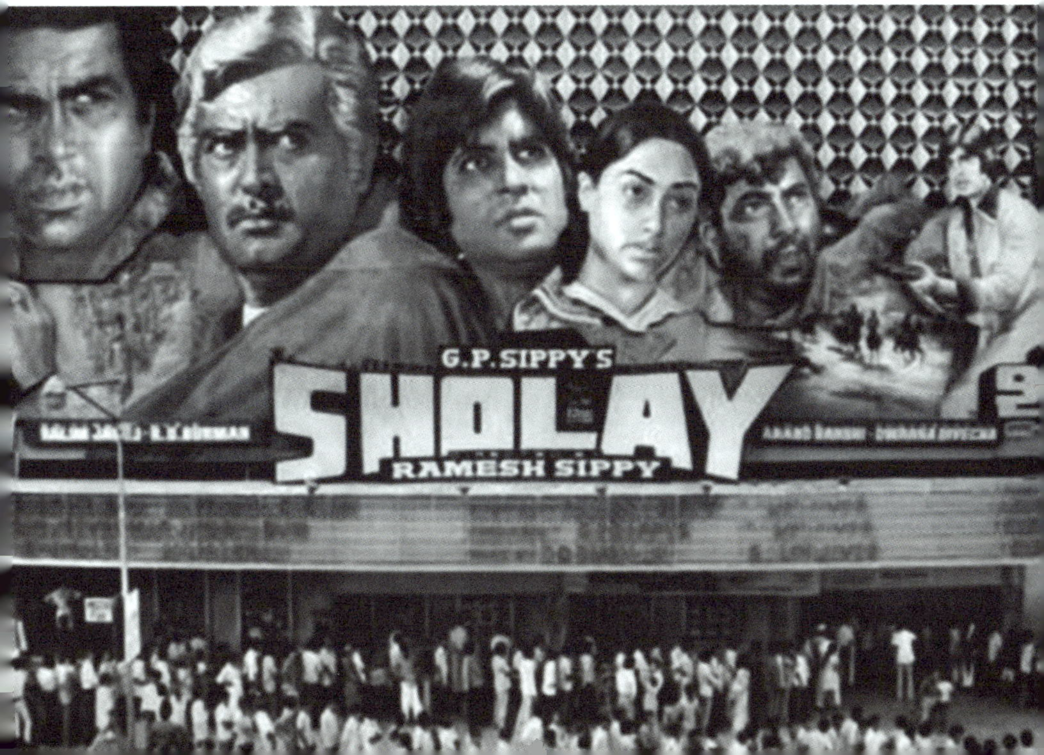
G.P.SIPPY'S
SHOLAY
RAMESH SIPPY

'Tumhara naam kya hai, Basanti?'

AMITABH BACHCHAN IN THE ROLE OF JAI

Considered the biggest blockbuster of Hindi cinema, when *Sholay* completed forty years, the BBC, through its Facebook page, asked viewers to list their favourite dialogues from the film. In this survey, the dialogue that was mentioned as being the favourite by the maximum number of viewers was the line, *'Tumhara naam kya hai, Basanti* (What is your name, Basanti)?' Amitabh Bachchan, who played the role of Jai in the film, had addressed this question to Hema Malini, who had essayed the role of Basanti.

A week after its release, film pundits and critics declared *Sholay* to be a flop. That is when Salim–Javed put in this advertisement in *The Trade Guide*. Such an advertisement had never appeared before, nor has one like this ever appeared again. This advertisement captivated the entire film industry.

The records and audio cassettes of *Sholay* witnessed an unprecedented sale with over 5,00,000 copies sold; this included cassettes of the film's most popular dialogues. *Sholay* was the first Indian film to gain a 'platinum disc', which used to be given those days when a record sold more than 3,00,000 copies. *Sholay* did a business of ₹ 10 crore in the music market, of which 50 per cent came from the sale of the film's dialogues. *Sholay* earned ₹35 crore in the first run itself, a record it maintained for the next nineteen years at the box office.

786
THIS IS A PREDICTION
BY
SALIM-JAVED
THEIR PERFECT DREAM
SHOLAY
EXACTLY AND BEAUTIFULLY CONVEYED TO THE
SCREEN BY THESE GREAT FILM MAKERS
Mr. G. P. SIPPY
Mr. RAMESH SIPPY
AND
THE UNIT
WILL BE A GROSSER OF
RUPEES ONE CRORE
IN EACH MAJOR TERRITORY OF INDIA

Polydor
MAXIMUM RETAIL PRICE Rs. 30/- ALL INCLUSIVE
ECONOMY SERIES
G.P. SIPPY'S
SHOLAY
RAMESH SIPPY
Music:
R. D. BURMAN
Lyrics:
ANAND BAKSHI
SHOLAY (SONGS)
ECO SERIES
MC-A
3227 011
STEREO
PKD 3/96
G.P. SIPPY'S
SHOLAY

GUFTAGU

In conversation with Javed Akhtar

Arvind Mandloi

It is necessary that you must possess a very large vocabulary, something that you gain from listening to and reading good writers.

Javed Sahab, we were talking about the language used by your characters, this simple language that came into films, that has today become a part of the popular idiom... For instance, when someone carries tales, people call that person a Hariram Nai. Or when you want to praise someone, you say that '*Ye lambi race ka ghora hai*'. So, this language that has come from films and entered society, tell us how this happened? How did you create this language? What was its process?

Look, I have read a great deal of fiction, both in Urdu and in English. When you read a lot of fiction, especially when you read good writers, your vocabulary increases. Regardless of whether you are a songwriter or a dialogue writer, it is not necessary to be a great writer. If you are a great writer, it is wonderful. What is most important is that the vocabulary that you have at your command should be a vast one and that you must know how to write in every tone and tenor, every shade and colour. For example, if you have a character like Gabbar, how will he speak? I want to speak about Gabbar here because I feel we got a new language thanks to Gabbar. Gabbar's style of speaking, his slang and idiom, his behaviour, his language itself were entirely new and different. That can only come from listening to and reading good writers. With time, your ears become attuned; the moment you read or hear a good word or a new expression, the moment it enters your ear, it reaches your memory and it comes handy when you need it. So, I believe that I am very indebted to those writers whom I read for years. If you want a good Hindustani vocabulary, you can get it only if you read a great deal of Urdu–Hindi literature.

The secret of a film's success

The film *Trishul* depicted certain things that had never been shown before. Today when we talk about that film, those things might appear very insignificant. But anything that has not been tried and tested before appears dangerous and perilous to an Indian film-maker. The hero of *Trishul* was, in the truest sense, the first illegitimate child in Hindi cinema. His parents were Sanjeev Kumar and Waheeda Rehman. Let alone the world's eyes, even in the eyes of God they were not shown going to a temple and exchanging garlands to prove themselves a married couple. Also, they don't sleep together just because it is raining outside! In fact, they have a mature physical relationship and this has been shown very clearly in the film. The hero's mother becomes pregnant. Such a thing has not been shown in Hindi films ever before. Years later, it is the hero's mission to destroy his own father. This too, has never been seen before. When *Trishul* was released, S. Mukherji had said to me, 'I watched this film three times to understand the reason for its success. But let me tell you that had you come to me with this script, I would not have taken it.'

'Zindagi mein kuch baatein fayde aur nuqsaan se upar hoti hai.'

AMITABH BACHCHAN IN THE ROLE OF VIJAY KUMAR

FILM *Trishul*
DIRECTOR *Yash Chopra*
1978

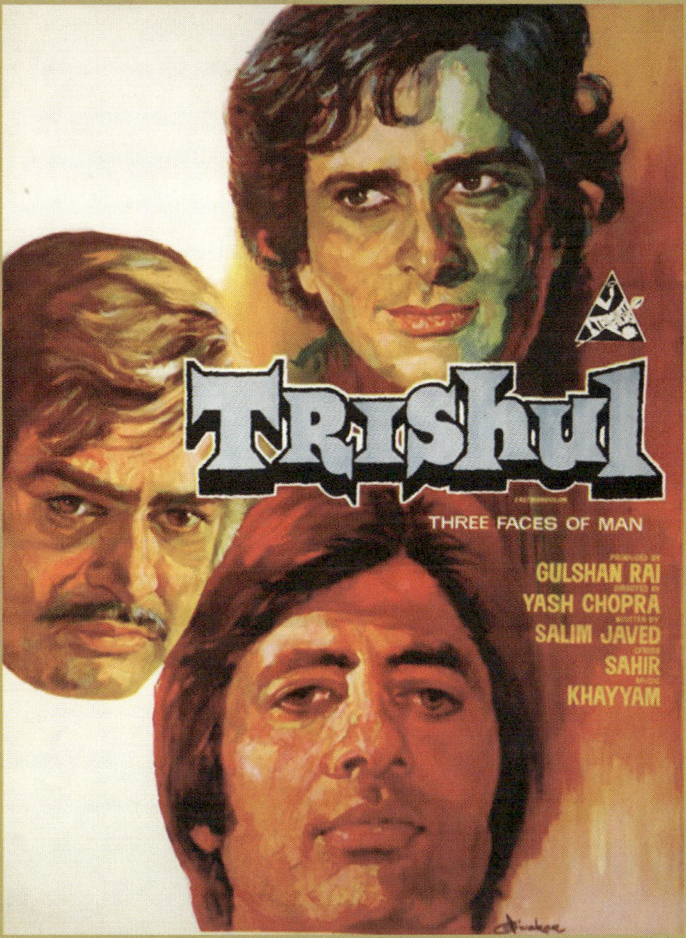

The genre of urban crime thrillers gets a new identity

By 1970, the making of films on the theme of crime had reached its peak. In the years ahead, the film *Don* helped this genre scale new heights. Made as an urban crime thriller, this film went on to create its own unique place. Film historians agree that before *Don*, crime had never been presented in such a sleek and sophisticated way. The screenplay of *Don* proved to be so successful that it gave birth to a *Don* franchise. Javed Akhtar's son, Farhan Akhtar, made a remake of this film under the name *Don: The Chase Begins Again* (2006), followed by its sequel *Don 2* (2011). Keeping Salim–Javed's basic plot intact, he co-wrote the screenplay with his father Javed Akhtar.

'Don ko pakadna mushkil hi nahin,
naa-mumkin hain'

AMITABH BACHCHAN IN THE ROLE OF DON

FILM *Don*
DIRECTOR *Chandra Barot*
1978

GUFTAGU

In conversation with Javed Akhtar

Arvind Mandloi

Was there any special reason why your professional partnership with Salim sahab ended? Was there any point at which it was decided that the two of you would not work together anymore?

Look, first of all, I wouldn't call the relationship that I had with Salim sahab a professional one. It is a different matter that we were writing films together, our names would come together. But this was happening because there was a bond of love, of belonging, of trust... a deep bond, a very deep bond. I would say that for a long time Salim sahab was a father figure in my life. Salim sahab's wife, Salma, whom I call Bhabhi, was like a mother to me even though she might be the same age as me. In fact, I wouldn't be surprised if she is a year older or a year younger than me. That has been my relationship with these two people. My relationship with Salim sahab or with Bhabhi was never one of equals, nor is it one today. They are my elders and even today I consider them my elders. There was such love and such closeness between us, and that was the reason we could work together, and work so splendidly well together. Because you see, it isn't difficult to be a partner in a cement factory; it doesn't matter if you are well matched or whether you love each other or not because this is the cost

That bridge had broken somewhere along the way, the bridge through which we used to reach each other's thoughts and hearts

of cement in the market, this is the price it sells at, this is the cost of manufacturing it, this is the expenditure, this is the profit – let us divide everything equally. You can say the same thing for a steel factory or a textile factory, but it isn't the same when you are making a script. There is no weighing scale, nor any measuring tape with which you can weigh a scene or measure it. When two people sit down to make a scene, they have complete faith in each other, that if I am saying something else it isn't because I want to say something different, or if he is not agreeing with me then it isn't because he wants me to go along with him. No, we were both thinking about the scene. And if you don't have that faith, that trust in each other in your real life, then it won't come in your work. It isn't easy to work like this. Till we had such a relationship, we worked together. And then it so happened that life caused our friend circles to be different. I began to have a different set of friends, so did he. There was a time when it was not possible that we would sit separately from each other in the evenings. Then, our evenings began to be spent separately and a distance crept in between us.

I can't recall how that happened or because of whom it happened, nor would I ever be able to understand why it happened because these changes occur so slowly that you barely notice them as they are happening. But one day I could see that the relationship we had between us, whereby we could understand the unspoken words between us, was no longer there. We could no longer work together. Not because he was dishonest with me or because I cheated him. Nothing of that sort happened. Not on our name or our work or our price, we never had any difference on any of these issues. Not for a moment. But that bridge, that bridge had broken somewhere along the way, that bridge through which we used to reach each other's thoughts and hearts.

Kaifi Azmi and Shaukat Azmi

I never found any difference between what he said and what he did

Ajeeb aadmi tha woh
Mohabbaton ka geet tha
Baghawaton ka raag tha
Kabhi woh sirf phool tha
Kabhi woh sirf aag tha
Ajeeb aadmi tha woh...

A strange sort of calamity befell on Urdu after 1947. Although I cannot say with complete certainty, but there has been a tradition of IPTA making some films too, and after that all the progressive poets and writers flocked to the film industry and, with the help of mass media, they took their message to the ordinary people of Hindustan. Among these writers were people such as Khwaja Ahmad Abbas, Krishan Chandar and Ismat Chughtai who became scriptwriters and Sahir, Kaifi, Majrooh, Shailendra who became songwriters. If you were to see their films and songs, you will find that the publicity they did for socialism through commercial films would not have been possible anywhere else. If you were to carefully see their many films and songs, you will find that they are presenting a clear political and social message.

I think that all these progressive poets, with the exception of Majrooh, were essentially writers of the nazm and not the ghazal. It isn't as though they did not write ghazals or did not write good ghazals, but the nazm was closer to their poetic temperament. You might recall that the All India Progressive Writers' Association held its first meeting in Lucknow in 1936, presided over by Munshi Premchand; at this meeting, a message was also sent by Gurudev Rabindranath Tagore. In his presidential address, Munshi Premchand had pointed out that this was not the time to talk of the nightingale and the rose (*gul-o-bulbul*) and the lover's street (*kuu-e-jaana*). Poetry today must be about social and political inequalities; literature and the power of the pen must be used to speak against the chains that have shackled society. And naturally, the progressives' attention was diverted to the nazm that was better equipped to carry this message in comparison to the ghazal which spoke through allusions and metaphors. Kaifi sahab's first collection contained absolutely no ghazals. Later, he wrote ghazals, but essentially, he, along with all other progressive poets, be it Jafri sahab or Sahir, they all made their mark as a poet through their nazms. And they show their true talents in the nazm, except Majrooh sahab. Faiz sahab too, has written ghazals, but his nazms are far more powerful than his ghazals. Makhdoom has also written ghazals, but his nazms are weightier than his ghazals.

It is often said for poets that there's a huge difference between what they do and what they say. It is true; indeed, there is a difference because what they say is so exceptionally good that it is difficult to be just as exceptionally good. So, naturally, there is some difference. But I can say with complete certainty that whoever said this had not met Kaifi sahab. If Kaifi sahab spoke about peasants and workers, it was not from the comfort of his own home; he, in fact, went to live with peasants and workers and worked in close proximity with them. If Kaifi sahab spoke of secularism, then it was not merely a slogan or a fad for him; if anything, it was a way of life. That is how he lived. You could see it in his everyday life. If Kaifi sahab spoke of women's empowerment, then it wasn't as though this talk came and stopped at his doorstep; these things were a part of his family's value system. And so, I never found any difference between what he said and what whe did. He did exactly what he said and wrote exactly what he did. The interesting thing is that when he wrote romantic poetry and when he began to write revolutionary poetry, he did them with equal gusto. Both these colours—of romance and revolution—are found in ample measure in his poetry.

'Kaifi aur Main' things fell into place so well that a story was formed

I was suddenly called upon to write the play 'Kaifi Aur Main'. Had I been told earlier that I have to write a play, one that would be staged over and over again, I would have offered my apologies to Ramesh Talwar and others from IPTA because I don't know how to write a play.

Actually, it began with just a programme. It so happened that on Kaifi sahab's third death anniversary, something new had to be done for IPTA. It was decided that some quotations culled out from Shaukat Azmi's book, along with some quotations by Kaifi sahab would be narrated on stage, interspersed with some of his *nazms*. But when I sat down to write, things fell into place so well that a story was formed.

It wasn't even ready by the afternoon of the day we had to present the play in front of an audience. It was completed just two hours before the performance. Some chopping and pruning kept happening till its first reading finally took place in front of a live audience. The play is based on Shaukat Azmi's memoir *Yaad ki Rahguzar* (*The Pathway of Memory*). Extracts from Kaifi's interviews, articles and prefaces of books have been strung together in such a way that a beautiful story comes alive on stage. Two characters are sitting on two tables on the stage, there is no movement, and the story is told only through the tone and tenor of the spoken word. The storyline of the play begins in Hyderabad where Shaukat meets Kaifi for the first time at a *mushaira* when she comes to take an autograph; this first meeting, then, turns into love.

A scene from the play 'Kaifi Aur Main', Indore (2010)

Khush-shakal bhi hai woh ye
alag baat hai magar
Humko zaheen log
hamesha azeez the

Javed Akhtar and Shabana Azmi

We grew up in the same milieu

Believe me, I can't even remember when I met Shabana for the first time. We were born in the same milieu. In Mumbai, the progressive writers of those days, like Sardar Jafri, Kaifi Azmi, Ismat Chughtai, Krishan Chandar, Jan Nisar Akhtar, Majrooh Sultanpuri, Rajinder Singh Bedi, were all part of a tribe. Or you could say they were all part of an extended family. They would be in and out of each other's homes, they knew each other's children, and their children too knew each other. And so, Shabana and I would have met each other thanks to this extended family.

I don't remember, but perhaps she would have been a year old and I four years old. I can't recall when I met her parents—Kaifi sahab and Shaukat aapa—for the first time in my life. Nor would Shabana know when she met me for the first time. All I know is that we both grew up in the same milieu.

Sometimes people joke and say that we should have had an arranged marriage because our backgrounds are so similar. My father and hers were very dear friends. My mother was older than Shabana's, and so she regarded her as a younger sister. So you can say our relationship precedes our birth.

A new edition of my ghazals and nazms, *Lava*, has appeared. It contains a poem entitled 'Shabana'. Some of its lines are as follows:

Yahan jaana wahan jaana, isse milna usse milna
Hamare saare lamhe aise lagte hai
Ke jaise train ke chalne se pahle railway stationon par
Jaldi-jaldi apne dabbe dhoondhte koi musafir ho
Jinhein kab saans bhi lene ki mohlat hai,
Kabhi lagta hai tumko mujhse mujhko tumse milne ka khayal aaye
Kahan itni bhi fursat hai
...
Magar jab sangdil duniya mera dil torhti hai toh
Mujhe uss morh par bas eik tumhari hi zarurat hai

GUFTAGU

In conversation with Javed Akhtar

Arvind Mandloi

Apart from love, what were the other factors that turned your friendship into marriage?

What is love? It's very difficult to define it, my friend. What happens is that the lack or deficiency you find in your heart or in your feelings or when you say that such and such space is empty in my life and someone comes and fills those empty spaces, then you are in love with that person. Everyone has some spaces in their hearts that are empty, and so people love different people. Writing about Shabana, I once used this line from Majaz: '*Main jis duniya mein rahta hoon, woh uss duniya ki aurat hai* (the world I live in, she is a woman of that world)'. I believe that the incompleteness I felt within me, which was inside me, in my personality, that incompleteness was removed only when I met Shabana. The bond I have with Shabana is not at all like the one shared between a regular husband and wife. We are friends who live together. She has her own life, her commitments. She is doing a great deal in her life; she keeps herself very busy. I too am busy and so we are both leading very hectic lives. But the thing is that whether it is her or me, when either of us feels anxious or faces a hardship, we rely on each other's opinion, and it invariably turns out to be right. So I always say that our friendship is such that even marriage could not ruin it.

I believe that the incompleteness within me was removed when I met Shabana.

GUFTAGU

In conversation with Shabana Azmi

Arvind Mandloi

When did you first meet Javed sahab and where?

I don't remember when I first met Javed sahab. He says that when he was five years old, he had come with his mother, Safiya aapa, to Red Flag Hall (the Communist Party commune) where we used to live in a 200-square feet room. Actually, Jadu's parents and my abba-amma were close friends because both Akhtar sahab and Abba were associated with the Progressive Writers' Association and both were members of the Communist Party; so we went to each other's homes. But we really met, properly, at Sai Paranjpe's house. Javed saw *Sparsh* and he liked it so much that he insisted Sai introduce him to the people from her unit. I found that he had watched the film very closely and knew the film's dialogues nearly by heart. I was quite surprised that such a big writer from the world of mainstream cinema should so like this small film. I had heard that Salim–Javed had a reputation of being arrogant. But the person I was meeting was a very intelligent man with a great sense of humour and terrific repartee. He used to come to meet Abba because

Javed should certainly write his autobiography because his life can inspire many people.

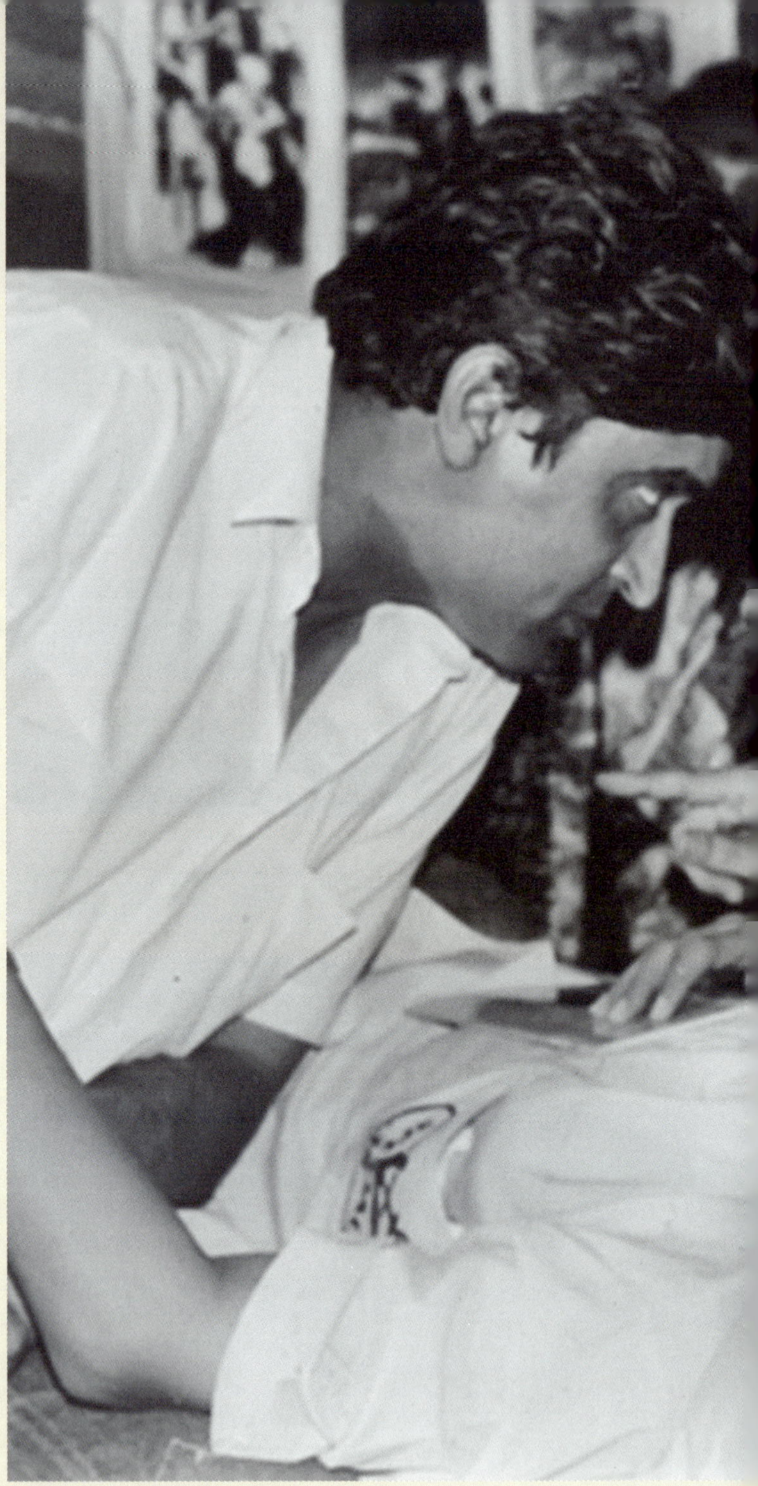

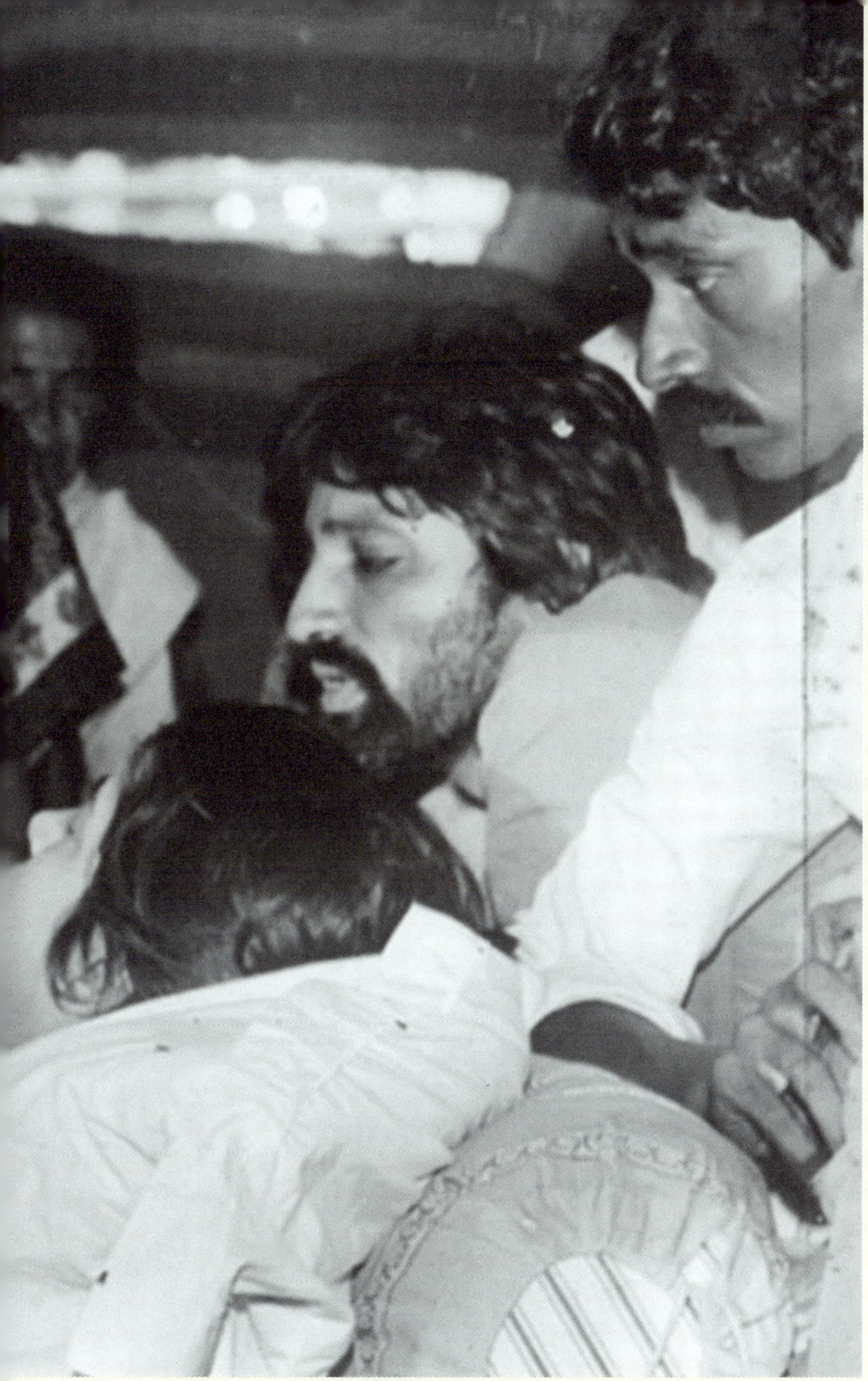

Shabana Azmi sitting on a hunger strike in favour of the Mumbai slum-dwellers; talking to her are Javed Akhtar and documentary film-maker Anand Patwardhan (1986)

those days he had begun to write poetry and used to recite it for my father. I too, began to sit with Abba and I began to sense that Javed was a lot like my father in many ways. Respectful towards elders, his great love for Urdu, his interest in politics, even their preferences in food were similar – arhar dal, shaami kebab, alu-gosht in a thin runny curry. As my friendship with Jadu deepened, I felt as though I was being acquainted with my own roots. It is no wonder that people began to say that we had an arranged marriage.

How do you see Javed Akhtar's work in films? As an actor, how do you view his contribution to cinema?

I think that whenever there is any discussion about the history of Indian cinema, Javed Akhtar's name will always be written in golden letters. Salim–Javed appeared at the beginning of the 1970s and re-fashioned and moulded cinema anew, delivering hits after hits. They changed the essential character of our hero. And I think that Javed sahab has himself experienced, at first hand, much of the struggle that his heroes have gone through. The struggles that Javed sahab experienced became a part of his characters. I always feel that when something emerges from within an artist, from a wellspring deep inside him, it is always more effective.

What I like most about Javed's writing is the fact that when he writes a character, he speaks in that character's voice.

Javed sahab had written the script for *Main Azad Hoon* in which you had acted. How was that experience?

It was great. I wanted us to work together again but, unfortunately, we never got the chance to do so. I do feel that *Main Azad Hoon* has been an under-rated film. It did not get the sort of attention it deserved. It was an important film.

As an actor, did you notice any special quality in Javed Akhtar sahab's script writing that sets him apart from others?

Among his earliest films, when he had just begun work, his women, his heroines are very different from the way women were depicted at the time. The character of the mother is very important because his own

Shabana and Javed Akhtar with the famous film-maker Satyajit Ray

mother was very important in his life. Girls didn't have very large roles as compared to the heroes at the time. People often fail to notice that the girls in Salim–Javed's films were very different from the way girls were depicted in contemporary Hindi cinema. In all their films, Salim–Javed's heroine is a girl who takes her own decisions, earns her own money, who works for a living. If you were to see the other films of that period, you might think that Indian girls do nothing else in their life except run around and dance wearing a yellow chiffon sari; they are never shown having a real life or a job. What I like most about Javed's writing is the fact that when he writes a character, he speaks in that character's voice. And the most important thing is that Javed's value system is a morally correct one. So even if his hero goes against the law, there is usually a very good reason for it. I feel that in the present day, when we try to create an anti-hero, we go wrong somewhere because the anti-hero's morality is somehow wrong. If you look at Amitabh Bachchan's character or Dilip Kumar's character in Ramesh Sippy's *Shakti*, these characters are very beautiful. In that big scene in *Deewaar* with Amitabh Bachchan, Shashi Kapoor and Nirupa Rai, all three characters give their own version of things and all three arguments are so good that when you hear each side you feel that that person is right. This is a special quality of Javed's.

Which quality of Javed sahab's do you like the most?

At a cursory level, it might appear as though Javed is very careless, but he is a very responsible human being. He never forgets those who supported him during his bad days. He is a very grateful person. But he also says that if you have ever done good for a person, you should never remember it, nor should you raise your hopes that that person will do you good in return. Never make a person feel beholden to you. I will always remember a few things.

I had a nephew; his name was Kamran Rizvi. He was struggling to find work in films. Whenever he came home, Jadu had instructed our cook to serve food for him no matter what time he might arrive, be it four in the evening or eleven at night. When I said, 'Who eats at 4?' Jadu answered, 'I have been hungry; I know how difficult it is to eat to your heart's content. If you ask him he will lie and say I have eaten. I used to do that. Even if I had been hungry for three days, if I went to someone's house where people were eating, I would say I have eaten but I will have a cup of tea.'

He has bought a house for every member of our household staff. He helps many people without letting anyone know. During the lockdown, when he would see the exodus of migrant workers trudging in the heat with all their belongings on their head, his heart would break. He cannot bear to see others in pain. One day, a cat had climbed the roof of Janki Kutir; it snatched the roti from our plate and was running off with it. When a member of the staff tried to shoo it away, Jadu shouted and said, 'Let her take away the roti; she's taking it for her children.' He might look tough from the outside, but he is very tender-hearted.

You are very successful in your career; so is he. Has there been any ego or any issue on which the two of you have disagreed?

No, no, never. There is no question of ego because the two of us have enormous respect for each other, for each other's work. And when we do disagree with each other, there is no ego between us. Let me tell you something very interesting. We have a beautiful house in Khandala; its name is 'Sukoon'. When we were making it, we used to have a lot of fights because I was thinking of a very different kind of house and he had something totally different in mind. We would fight over everything. He and I used to have a very dear friend, Farhan Mujib, who is unfortunately no longer alive. Farhan said to me, 'Look here,

Shabana, Javed has slept on the streets, he has been homeless, he has gone without food for many days. You have not seen the struggles he has been through. He has a dream and to make that dream come true it is important that you should let him make exactly the sort of house he wishes to make. Understand one thing: You are *Ankur* and he is *Sholay*.' I liked this and I understood it. So, now, we complement each other.

Is there any incident or anecdote regarding Javed sahab that you might wish to share with the present-day readers?

There are many such incidents. Javed and I are husband and wife, but we don't burden each other with the roles that are expected of a husband and a wife. We lead very busy lives. Sometimes it happens that I wake up in the morning and ask, 'Where is Javed sahab?' and I am told, 'He has left.' Or he gets up and he asks where I am and he is told, 'She has gone to Hyderabad.' In fact, he has a poem entitled 'Shabana'; it is precisely about this. We are both very busy, but our company is special for each other. There is no role play between us, that a husband should do this or a wife should do that. Today's generation has got the idea of equality all wrong; they think they can legislate equality. But this causes too many problems. For instance, I was in America once and I was ironing Javed's *kurta* when someone we knew came in and asked, 'What are you doing?' I replied, 'I am ironing Javed's *kurta*.' She said, 'What sort of feminist are you that you are ironing your husband's *kurta*? Will he iron your kurta?' I replied, 'This has nothing to do with feminism. I will not give him my *kurta* to iron because it would surely get burnt. He hasn't asked me to iron this *kurta*. I want him to wear it and so I am ironing it.' When we start measuring such things on the scale of equality, I think we are being childish. Real equality is when he gives the same respect and importance to what I am saying as he does to his own words, as I do to his.

I do believe Javed must write his autobiography because his life can inspire many people. He is a very extraordinary person. I think it's important that there should be a book on his personal life.

Once, you had been taken ill and you were admitted in the hospital. I had phoned Javed sahab and he was very emotional. His voice was trembling and he had said to me that only when you pull at a hair do

you know how deeply embedded it is in your skin. When something happens to Shabana, I realise how much I love her. What do you think?

There are many such incidents, but let me tell you something. Recently, I had gone with Javed for Safdar Hashmi's thirty-first death anniversary. The incident is a recent one so I remember it well. In 1989, I had read a pamphlet from the stage of the International Film Festival with HKL Bhagat, who was then a Congress minister, sitting in front of me. In my speech I had held the Congress responsible for Safdar Hashmi's murder and said that it makes little sense to hold such festivals when we can kill our cultural activists in such a manner. There was a huge outcry and I was wondering what was going on. Javed called me from Mumbai and said, 'I am so proud of you. You have been so brave.' He caught a plane and came straight to me… in Delhi. That gave me strength. When Javed is beside me, I am not scared of anything.

Is there anything you feel Javed sahab absolutely must do now?

I do believe Javed must write his autobiography because his life can inspire many people. He is a very extraordinary person. I consider him to be a very 'wide' person. I think it's important that there should be a book on his personal life. And if only he were to direct a film, I would be very happy.

Is there anything you would like to say to Javed sahab publicly?

There is a permanent dialogue of his that runs through my life: 'Wait, stop, let's think about it.' If only he were to abandon this 'wait, stop, let's think about it' and do what I want him to do at any given moment, it would be the most priceless and rare gift of my life!

Javed Akhtar with brother Salman Akhtar

We are psychological, not biological twins

Salman Akhtar

We are elder–younger from each other by seventeen months. We are psychological, not biological twins. I became a mother-oriented child whereas he became a father-oriented child. But life is not straight as an arrow because when you experience a closeness to one parent, the other parent is hidden somewhere inside you and comes out some time later in your life. First, Javed goes on the path of his father, then he returns to his mother. I go first towards my mother, then I return towards my father. Our lives are braided like a woman's plait.

Though Javed was active on the stage, doing acting, mimicry, debate, etc., I think at the age of eighteen, when he was in Bhopal, he developed a keen interest in joining films. He was constantly reading about films. I remember him reading James Michener's novel *Caravans*. He asked me to read it too. I read it. He asked me, 'Do you know why Michener wrote this book?' I said, 'No.' Then he told me, 'Michener wrote this book because one day I will make a film on it.' So Javed had this intense desire to join the film industry.

He is about a year and a half younger than me in age, but when it comes to poetry, he is a full ten years older than me.

On the occasion of the release of Dr Salman Akhtar's first collection of poetry, 'Ku-ba-ku', published in Hindi–Urdu in 1976

GUFTAGU

In conversation with Shahid Akhtar

Arvind Mandloi

Daddy's memory was such that he knew thousands of sher; Jadu is the same, his memory is incredible

When you saw your elder brother, Javed Akhtar, for the first time, when you spoke to him for the first time, what was that moment like? Did you witness his days of struggle?

I don't remember exactly, but I think we were at Rahi Masoom Raza's house. We were very young, so young that we had no idea of what was going on or who was who. All we knew was that he was our brother. I have seen each and every aspect of his struggle. From his days at Bhopal's Hilal Manzil to the time when he lived in a tiny flat in Horizon Building on Pali Hill, behind Horizon Hotel and, later, the apartment at Bandstand. When he bought his black Ambassador, he didn't have money to buy petrol for it. He managed to scrape together some money to buy petrol. Once, he said to me: 'If you want to move ahead in life and do something in life, you should buy a car. That will bring you confidence.' I bought a car right away. He helped me buy a house. He has been beside me at every step, in every stage of my life.

What similarities do you find between Jan Nisar Akhtar sahab and Javed sahab?

Daddy's memory was such that he knew thousands of sher; Jadu is the same, his memory is incredible.

Javed with his brother Shahid Akhtar and sisters

GUFTAGU

In conversation with Baba Azmi

Arvind Mandloi

You have worked with Javed sahab. What difference do you find between his personal and professional life?

A common factor between his personal and professional life is his humour, which you also see in his writing. People might think that he is a very serious person, but no. If he is in a group, he is always the centre of attention. His humour is not such that only people of his own age can appreciate it. In our family or during any get-together with friends, all the young people are always sitting around him and there is always something witty being said. I have worked on some of his films, such as *Mr India*, *Roop Ki Rani Choron Ka Raja*, *Arjun* and *Prem*. I have worked on the scripts of many other people too, but the great thing about Javed sahab's writing is that you just have to pick up the script and go to the set and start shooting. One seldom sees such detailed observation and writing.

Javed sahab has written some incredible songs.

Yes, '*Mameya kero kero kero mama*' from *Arjun* and '*Eik, do, teen...*' from *Tezaab* are my favourites. Now when we hear '*Eik, do, teen...*', and it was a superhit in its time, it seems easy, but to make it fit the music in that way was incredible. '*Eik ladki ko dekha to aisa laga...*' is an iconic song. People think that Javed sahab won't be able to write rap, but I am sure that he will and the remarkable thing will be that there won't be any mistakes of language in it. Look at the songs of *Rock On*. The lightness in these songs and the contemporariness is incredible! So, it isn't as though Javed sahab cannot write the songs of today. The songs of *Rock On* are in the language of the youth, in today's language. And there isn't any single word that you will find awkward.

How do you see his contribution to cinema?

If the script is by Javed sahab, 70 per cent of the director's work is done because the shot division, that is the way a scene has to be mounted, where the scene has to begin, to which pitch it has to be taken, everything is printed on paper. This is the hallmark of a good writer. My request to Javed sahab is that he should write a script with a political background. If Javed sahab were to write on political background with real earnestness, I feel that there cannot be a better film and it would be a 100 per cent success at an international level.

Javed Akhtar and Shabana Azmi with Tanvi Azmi and Baba Azmi

GUFTAGU

In conversation with Tanvi Azmi

Arvind Mandloi

Is there any incident or memory related to Kaifi sahab and Javed sahab that you can share with us?

I can't think of any incident concerning the two right now, but what used to happen was that even if there were no visitors, the six of us would sit down together, that is Shabana, Javed sahab, Mummy-Abba, Baba and I. Someone or the other would invariably join us at some point and a round of poetry recitation would begin. Abba would make a request and then Javed sahab would recite something. It would be a very enriching experience for us. When I got married, Shabana and Javed used to live with Mummy and Abba in the Janki Kutir house. Now the thing is that since both are from U.P., both would observe the most immaculate etiquette. If, for instance, I said, 'Come, the food has been served,' and if perchance both came out of their room together, both would expect the other to precede him to sit down for the meal. Javed sahab and I have a private joke; we both say that we are still not a part of the family. Though we are now related by a bond, no matter what one says, we remain outsiders. He came from outside the family and so did I, and so we are outsiders. Sometimes, we get united and then we 'criticise' them, our in-laws that is. Actually, all this is in good humour and none of us take it seriously.

Abba would make a request and then Javed sahab would recite something

Javed Akhtar with Anand Bakshi

There was a time when a Hindustani film song meant Anand Bakshi

While he gave wonderful lyrics for several films, many of his ghazals were also used in films

There was a time when 80 per cent of the songs in Hindustani films were being written by Anand Bakshi. During that time, the very meaning of a Hindustani film song was Anand Bakshi. In 1965, the film *Himalay ki God Mein* was released; it gave Bakshi sahab his due recognition. But the same year another film appeared that was beautifully adorned with his songs; this was *Jab Jab Phool Khile*. Every single song from this film became such a huge hit that Bakshi sahab began to rule the market. He has written songs for 636 films in his career, with over 3,500 songs. While he gave wonderful lyrics for several films, many of his ghazals were also used in films. Yet, he never made any claim about being a poet. He would always say, 'Look here, I am not a poet; I am a lyricist, that too, a film lyricist.' I have no hesitation whatsoever in saying that Bakshi sahab was one of those people who encouraged me to write film lyrics. Once, at a party at Pyayrelal ji's house, I recited some of my poetry to Bakshi sahab which he liked very much. Afterwards, whenever he met me, he would always say, 'You should write lyrics; I am convinced you will write excellent songs.'

A song by Bakshi sahab that I liked very much was '*Zindagi ke safar mein guzar jaate hai jo maqaam...*' Once I met him at a party. Those days I hadn't begun writing songs; I was only writing scripts. I said to him, 'Bakshi sahab, I liked this song of yours so much that I want the pen with which you wrote this song.' Bakshi sahab was very pleased to hear this; he smiled and said, 'That pen was presented to me by Asha Bhosle ji. How can I give it to anyone else? It doesn't seem right, but because you have given me this love and respect, I will certainly present you with a pen.' I got that present the very next day.

I have kept it very carefully till this day.

This song is among my favourite film lyrics. If you were to ask me to make the smallest possible list of my favourite songs, starting from the time films began to be made, this song would feature in that short list.

It is a 'word heavy song'; there are too many words in it, but its tune is such that the words don't weigh heavily on you. If there are too many words, the listener begins to ponder and there is a fear of 'dryness' seeping into the tune. But the 'orchestration' and composition of this song are as remarkable as the words. The song is such that I am as impressed by it today as I was all those years ago.

Javed Akhtar with Lata Mangeshkar

My very first song was sung by Lata ji and Kishore Da

One day, Yash Chopra sahab came to my home early in the morning. I had written many films for him as a scriptwriter. He said, 'I am making a film called *Silsila*. Please write the songs for it.' Till this point, I used to write poetry, but I had kept it close to me; only four–six people knew that I also wrote poetry. Yash Chopra was among the people who had heard it. I told him I didn't want to write for films; I only wrote poetry for myself. I wrote scripts and that was enough. But he got after me and wouldn't let me be till I wrote the songs for his film. I tried my best to put him off so that he would take offence, but he refused to get angry. I came to know much later about why Yash Chopra sahab was so insistent that I write for his film. Though there is no doubt that he had a sense for poetry. He used to get Sahir sahab to write for his films, but Sahir sahab was unwell and couldn't write. He went to Lata ji and asked her, 'Didi, Sahir sahab is not available; who should I ask to write now? I need poetry for this film.' To this Lata ji replied, 'I have a friend, Padma; she has heard Javed sahab's ghazals and nazms. She praises him. She is a fine poet herself. You have good relations with him, so you shouldn't ask anyone else; you should only ask him.' So it is Lata ji who is hidden behind the reason I began to write film lyrics. And look at what destiny had in store for me: my very first song was sung by Lata ji and Kishore da. Lata ji has sung thousands of songs. The Hindustani language is deservedly proud of itself because of her.

I am a writer and I can say this with complete assurance: I have heard Lata ji's songs and so have you, but I have never heard her mispronounce a word, ever! Others have made such mistakes. It is not as though people don't make mistakes. The biggest singers have occasionally mispronounced words. But in Lata ji I have never found this mistake... her accent is always perfect, always flawless.

Once, Pandit Jasraj narrated a very interesting incident to me. He said, 'Many years ago, when I had just begun to make a name for myself as a classical singer, Bade Ghulam Ali Khan was among the great utsads; he was my senior and my elder. I was in Amritsar and I came to know that Bade Ghulam Ali Khan was visiting. I went to see him, touched his feet, talked for a while. He was talking to me when suddenly he signalled to me to be quiet. Scared, I fell silent. I found that he was listening very carefully; from somewhere downstairs in the hotel the song from the film *Anarkali* was playing: '*Ye zindagi ussi ki hai, jo kisi ka ho gaya...*' I was astonished that a great ustad as Bade Ghulam Ali Khan was listening to a film song and, that too, with such utter absorption. When the song finished, he smiled with great surprise and said, 'The wretch is never out of tune.'

Javed Akhtar with Yash Chopra

I am a fan of his poetry

Yash Chopra

We met for the first time when the film *Deewaar* was being made. I believe that *Deewaar* is the best script he's ever written. From then till now, the three of us—that is, Salim sahab, Javed sahab and I—have been friends. We used to hear his poetry in our gathering of friends and I would always say, 'Why don't you write songs for films?' And he would always brush it aside. When I was making *Silsila*, I again requested him to write for this film, and he agreed.

After this, he wrote songs for many films, and he proved that he's the best songwriter. I am a fan of his poetry. He's a modern poet. He wrote wonderful songs for *Border*. When he used to write scripts, he always gave a 'complete' script. Before him, I had only ever seen Pandit Mukhram Sharma doing that. His memory is amazing; it's one of his greatest assets. We have spent many evenings together. He is always the life and soul of any gathering.

Though This Song Was....

'*Dekha ek khwaab to ye silsile huye...*' It was the first song of my career and that of Shiv–Hari. Though this song was written on a tune, I think they had to slightly alter the tune to make the words fit it. I didn't have any experience of writing songs at that time. The thing is, there was a slight twist at the end of the tune, but there was no such twist in the words I had written. Had I written '*Dil ne tera naam gungunaya hai...*' it would have worked. But he liked the first line so much that he changed the tune to fit the words.

Main aur meri tanhai
Aksar ye baatein karte hai
Tum hoti to kaisa hota
Tum ye kehti tum woh kehti
Tum iss baat pe hairaan hoti
Tum uss baat pe hansti
Tum hoti to aisa hota
Tum hoti to waisa hota

SINGERS Lata Mangeshkar, Amitabh Bachchan **MUSIC** Shiv-Hari

FILM *Silsila*
DIRECTOR *Yash Chopra*
1981

The highest number of cassettes sold in the history of HMV

After *Silsila*, I worked with a new music composer, Kuldip Singh, on a very small film. This was *Saath Saath*. Its songs were sung by Jagjit Singh and Chitra Singh. These songs were a big hit. They are heard even today. The combination cassette of *Arth* and *Saath Saath* was the highest selling cassette in the history of HMV.

Ye tera ghar ye mera ghar, kisi ko dekhna ho gar
To pehle aake maang le, meri nazar teri nazar
Jo chandni nahi to kya, ye roshni hai pyaar ki
Dilon ke phool khil gaye, to fikr kya bahaar ki
Hamaare ghar naa aayegi, kabhi khushi udhaar ki
Hamaari raahaton ka ghar, hamari chahaton ka ghar

SINGERS Jagjit Singh, Chitra Singh **MUSIC** Kuldip Singh

FILM *Saath Saath*
DIRECTOR *Raman Kumar*
1982

SAN FRANCISCO

The name Dilip sahab is a complete introduction

It is very difficult to say something about a great artist, and also easy; easy because the name Dilip sahab is a complete introduction in itself. And difficult because how does one explain how much light the sun contains? How does one explain how many waves are there in the ocean? How does one explain how vast, how immense the universe is? And how does one explain the heights and depths of Dilip sahab's art? I too, am one of those crores of people who were his fans, are his fans, and will always remain his fans.

Javed Akhtar with Dilip Kumar and Amitabh Bachchan

Shakti is a question mark on ethics

I think *Deewaar* is my most ethical film. I am not using the word 'ethics' in its narrow sense; rather, I am taking it to the level of the unconscious mind. Another such film that poses a question mark on ethics by asking questions about what is right and what is wrong, is *Shakti*. It doesn't answer in black and white because perhaps there were no easy answers. Perhaps *Shakti* is the best example of such a dilemma. It is based on three different ethical persons, all three of whom are right in their own way.

FILM *Shakti*

DIRECTOR *Ramesh Sippy*

1982

Shatrughan Sinha with Subhash Ghai, Javed Akhtar and Rehana Ghai

He is not just my friend, but also my guru friend

Subhash Ghai

We have been friends since our days of struggle in Mumbai. He is my first friend from the film industry. He told me a great deal about the industry. He is not just my friend, he is my guru friend. He and I share an emotional bond. His oratory is his greatest asset. He can mimic Kishore Kumar, he can speak in Parliament, in the UN, in any world forum. There is a child in his heart that creates his sense of humour. One can still see the anger that was in him in his days of struggle. But he took his success forward with great good sense. He has never run away from his responsibilities. He has always thought that if I move ahead, my family members should not be left behind. This is a great human quality. We have worked together only twice: in *Meri Jung* and *Krishna*. Perhaps I expect a great deal from him; perhaps I think it is my right that he should give greater preference to my work. I have some unjustified demands, as one friend from another, and that is why we have not been able to do more work together. But we have always been friends. But there is also a fear that this sweet relationship we share might get snarled if we work together. I am scared. I don't want to lose him. Our friendship goes back to our days of struggle. The fact that he has won many awards is one thing, but he has given a special place to scriptwriters. That is a great achievement. He is an atheist; he has had faith in himself and not in God.

'Shatranj ke mohre wahi hain,
lekin baazi palat chuki hai'

ANIL KAPOOR IN THE ROLE OF ARUN VARMA

FILM *Meri Jung*

DIRECTOR *Subhash Ghai*

1985

Footpathon ke hum rahne wale
Raaton ne paala hum woh ujaale
Aakaash sar pe
Pairon tale hai duur tak ye zamiin
Aur to apna koi nahi
Footpathon ke hum...
Ho bachpan mein khele gham se
Nirdhan gharon ke bete
Phoolon ki sej nahi
Kaanton pe hum hain lete
Bhookhe rahe, sau gham sahe
Dil ye kahe
Roti jahan, hai swarg apna wahiin
Aur to apna koi nahi
Footpathon ke hum...

SINGERS Anup Jalota, Hariharan, Shailendra Singh, Suresh Wadkar
MUSIC Hridyanath Mangeshkar

FILM *Mashaal*

DIRECTOR *Yash Chopra*

1984

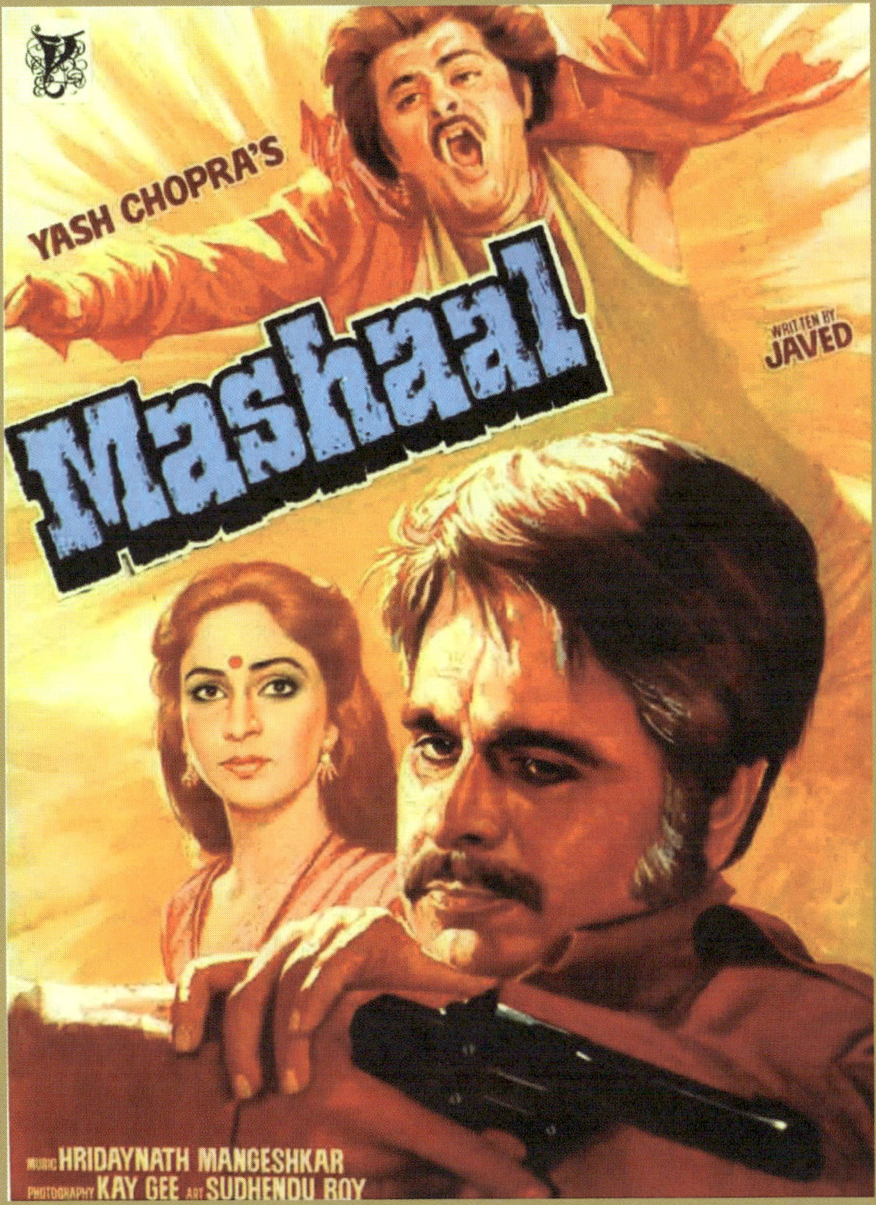

The character of Arjun was new to the Hindi screen

Sometimes it so happens that you do many things right but go wrong in one thing, and that one thing reduces everything. I feel that *Arjun* was an excellent script and even though you cannot count it among superhit films, it was a hit film. It was a successful film, like *Deewaar* was or *Trishul*, *Sholay*, or *Don*, but it was not in the same league. Yet years later, people still remember it. People often tell me that it should be remade. Its first half was incomparable. In the second half, I think I stumbled somewhere as a writer. Had I known the mistake that I later realised, and done what I should have done to rectify it, this film would have been ranked amongst the great superhits that I had earlier mentioned. Despite all this, look at the character of Arjun; it was a new character for the Hindi screen. Many films have been made subsequently that have been modelled on a character such as Arjun.

FILM *Arjun*

DIRECTOR *Rahul Rawail*

1985

Sach mere yaar hai, bas wahi pyaar hai
Jiske badle mein koi to pyaar de
Baqui bekaar hai, yaar mere...
Jis haath mein eik haath hai
Uss haath ki kya baat hai
Kya manzile, kya faasle
Eik humsafar gar saath hai
Jiski qismat koi yuun sanwaar de
Wohi dildaar hai, yaar mere...

SAAGAR (1985)
DIRECTOR Ramesh Sippy
SINGER SP Balasubramanian **MUSIC** RD Burman

Theek hai,
Samandar hamari jagir nahi hai,
Lekin uski lehron par
Tumhari company ka
Thappa bhi nahi laga hai

KAMAL HAASAN IN THE ROLE OF RAJA

FILM *Saagar*
DIRECTOR *Ramesh Sippy*
1985

Javed Akhtar with Kishore Kumar

GUFTAGU

In conversation with Javed Akhtar

Arvind Mandloi

There was an incomparable magic in Kishore Kumar's voice

What do you have to say about Kishore Kumar?

As far as Kishore Kumar is concerned, what can you say about a man who takes one *alaap* and his voice immediately enters his listeners' hearts? His alaap before the song *'Kora kaaghaz'* in the film *Aradhana* has neither *murki* nor *taan*. It is a simple, straightforward alaap; in fact, there can't be a simpler alaap. But why do you remember it today even fifty years later? Simply because of Kishore Kumar's voice, that magical voice! There have been many great singers before him. I consider Rafi sahab to be a great singer. In fact, I think he is the first great playback singer. There were playback singers before him, but Mohammed Rafi was the first to note who was singing the song on the screen and modulated his voice accordingly. This is a difficult thing to do. When he sang for Dilip sahab, it was a different style, when he sang for Dev Anand, it was a different style. His style of singing, when it came to Shammi Kapoor or Johnny Walker was also different. He would even change his voice for the actor he was singing for. For instance, Rajinder Kumar had a somewhat choked voice. You will find that the songs Rafi sahab has sung for Rajinder Kumar have that choked quality. This is a remarkable ability. Manna De displayed the same control over comic songs that he had over classical music. Look at the songs he has sung for Mehmood. And on the other hand, look at some of his intensely sombre, classical songs. Yet all are great in their own place. The pain, the ache in Mukesh's voice... can that be found elsewhere? But there was one man, Kishore Kumar, who had magic in his voice. It was there from birth and there is no comparison for it.

I want to say something with great hesitation, even trepidation, but I will still say it because I am a hardcore fan of Kishore Kumar's. Whenever he has sung with someone else, you would have noticed a difference. It could be him singing alongside anyone: a male or a female singer. All these singers are great singers; that is why they are where they are. But Kishore Kumar had an altogether different quality. Please note the fact that whenever Kishore Kumar has sung along with someone else, your attention remains on only Kishore Kumar's voice.

Mai khwabon ki shehzadi
Mai hoon har dil pe chhai
Baadal hai meri zulfein
Bijli meri angdai
Bijli girane main hoon aayi
Kehte hai mujhko Hawa Hawai
Samjhe kya ho naadaanon
Mujhko bholi naa jaano
Main hoon sanpon ki rani
Kaanta mange na pani
Saagar se moti chhinoon
Deepak se jyoti chhinoon
Patthar se aag laga loon
Seene se raaz chura loon

MR INDIA (1987)
DIRECTOR Shekhar Kapur
SINGER Kavita Krishnamurthy **MUSIC** Laxmikant Pyarelal

'Mogambo Khush Hua'

AMRISH PURI IN THE ROLE OF MOGAMBO

FILM *Mr India*
DIRECTOR *Shekhar Kapoor*
1987

And Sridevi became the 'Hawa Hawai' girl

I had written the script of *Mr India*. There is a scene where the heroine, Sridevi, says that she is a cabaret dancer from Havana and that her name is Miss Hawa Hawai. We have an idiomatic expression: 'Bhai, why are you roaming around in this hawa hawai manner?' It is used in UP for someone who is flighty and breezy. The expression '*hawa hawai*' has a very interesting sound. And so, Sridevi became Miss Hawa Hawai from Havana. When I wrote the song for this situation, I used the name too: '*Kehte hain mujhko Hawa Hawai*.' Do you know that when *Mr India* and *Tezaab* were released, Sridevi and Madhuri Dixit were in competition with each other? The media had dubbed them 'Miss Hawa Hawai' and the '*Eik, Do, Teen Girl*'. And the interesting thing is that both these songs were written by me.

Javed sahab and the late actor Satish Kaushik

GUFTAGU

In conversation with Satish Kaushik

Arvind Mandloi

I would like to call Javed Sahab my guru because I have learnt the gurumantra of living my life from him.

In the gap between writing the script of *Jaane Bhi Do Yaaron* and establishing yourself as an actor in films, you were active in theatre and plays. When did you meet Javed sahab?

I got my break in commercial films through Javed sahab. The film *Saagar* was released after *Jaane Bhi Do Yaaron*. *Saagar* was a mega film. At its premiere, Shabana, Javed sahab and I had gone together. After that came *Joshilay*, then *Mr India*. In *Mr India*, he felt that I should be the assistant director. But I said, 'Sarkar, you will have to be in the film.' He came to narrate the story to me in my one-bedroom flat in Santa Cruz East. He narrated the story and said, 'You will have to be the assistant in this film.' Both he and Boney had come. His sense of humour and his writing are par excellence, and the script of *Mr India* was incredible. So, in the course of his writing the script and me assisting in the film, we forged such a deep bond that he decided that after *Mr India* we have to turn Satish into a director.

You were closely involved in the writing of *Mr India* and in the making of the film. Tell us about the character of 'Calendar' that has given you such an enduring identity. How did he come to be created?

The thing is that one day we were just sitting and talking, our usual light-hearted nonsense that was so typical between us. We selected many characters, some based on people we knew in alleys and lanes. My father, Banwarilal Kaushik, was a salesman. He had a dealer and I was narrating an incident about him to Javed sahab: 'Javed sahab, my father once told me about a man who would use the word "calendar" several times in the middle of his conversations.' But Javed sahab said, 'Calendar, yaar, how did he use the word in his sentences?' So I said, 'Bauji used to tell me that the man would say: "Pandit ji! Five boxes have come. Out of these five boxes, Calendar, four boxes, Calendar, turned out to be ruined. So you see, Calendar, out of goods worth ₹10 lakh, only goods worth ₹2 lakh are left. If it goes on like this, Calendar, what will happen to us?"' And Javed sahab said, 'Calendar, yaar, this is amazing!' At the time the character of the cook was being worked out and I was trying to figure out how to tell Javed sahab to give this role to me. Javed sahab said, 'Yaar, let's give him the name Calendar.' And so the cook was named Calendar. Then his 'get up' was decided. And so the character of Calendar came into being. But Javed sahab said, 'Yaar, we will have to give some sort of justification for the name.' That is when Javed sahab inserted this dialogue: '*Eik to samajh mein nahi aata tera naam Calendar kis ne diya* (I can't understand who gave you the name Calendar)'. In response,

Calendar says, '*Kuchh nahi, mere Mummy-Daddy hai na, kuchh angrezi mein naam rakhna chahte the* (It's just that my Mummy-Daddy wanted to give me an English name)'. And that's how Javed sahab linked the name of my character to the situation.

And then *Roop Ki Rani Choron Ka Raja* was made?

Roop Ki Rani Choron Ka Raja turned out to be a huge disaster. It was a terrible shock for all of us. Javed sahab and the rest of us were numb. There was nothing wrong in the film, but it took five years to make. No one knows what the reasons for its failure were. No one was expecting this outcome. Even today when people see the film, the reactions are: 'Yaar, what a film!' It is a hit on TV; it is shown repeatedly. So many directors say, 'Yaar, I want to remake the film.' Especially young directors want to make it again because its script was unbelievable!

If you had to describe Javed sahab in one line, what would you say?

I will call him a sant, a saintly man, a good, virtuous person. At least in my life he is a sant because I have only ever received good things from his company. The changes I see in my personality are because of him. I would like to call Javed sahab my guru because I have learnt the gurumantra, not about the film industry, but the gurumantra for leading my life.

Is there any incident from your life that you would like to share with us that you think should happen again?

The most important thing is that we should work again as a writer and as a director. The work we do now will be truly very mature. I want to double prove him and his writing; I want to do now what I couldn't do then. We should come back as writer and director. I had met him in 1984–85 and as you can see, it's been thirty–thirty-five years now, and in these thirty–thirty-five years we have spent at least twenty years in close association.

FILM *Tezaab (1988)*

DIRECTOR *N. Chandra*

Chaudah ko tera sandesa aaya

Pandrah ko aaunga ye kahlaya

Chaudah ko aaya na pandrah ko tu

Tadpaake mujhko tune kya paaya

Solah ko bhi

Solah ko bhi solah kiye the singhar

Aaja piya aayi bahaar

Eik do teen char paanch chhe saat aath nau

Das gyarah barah terah

Tera karoon din gin-gin ke intezar

SINGER Alka Yagnik **MUSIC** Laxmikant Pyarelal

In writing *'Eik Do Teen',* I wrote a Barahmasa in miniature form

A lot of people expressed their criticism for this song, saying, 'You are a poet and you have written *"Eik do teen char panch chhe saat aath nau das gyarah barah terah"*.' Actually, Lakshmi ji (of Lakshmikant Pyarelal fame) told me of this tune by singing it from one-thirteen. I was struck by an idea. I said, 'Let it stay exactly like this from one-thirteen; don't change this. I will write on the rest of the tune after this.' Lakshmi ji heard this and became somewhat nervous. He said, 'Bhai, it was fine till we had heard *"Eik do teen aaj mausam hai rangeen* ..." but it will sound very odd if the song is sung right up till thirteen.' I said, 'You don't worry about that. I will justify that in what I write after it.' And so it happened: *'Gyarah baarah terah, tera karoon din gin-gin ke intezar, aaja piya aayi bahaar, chaudah ko tera sandesa aaya, pandrah ko aaunga ye kahlaya, chaudah ko aaya na pandrah ko tu, tadpaake mujhko tune kya paaya, solah ko bhi, solah ko bhi solah kiye the singhar, aaja piya aayi bahaar...'* We have a tradition in Urdu–Hindi poetry called the Barahmasa, referring to the twelve months in a year. These are songs of separation (virah) in which a virhan (a woman who is separated from her beloved) gives a description of the twelve months in which she is far away from her lover and how she spends those twelve months. So I wrote this as a barahmasa in a miniature form showing how she spent each day of the month. And in this way the numbers were justified and the song too, became hugely popular.

'Unn saari nafraton ke andhere se jo insaan ko insaan se duur kartin hain kaho ke – Main azad hoon.'

AMITABH BACHCHAN IN THE ROLE OF AZAD

FILM *Main Azaad Hoon*
DIRECTOR *Tinnu Anand*
1989

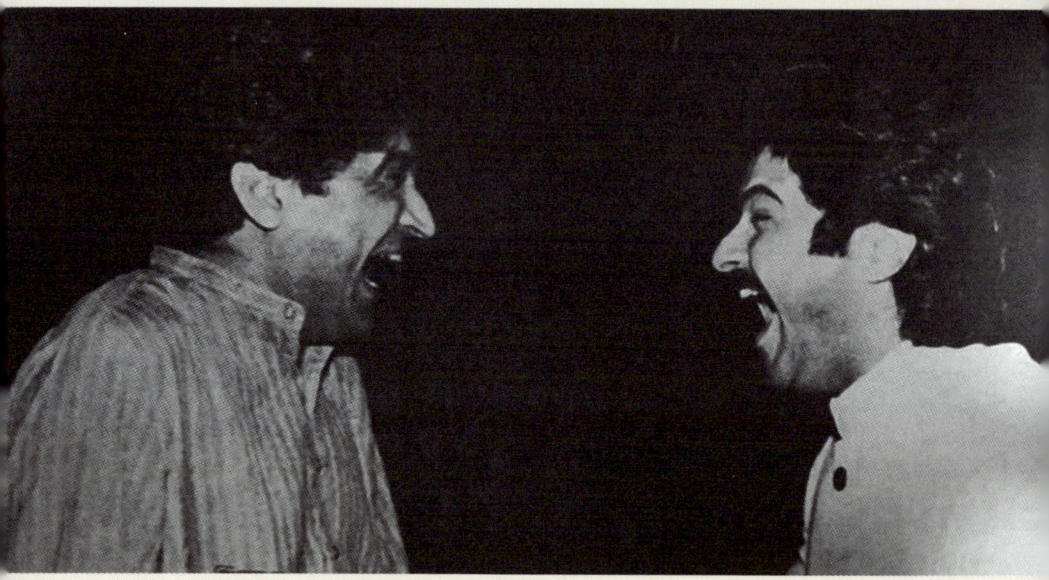

GUFTAGU

In conversation with Anil Kapoor

Arvind Mandloi

Javed sahab is like the book that reveals something new and different each time you read it

When and how did you meet Javed sahab for the first time?

I met Javed sahab for the first time with Shabana ji. She has always encouraged me. I used to think that Javed sahab didn't quite like me though we would talk to each other. Then he saw my work and then a sort of bond developed between us. I think he has recommended me in two–three places. And that is how it started.

When you look back at your journey as an actor, what role do you see being played by Javed sahab in it?

It was Shabana ji who started my journey as an actor; that is something I can never forget. Then Javed sahab began to suggest my name and *Shakti* was made, but the turning point in my career was the film *Mashaal* for which Javed sahab had recommended my name to Yash ji.

Your journey began from there, then came *Mr India* and after that would you say the next turning point was *Meri Jung*?

I feel, and so does the rest of the industry, that these two films were my turning point, and I must give credit to Javed sahab for both. He had a terrific role to play in my getting both these films. Had I not been in *Meri Jung* and *Mashaal*, I would certainly not have been in *Mr India*.

What was special about the script of both these films? What gave you satisfaction as an actor?

When Javed sahab creates a character, they are then, and even years later, landmark characters. As he did in *Zanjeer*, *Deewaar*, *Meri Jung*, *Mashaal*. When you talk of the character of the angry young man, you must understand that at the time he himself was an angry young man. And such is the power of that character, which one can only dream about now, an actor or an artist cannot hope for a better role in his career. So these two films, in fact the script of these two films, paved the foundation for my roles in the films I did subsequently.

As an actor what have you learnt from Javed sahab?

I learn something every day. I am still learning. Whenever I meet him, I learn something when I return. This is a daily journey for us. I mean I learn something every day even by remembering his words. There is always something happening at the subconscious level and that is an ongoing process. There are some books that you read and forget. Then there are the other sort of books that you pick up again, you read them again, you derive pleasure from them yet again. You read them after ten years and you enjoy them again. You read them yet again after thirty years and once again you derive pleasure from them. Javed sahab is like one of those books; every time you meet him the pleasure is the same. Every time you find something new and different about him. I didn't understand all this about him back then; now I am beginning to understand it.

Is there anything special about Javed sahab that you want to share with us, something that you have noticed and that you think you would want people to know about him?

I think the message should reach this present generation that there is no younger person than Javed sahab. He will always be young in his thoughts and ideas and in every which way. You can be anyone—a filmmaker, a poet, a politician, leader, anything—you will gain something from meeting Javed sahab. And those who have not met him or spoken to him, it is their misfortune. Or so I think.

Ghar se nikalte hii, kuchh duur chalte hii
Raaste mein hai uska ghar
Kal subah dekha to baal banaati woh
Khidki mein aayi nazar
Masoom chehra, neechi nigahein
Bholi si ladki, bholi adayein
Na apsara hai, na woh pari hai
Lekin ye uski jadugari hai
Diwana kar de woh, ik rang bhar de woh
Sharma ke dekhe jidhar...

FILM *Papa Kahte Hain (1996)*
DIRECTOR *Mahesh Bhatt*

SINGER Udit Narayan **MUSIC** Rajesh Roshan

Woh Krishn Kanhaiya murlidhar
Manmohan kunj bihari hai
Gopal manohar dukh bhanjan
Ghanshyam atal banwari hai
Woh kans vinashak maharathi
Sudarshan chakradhari hai
Ban kunj birhaiya saawariya
Nandlala kanha murari hai
Har roop nirale hain uske
Har leela uski nyaari hai
Woh gopinath madanmohan
Woh shyaam pitambar aayega
Aayega yugandhar aayega

SINGERS Amit Kumar, Kavita Krishnamurthy
MUSIC Laxmikant Pyarelal

FILM *Yugandhar*

DIRECTOR *N. Chandra*

1993

There is no end to the amount of poetry written on Krishna in Urdu

There was a film by N. Chandra sahab called *Yugandhar*. It had my songs and music by Lakshmikant Pyarelal. One day, I went to meet Chandra sahab; I realised it was a music sitting that Lakshmi ji had organised. Chandra sahab was also present there. It looked like both wanted to say something to me but did not know how to say it. I asked them what the matter was. So they said, 'There is a situation that requires a Krishna aarti, and that has to be written in the song.' At that moment, when I saw the discomfort on their faces, I understood. They probably felt, 'It is all very well that he can write poetry, but can he write a Krishna aarti? That will be a tough call.' So I said, 'Please give me the tune. We will meet tomorrow; till then, I will try and do something.' They gave me the tune. I came home and wrote the song. The very next day, I went to them and said, 'I have written the aarti, but look here, an aarti has a crescendo. That was missing here; your tune was just the tune of a song. It needed a crescendo which I have added on my own. You can hear the rest of the song on your own, but let me recite the crescendo for you; it comprises entirely of the names of Shri Krishna.'

They were amazed. They said, 'We didn't know there were so many names. How did you know?' I said, 'There are two reasons for this. First, I am from Awadh and the entire Awadh region is resplendent with the glory of Krishna. Second, I have read Urdu literature and I know old Urdu poetry. I have learnt all these names from Awadh and Urdu poetry. Few people know that there is no end to the poetry written on Krishna in Urdu a 100, 150 and even 200 years ago. I have read it and that is how I know all these names. Look here, most people seem to think that Urdu poetry is about the goblet and wine or the lover's lane. This kind of poetry has been popularised by singers whereas the truth is that there is no end to the poetry that has been written on our ancient culture and mythology in Urdu.

FILM *1942 A Love Story*

DIRECTOR *Vidhu Vinod Chopra*

1994

Kuchh na kaho, kuchh bhi na kaho
Kya kehna hai, kya sunna hai
Mujhko pata hai, tumko pata hai
Samay ka ye pal, tham sa gaya hai
Aur iss pal mein koi nahi hai
Bas eik main hoon, bas eik tum ho

SINGERS Kumar Sanu, Lata Mangeshkar **MUSIC** RD Burman

'Ek Ladki Ko Dekha' was written like this

My songs were doing fine, but sometimes you get a springboard for you to write a 'big' song. For this springboard I shall be grateful to Vidhu Vinod Chopra till the last day of my life. During this time, a certain phase had come in when songs had become very pedestrian, very banal but they were doing well too. People had begun to believe that only such songs will work. At such a time, if a producer-director asks for a totally different kind of song and accepts the kind of songs I write, it might seem like an ordinary thing today, but at that time it was indeed a very courageous thing to do. It was Vidhu Vinod Chopra's conviction that he accepted such songs from me.

It so happened that one day there was a sitting in the music room of RD Burman where Vidhu Vinod Chopra narrated his script. I heard everything and then I made the request that there should be a song at one particular scene where the boy sees the girl for the very first time, and is searching for her. He couldn't agree with me, but I insisted that there can be a very good song at this juncture. He heard me and said, 'Okay, all right, you write the song and we will keep it if it is good. There is no problem in that ... So when shall we meet next? Let's meet on Wednesday at 4 pm.' I agreed, but it so happened that I had written nothing by Wednesday. I was driving the car myself as I was going for the 4 o'clock meeting. On the way I was thinking: What will I say when I reach there? I had argued with all of them. They were saying there can be no song at this place and I was insistent. What will I go there and say? That I haven't written the song at all? They will think I am a fool! There used to be a Lido cinema hall in Juhu. I was thinking of all this as I was driving. I went in and they said, 'What about the song?' I said, 'There is a terrific

RD Burman and Javed Akhtar

angle and I was thinking that if all of you agree then I will do it; there is no problem. The angle is *"Eik ladki ko dekha to aisa laga"* and then there will be similes, as in "I saw a girl and felt like this, or like that".'

Now, the thought had occurred to me only to save my skin because I had to say something. RD said, 'It's a great idea; why don't you do one thing? Why don't you write out the first antara here right now?' I wrote the first antara and RD kept it in front of him and started to sing. It didn't take him even a second. He sang it in the tune that you have heard the song in. He said, 'There won't be anything else in this song; there will only be three antaras. Now, you write two more antaras.' I said, 'All right.' And I wrote the second antara too, with ease. But I began to pant a bit by the time I reached the third antara. Normally, I complete a song in one sitting, but it took me two days to write this song. Ordinarily, I take thirty minutes to an hour to finish a song, but it took me two days to finish this because I didn't want to use certain similes. I wanted to have a certain purity in the song, a certain innocent quality. I could also have said, '*Jaise chhalka ho jaam* (like brimming goblets)'. But I didn't want any simile that indicated lust or any sin. I wanted to maintain a purity. Anyhow, the third antara was completed. The song has twenty-one similes. It was appreciated a lot and it became very famous. For the first time in my life, I won awards for a song. I got trophies for this song.

1942: A Love Story– RD's knock-out punch

RD Burman came into the industry with a new sound, a new rhythm, a new sensibility. He was a very sophisticated man. It's unfortunate that in the end people rejected such a genius. Mohammad Ali has written something very wise in his autobiography; he has said that a champion is one who, when he is about to fall to the ground, finds the energy from somewhere in his system and gathers all he has to deliver a knock-out punch to his opponent. And this is what RD Burman did. Circumstances in his life had completely wounded him, almost broken him, but he was RD Burman, he was a champion. He gathered all the energy in his system and delivered a knock-out punch in the music of *1942: A Love Story*.

As time passes, I think more and more people are beginning to respect RD Burman. That is the sign of a great man. Time makes a great man even greater... Time is kind to great people.

1942: A Love Story was important to Pancham and me in many ways. Had he been alive, he would have regained his lost position with this film, the position he deserved. The song from this film that everyone talks about is *'Eik ladki ko dekha...'*, but if you were to ask me, the song I like the most in this film is *'Kuchh na kaho, kuchh bhi na kaho...'* Not just Pancham's, but the values and traditions of the entire Burman family, I feel, have seeped into this song. This song has his father's touch and his own too. It has stability and depth, and by stability and depth I don't mean that you end up boring someone. There is a magic in this tune. This song is my favourite among all the songs I have written whose music has been composed by Pancham.

Pancham had worked with many singers and lyricists, but there was this team comprising RD Burman, Kishore Kumar and Anand Bakshi. Together, they have given many exceptional songs such as:

'Kuchh to log kaheingey, logon ka kaam hai kehna...'

'Zindagi ke safar mein guzar jaatey hain jo maqaam...'

Pancham was ahead of his times. We are gradually moving towards Pancham. He is coming alive once again for us. Pancham didn't have to try; music simply came out of him. He could make the tune for a song in just about a minute or two. It's my greatest good fortune that I have worked with Pancham.

RD Burman had left school at a very young age and come to Mumbai where his father, Sachin Dev Burman, was a very successful music director. There are many advantages to being the son of a great man, but believe me, there are some disadvantages too. Sometimes people have a certain reservation, or even hostility. 'Arre bhai, he is the son of a great man... what does he think? That he can also become a great man?' But the fact is that he was very talented. He was the worthy son of a worthy father.

He began to make his contribution from a very young age. A film called *Solva Saal* was released in 1958. It had a very famous song: *'Hai apna dil to awara, na jaane kis pe aayega...'* The mouth organ you hear in this song was played by this young boy. The mouth organ in the song from *Dosti* (1964) is also played by RD Burman: *'Jaane waale zara murh ke dekho mujhe...'*

There was a time when almost half the music in the Hindi film industry was with RD Burman and the remaining half with Lakshmikant Pyarelal and whatever little remained went to other music directors. Those were the days.

I am reminded of an incident that was narrated to me by RD Burman. His father SD Burman had suffered a very severe heart attack. He was in the ICU. The doctor gave Pancham permission to meet his father briefly. He went in and found his father lying down. A cardiogram was attached to his father and on the screen the heartbeat could be heard: Tik-tok tik-tok tik-tok tik-tok tik-tok. His father signalled to him and, in a very faint and weak voice, said: 'See, this is the real beat of life. As long as this heartbeat is there in your songs, your songs will be all right.' What a beautiful thing Sachin Dev Burman said, and it seems to me that RD Burman took note of it. The heart's beat was always heard in RD Burman's music because his songs were made in the most heartfelt manner. Now, the heart feels differently at different times. Sometimes it brims over with mischief, sometimes with grave thoughts, sometimes with love or with sorrow, but no matter what the feeling, emotion, mood or sentiment, when RD Burman captured it, it would seem as though it had come from the wellspring of his heart.

Sandese aate hain, hamein tarhpaate hain
Jo chitthi aati hai woh poochhe jaati hai
Kisi dilwali ne, kisi matwali ne
Hamey khat likha hai, ye hamse poochha hai
Kisi ki saanson ne, kisi ki dharhkan ne
Kisi ki choorhi ne, kisi ke kangan ne
Kisi ke kajre ne, kisi ke gajre ne
Mehakti subhaon ne, machalti shaamon ne
Akeli raaton ne, adhoori baton ne
Tarsati baahon ne
Aur poochha hai tarsi nigahon ne
Ke ghar kab aaogey, likho kab aaogey
Ke tum bin ye ghar soona soona hai

FILM *Border*
DIRECTOR *J.P. Dutta*
1997
SINGERS Sonu Nigam, Roop Kumar Rathore
MUSIC Anu Malik

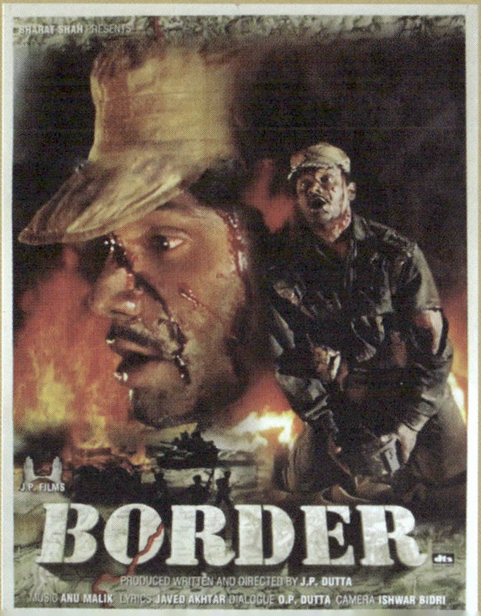

In many ways, Javed sahab's writing is ahead of its time

Anu Malik

Anu Malik on Javed Akhtar

I met Javed sahab for the first time in connection with one of his films when I was a child. He has been a great storyteller. His team of Salim–Javed was incredible. I am remembering *Zanjeer*. I came to know him through his songs for *Silsila*. I like *'Dekha eik khwaab...'* I have always respected him because of his writings. Whenever I met him, I found him to be an open-hearted pleasant person who does not carry his success on his shoulders, one who is aware of his contribution to the film industry but doesn't go around bragging about it. He is one of those people who always wants to move forward, to do something new.

We were working on films like *Duplicate* and a few other projects, but I will give extra brownie points to the film *Border*. I want to express my gratitude to JP Datta because he had the belief that our pairing would be a successful one. I have won many awards thanks to Javed sahab's poetry. People tell me that when I work with Javed Akhtar sahab I produce good work such as the song '*Kiska hai ye tumko intezar, main hoon na...*'

Javed sahab is a talented writer. He can sit here and create a line on the spot and we would not even know how it happened or how he did it... Bingo! It just happens! He welcomes criticism, but only when he feels it too. You have to prove that, 'See, this is not correct,' and he will ask 'Why?' If you criticise only for the sake of criticism, he will get angry because you are criticising without any good reason. He is very careful, very principled. He knows exactly what he is talking about. He can look into you. If he knows you are correct, then he will defer to you. You can't simply say that you didn't like it and get away with it.

There's much to be said for Javed Akhtar. He is like a child. He can take offence very easily, but he also becomes all right quickly. He looks as though he keeps everyone in control, but he doesn't always do that. He has an endless supply of jokes. In many ways, his writing is way ahead of his time. He and I work well together because he expects a vivid and melodious tune, and if the base is classical, he likes it even more. Take, for example, the song *'Gori gori'* from *Main Hoon Na*. It is very different from the song *'Aisa lagta hai'* from *Refugee*—both for the writer and the music composer, they are two very different songs.

◂ *Javed Akhtar and the music composer Anu Malik*

Maati re maati re maati re maati re

Rut aaye din aaye jo aaye dukh laaye

Dekh le humne kaise umariya kaati re, maati re ...

Desh chhoota, ghar chhoota, chhoote ghar aangan

Kaat hi daaley dukhon ne janmon ke bandhan

Dard ne hii dil ki khaii paati re, maati re

Main bhali ya buri thhi

Ab kahoon main kya

Har gharhi jaise bhanwar mein thi meri naiyya

Thak gayii hoon larhte larhte apne jeevan se

Gode le le mujhe maati meri maiyya

Hai andheri maut ki ye ghaati re

Maati re maati re maati re maati re

SINGER Lata Mangeshkar **MUSIC** Vishal Bhardwaj

FILM *Godmother*

DIRECTOR *Vinay Shukla*

1999

Film director and writer Vinay Shukla and Javed Akhtar

Names do not get inscribed in history just like that

Vinay Shukla

Vinay Shukla on Javed Akhtar

In the dialogues written by Javed Akhtar, words are not mere words; they are thoughts that have been flown into words. In *Deewaar*, when Vijay says, '*Main kisi ke phenke huwe paise nahi uthhata*,' then it isn't just Vijay's self-respect that glimmers through but that of all humanity. He gives the same respect to Anita, the call girl in *Deewaar*, that he does to Radha in *Sholay*. (Here I consider it appropriate to say that in all the films credited to Salim–Javed, while the script was written by both together, the responsibility for the dialogues was only Javed sahab's). Javed sahab's temperament speaks in his dialogues. When he speaks, the editor inside him has his finger on the 'Delete' button and that is why his scenes and his dialogues are so taut. His punchline is always incredible. He uses rhetoric too, but his word-play is not a mere display of word power like ordinary writers. His words carry the emotions of his characters and not mere sentimentality. While he knows how to play with words, you will find that in the scripts by Salim–Javed, silence is beautifully used as well. For example, the silent unspoken love between Radha and Jai in *Sholay*; Vijay coming home at the time of his mother's death in *Shakti* and expressing his grief without saying a word; in *Sholay*, the sound of the horse's hooves in the scene showing Ahmed's death, causing Imam sahab to ask, '*Itna sannata kyun hai, bhai?*'

It is said that literature is a mirror of society. Even a film can acquire the place of literature in the hands of a gifted scriptwriter. *Deewaar* is an excellent example. We see a reflection of the India of 1970 in this film. The soul of this India has moved from the villages to the city. The burden of the country rests as much with the worker as with the peasant. Social mores are changing rapidly. Rampant unemployment and ever-increasing inflation have filled the heart of ordinary people with anger. Salim–Javed turn this anger into a character and present it on the silver screen in the form of Vijay, who is neither black or white, nor is he a hero with all admirable qualities. Vijay is a human being like you or me. He is not entangled in the coiled tresses of the heroine, but in the daily strife and struggle of life. Indian films found a new hero in him.

There was a time when a film would go on the floor and the screenplay would keep getting changed according to the shooting schedule. The incredible thing is that even most writers didn't have any real understanding of precisely what a screenplay is. A screenplay meant the romance between the hero and heroine, the villainy of the villain, action, songs and melodrama. No matter what the story might be, it could be beaten and thrashed to fit a formula. If you recall the character of Amitabh in *Zanjeer*, *Deewaar* and *Sholay*, he does not sing a single song and the character has psychological dimensions too. There must be logic in a story. It took a Salim–Javed to sensitise the industry to the fact that writing a screenplay is a technical art. They gave one successful film after the other and proved that the story is not merely the spine of a film but also its heart. And this was made possible only when you have the script in your hand well before you begin shooting the film. Salim–Javed beat the drums of a film-writer's job so well that its sound could be heard not just by the producers and directors, but by the ordinary film-goers also. They gave respect to film writing and empowered writers to understand their own importance and their monetary worth. Names do not get inscribed in history just like that.

Ashutosh Gowarikar and Javed Akhtar

Javed sahab takes a song to an altogether different level

Ashutosh Gowariker

Ashutosh Gowarikar on Javed Akhtar

I saw the film *Zanjeer* when I was possibly nine years old. I found it special; it impressed me at several levels. At the time I didn't know Javed sahab's role in the film. I had turned into an 'angry young boy' after watching the film. Many years later, I saw a hoarding on Juhu beach which said 'Trishul by Salim–Javed'; it made no mention of the director or the producer or even the actors. But the names of these two writers were even above the film title. Then I saw *Zanjeer* with greater awareness. In Javed sahab's films, when it comes to the hero's relationship with his immediate family or girlfriend or wife or with society, his reactions are very different. At that time, the entire country was reflected in the image of the 'angry young man'. Disenchantment with the government, anger towards the administration, even opposition towards the powers-that-be—all this was reflected through the character of Vijay in these films. I often suspect, and I have shared this with Javed sahab, that he is Vijay, he is the 'angry young man', he is the romanticised version of the character of Vijay. He always laughs when I say this; he neither agrees nor disagrees.

When I was writing *Lagaan*, I had a 'wish list' in my mind: how wonderful it would be if AR Rahman were to give the music for this film and my joy would be doubled if Javed sahab were to write the lyrics. And as luck would have it, what I had hoped for came true. I got the opportunity to work with Javed sahab. I remember my first meeting with him very clearly, when I had to read out the script of *Lagaan* for him. He gave me four hours' time. He heard the script, expressed his views, gave his opinion and expressed his doubts. I was thinking he will not say 'Yes.' But I was surprised when he said, 'My doubts are only about the storytelling, screenplay, dialogue; they will not come between my writing the lyrics. This is simply my advice regarding the script, something I feel which I consider important to register.' Later, when I made *Swades*, things became easier for me. Javed sahab takes the song to another level when he writes the words. As soon as he finishes writing the lyrics, the scene before and after the song is elevated to another level altogether.

I have come to a big conclusion as far as Javed sir is concerned. And it isn't just about the way he works nor is it merely about his script writing or his song writing, but after seeing his views about the world around us. Imagine if you have a box, you will only look at its six different sides, but Javed sir can see the seventh side of that very box!

Baar baar haan, bolo yaar haan
Apni jeet ho, unki haar ho
Koi humse jeet na paave
Chale chalo, chale chalo
Mit jaave jo takraave, chale chalo
Bhale ghor andhera chhave
Chale chalo, chale chalo
Koi raah mein naa thham jaave, chale chalo
Toot gayi jo ungli utthi
Panchon mili to ban gayi mutthi
Eka badhta hii jaave
Chale chalo, chale chalo

SINGERS *AR Rahman, Shri Nivas* **MUSIC** *AR Rahman*

FILM *Lagaan*

DIRECTOR *Ashutosh Gowarikar*

2001

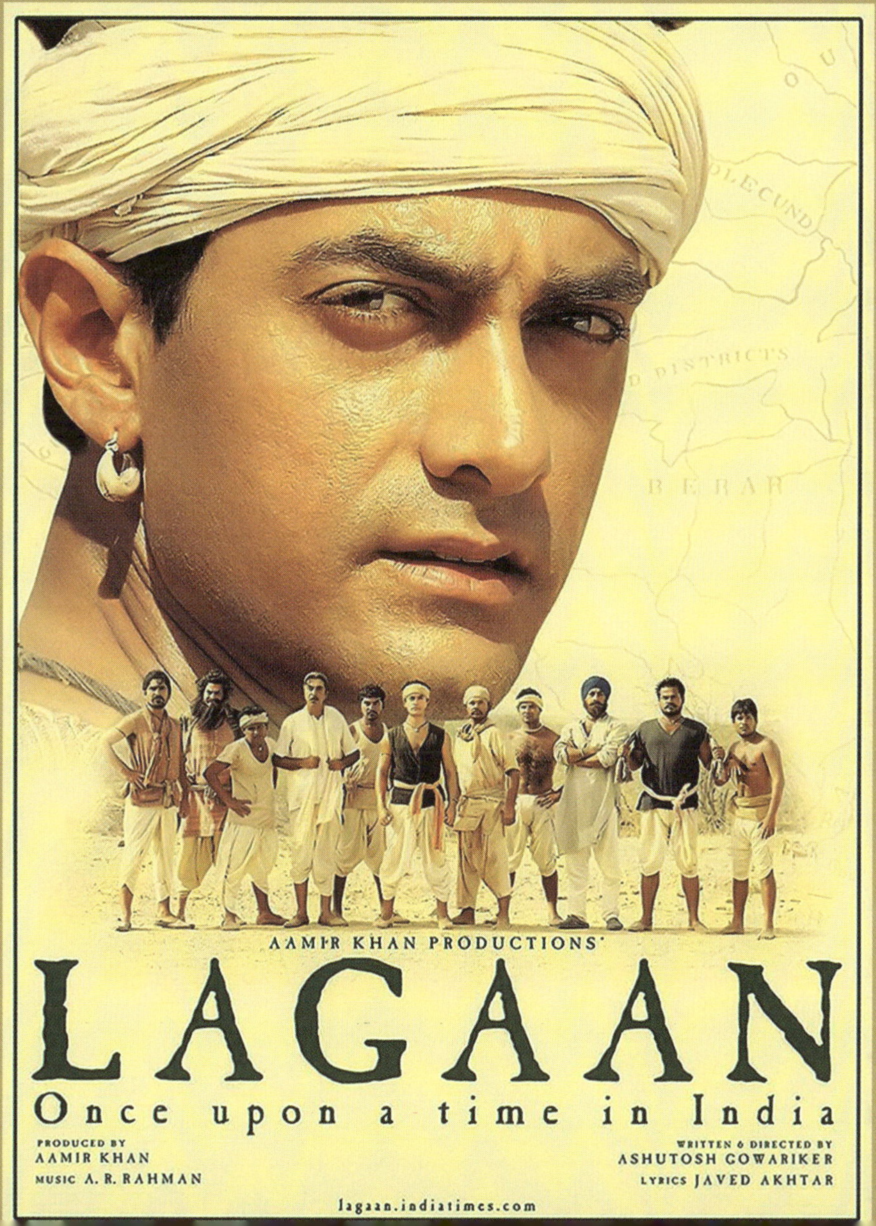

He always writes from two or three or four perspectives

Karan Johar

Karan Johar on Javed Akhtar

My parents were friends with Javed sahab and Honey aunty. I have grown up with Farhan and Zoya. I have a heap of memories of shootings during school holidays. My father had produced a film, *Dostana*, which was written by Javed sahab and Salim sahab. After this, the friendship between our families deepened. Javed sahab has been attached to us for a very long time. The other film made by my father was *Duniya*. By then Salim sahab and Javed sahab had separated as writers. Javed sahab has scripted this film entirely on his own, and also written its songs.

When I was directing my first film, *Kuchh Kuchh Hota Hai,* I asked him to write the songs. He wrote one song. There was a lack of dialogue between us that affected our thought processes. And so we went our separate ways amicably. I have the greatest respect and regard for his work and his talent in my heart. He is a genius. I think he is among the most intelligent people in the film industry and I was dying to work with him. So I called him and said, 'Look, you have to work with me on this.' And when he wrote the first four lines for *Kal Ho Naa Ho* I said to myself, 'So, okay, my genius has returned home.' Now I can't think of working with anyone else except him.

I was new when I was writing *Kuchh Kuchh Hota Hai*. I was a bit too hysterical, but I am calmer now. Today, he trusts me. My disagreement with him was only on the title of the film and I was adamant about using it. He had liked the script of the film. He believed I should go in for a more intense title, not a frivolous one which he thought *Kuchh Kuchh Hota Hai* was. I had said that this tile would become a 'buzz expression' and it did.

When we worked together on *Kal Ho Naa Ho,* we didn't have any disagreement on a single word. By then we had begun to understand each other better. When Javed sir feels comfortable with someone, when he trusts them, when he likes them, then the work atmosphere becomes very conducive.

Silsila was his first step in the world of lyrics writing. His best four lines are '*Dekha eik khwaab to ye silsile huye, phool bhi hon darmiyan to faasle huye.*' These lines say it all: love, romance, betrayal, infidelity. Despite being frugal with his words, he says a great deal. He always writes from two or three or four perspectives. While he writes for a specific context, his lines have a universal connect.

◂ *Film producer-director Karan Johar and Javed Akhtar*

Har gharhi badal rahi hai roop zindagi
Chhanv hai kabhi, kabhi hai dhoop zindagi
Har pal yahaan jii bhar jiyo
Jo hai samaa kal ho naa ho

Chhahe jo tumhe poore dil se
Milta hai woh mushkil se
Aisa jo koi kahin hai
Bas woh hii sabse haseen hai
Uss haath ko tum thham lo
Woh meherbaan kal ho naa ho
Har pal yahaan jii bhar jiyo
Jo hai samaa kal ho naa ho

SINGER *Sonu Nigam* **MUSIC** *Shankar Ehsan Loy*

FILM *Kal Ho Naa Ho*

DIRECTOR *Nikhil Advani*

2003

Javed Akhtar with Shah Rukh Khan on the sets of Main Hoon Na *(Film City, Mumbai, 2004)*

I have had the good fortune of working with Javed Akhtar

Shah Rukh Khan

I have known Javed sir since I came to Mumbai. The way my thoughts and ideas have formed, the many things that I have learnt, I have learnt from him. Javed Akhtar has given far more than those who claim to have contributed to Hindi cinema. Because of the songs he has written and the ideas we have shared, he has had a role to play in my success too. I feel the lack of not having worked with artists of the calibre of Sanjiv Kumar or Balraj Sahni or Madhubala. And I also miss the fact that I have not seen Raj Kapoor or K. Asif or Guru Dutt in their studios. But I will say that I have had the good fortune of working with Javed Akhtar.

It was both easy and difficult to write a good song for Yash Chopra

I worked on *Veer–Zaara* with Yash ji after *Mashaal*. Yash Chopra sahab was one of those people who understood language and poetry and the nuances of both. It was both easy and difficult to write a good song for him. It was easy because if you write correctly, he would understand, and difficult because if you have made the slightest mistake then, too, he would understand and spot the error! It is enjoyable to work with such people because you stretch yourself and you want to prove what is the best you can do. This also gives you an opportunity to expand yourself. There was a song that was sung by Roop Kumar Rathore and Lata ji... '*Tere liye...*' people liked this song very much. The strange thing about this song and this film is that the music director of this film was Madan Mohan who had left this world years ago.

Jaanam dekh lo mit gayiin duriyan
Main yahan hoon, yahan hoon, yahan hoon, yahaan
Kaisi sarhadein, kaisi majburiyan
Main yahan hoon, yahan hoon, yahan hoon, yahaan

Tum chhupa na sakogee main woh raaz hoon
Tum bhula na sakogee woh andaaz hoon
Goonjta hoon jo dil mein to hairaan ho kyun
Main tumhare hii dil ki to awaaz hoon
Sun sako to suno dhadkanon ki zabaan
Main yahan hoon, yahan hoon, yahan hoon, yahaan

SINGER *Udit Narayan* **MUSIC** *Madan Mohan*

FILM *Veer-Zara*

DIRECTOR *Yash Chopra*

2004

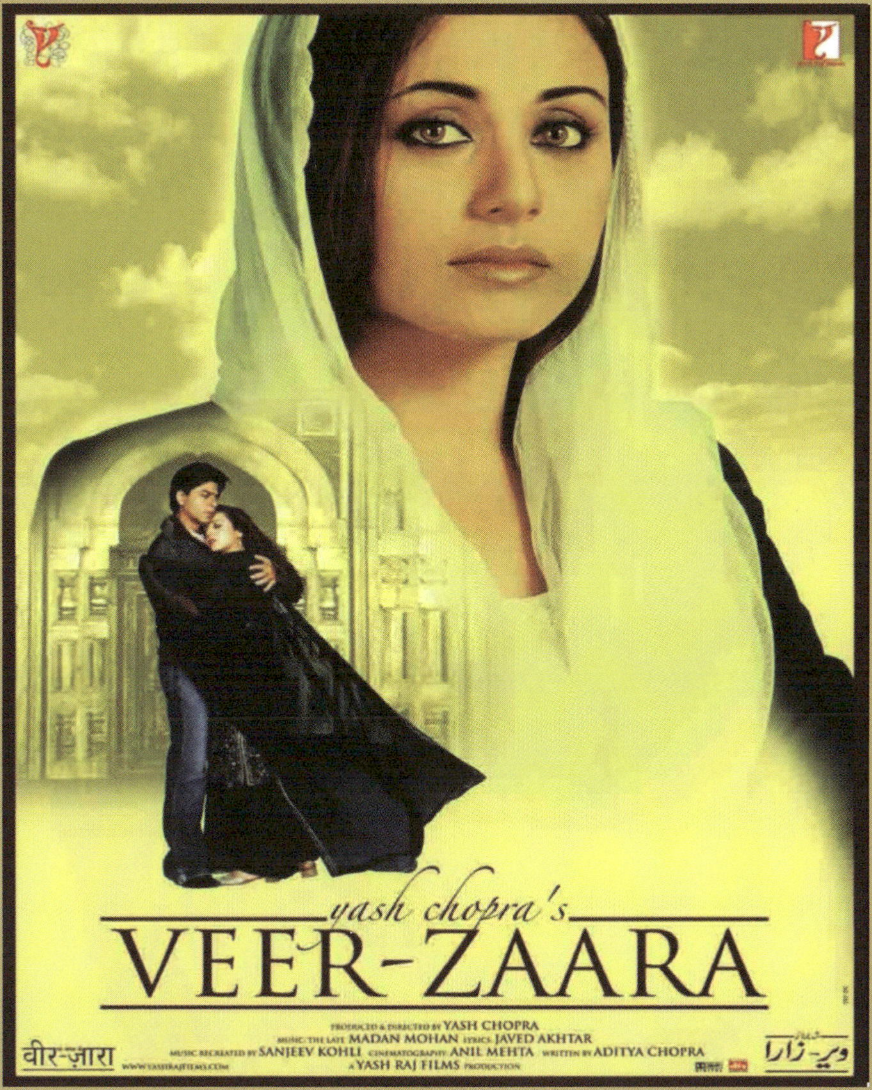

Madan Mohan

Years later, Madan Mohan's music was used in *Veer-Zara*

If one were to talk of the ghazal in Hindi cinema with anyone who knows even a little about the history of film music, the first name that is taken is Madan Mohan's. He played a long innings in film music and gave many memorable songs, such as:
- *Aapki nazron ne samjha pyaar ke qaabil mujhe (Anpadh)*
- *Do dil toote, do dil hare (Heer Ranjha)*
- *Aaj socha to aansu bhar aaye (Hanste Zakham)*

Madan Mohan, Kaifi Azmi and Chetan Anand formed a triangle and did some incredible work together, such as:
- *Main ye soch kar uske dar se utha thha (Haqiqat)*
- *Meri duniya mein tum aayiin kya kya apne saath liye (Heer Ranjha)*
- *Tum jo mil gaye ho to ye lagta hai ke jahaan mil gaya (Hanste Zakham)*

Madan Mohan sahab has a son, Sanjiv, who has done a huge favour to me. Let me tell you about it. It so happened that one day, Yash Chopra sahab called me and when we met he said, 'I am making this film and you have to write the songs. There are a lot of songs in this film.' I asked. 'How many songs?' Yash ji said, 'Ten songs.' So I said, 'All right, I'll write them. Who is the music director?' To which he said, 'I am taking the music of Madan Mohan in this film.' I asked, 'Whose music are you taking?' He said again, 'Madan Mohan.' I asked, 'How?' That's when he said, 'Look, he has a son, Sanjiv, who has a cassette and a tape on which Madan Mohan ji has left behind some tunes and those tunes are so beautiful that it would be a grave injustice if they remain within the confines of the tape. I have requested Sanjiv that I want to record these tunes and he is ready. Now, I want you to write the songs on these tunes.' I said, 'It is my great honour. I could never have dreamt that destiny would have this great good fortune waiting for me... that Madan Mohan ji has left us and gone away but I will be able to write songs on his tunes.'

Javed Akhtar with Jagjit Singh and Shiv–Hari

Chaley jaise hawain sanan-sanan
Urhe jaise parinde gagan-gagan
Jayein titliyan jaise chaman-chaman
Yoon hii ghoomoon main bhi magan-magan

Main diwani dil ki rani
Gham se anjani
Kab darti hoon
Woh karti hoon jo hai thhani
Chaley jaise hawain...

SINGERS Vasundhara Das, Kay Kay **MUSIC** Anu Malik

FILM *Main Hoon Na*
DIRECTOR *Farah Khan*
2004

Film director and choreographer Farah Khan

Javed uncle's house was a sort of FTII

Farah Khan

Actually, Javed sir is technically my ex-uncle. He was married to Honey Aunty who is my mother's real younger sister. So he is my 'Masa'. His marriage ended after a while, but it never occurred to me ever that he is no longer my Masa and that he be treated any differently.

Struggling actors, musicians and cameramen also lived in Honey Aunty and Javed Uncle's huge bungalow. Actually, this house was like the FTII. I know several people such as Satish Shah, Aman Kumar, Benjamin Gilani, Kamaljit Singh, Pankaj Parashar quite well because I met them at Javed Uncle's house when I was a child.

There is no doubt whatsoever that *Sholay* is my favourite film. If you were to see my film *Main Hoon Naa,* you will find dozens of tributes that I have given to *Sholay*. I like his other films such as *Majboor.* These were great scripts, especially those where the dialogues had been written by Javed Uncle. People still remember their dialogues and songs. I think that the 'Angry Young Man' is one of the finest creations of that time. The female characters in his films are always strong. Javed Uncle looks at women as being equal to anyone who has an independent view.

For me, he will always be Javed Uncle. When I was doing my film, if Javed Uncle had not written the songs, then it would have been made without songs. I fight a lot with him. But he has one of the easiest temperaments. If he thinks you are right then he will have no ego problems in admitting so. If you make a good suggestion, he will certainly adopt it. He is one of those people who can find something humorous in the worst situation. Once we had an argument over one, single word. His favourite words are *dharti–ambar (earth–sky),* which he later exchanged for the word *gagan* (sky). I want to be in a music sitting with Javed Uncle while a song is being written. He is one of the finest film lyricists in the country. When he writes the lyrics, he manages to capture the essence of the song. He needs a central point in a song, as in *'Main Hoon Naa' or 'Kal Ho Naa Ho'*. These songs are seemingly very simple yet they contain several profound meanings. You might think you are reading poetry, but these are commercial film songs that everyone can understand.

When it was written, *'Eik ladki ko dekha'* was an entirely new form. He wrote a rock qawwali for me. If I had to choose the Top 3 Interesting People, he would be one of them.

A perfect use of songs in the narrative

As a musician, I believe that Javed Akhtar has the perfect use of songs in a narrative. He has a huge storehouse of words and yet he is very careful in their selection. He is a great conversationalist and is always very interesting company. He is very good at expressing himself. At the time of recording a song, he knows instantly which word is working and which word needs to be changed. For instance, his song '*Chanda re chanda*' is very melodious despite being very simple.

Javed Akhtar and AR Rahman

Kehne ko jashn-e bahara hai
Ishq ye dekh ke hairaan hai
Phool se khushbu khafa-khafa hai gulshan mein
Chhupa hai koi ranj fiza ke chilman mein
Saare sehme nazaaare hain
Soye-soye waqt ke dhaare hain
Aur dil mein khoi-khoi sii baatein hain
Kehne ko jashn-e-bahara hai

SINGER Javed Ali **MUSIC** AR Rahman

FILM *Jodha Akbar*
DIRECTOR *Ashutosh Gowarikar*
2008

Farhan Akhtar, Javed Akhtar, Zoya Akhtar and Shabana Azmi

I want to see larger-than-life films made by Farhan and Zoya

I am extremely proud of the fact that there isn't even my shadow on Farhan and Zoya's work. They have their own tone, tenor and style. They are totally original. The films that these children have made are vastly different from their father's. That is the way it should be; instead of us being so impressed by our elders that we try to become like them, we should be better than them. I will not criticise them as writers and directors, but I want to see them make larger-than-life films. I want to see them make what is called a 'magnum opus'.

Father-son: Javed Akhtar and Farhan Akhtar; Zoya and Farhan on Rakshabandhan

GUFTAGU

In conversation with Javed Akhtar

Arvind Mandloi

Zoya and Farhan have their own voice and identity

Farhan and Zoya are both very successful today. How do you see their success? As a father, you must be happy, but as someone who knows and understands cinema, how do you assess them?

I am very happy at their success as any father would be for their children. But the other thing that pleases me very much is that they have a voice of their own; they are not an echo. Normally, what happens is that when children make a film, they try to make films like their father did. They try to adopt the same style. I can give many such examples. But these two have never done that, whether it was Farhan's first film, *Dil Chahta Hai*, or Zoya's debut film, *Luck By Chance*, or any of their subsequent films. You won't see even my shadow in any of Zoya's films. Both have their own voice, their own identity. The other thing is that both of them have never compromised for the sake of success such as, for example, occasionally inserting a vulgar song in their film, or putting in something in bad taste thinking it will please the public. They have both maintained a certain standard. How well or how poorly their films might do is a separate matter, but all their films have a certain class, there is a certain decency in them which is a very big thing. These days when people are so desperate for their films to succeed no matter what the quality of dialogues or songs or dances, I don't see that anxiety, that restlessness, that haste, or that greed in my children's work. I truly respect this.

Do you have a message for Zoya and Farhan? Is there anything that you have learnt in life that you would like to tell them?

I don't want to give them any message. Because I don't think they need any message from me. In my heart I know that they are both better human beings than me. Life has given them many privileges, but that ease, that privilege has not spoilt them; instead, it has made them better human beings. I am very proud of both. And the truth is sometimes, quietly, without telling them, I also learn something from them!

How do you see Zoya's oeuvre as a film-maker?

I think because I am a writer, my attention first goes to the writing and then to film direction. I respect her very much as a writer. I think she is a very, very good writer. She has brought something to Hindi cinema that never existed till now, that is, a character's multi-faceted quality. You can see what a character is on the surface, but she also shows you what is inside him or her, and under the layers. She tells you what is beneath the layers. The other thing is that she does not hate any character. She has no villains. The bad people in her films, or at least the ones we consider bad, show us a side of their personality as though she is telling us, 'Look here, it is not his fault. See the circumstances he has gone through, how he has been brought up, and what happened to him.' And you feel sympathy even for that 'bad' person. Take, for instance, the character of Anil Kapoor in *Dil Dhadakne Do*. Had an average film-maker made this film, they would have shown Anil Kapoor's character as a hard, selfish, opportunistic father who is using his children and wants to arrange his son's marriage so that it benefits his business. What a clever, selfish person he would have been! But she didn't do that. He is doing all of the above, and yet you have sympathy for the man. You say to yourself, 'What is the poor thing to do? He has his own problems.' So Zoya has this quality of seeing every human being with love and softness. It is a very big thing.

Have you ever shared a moment with Zoya that has made you very emotional? And very happy at the same time?

There must be many such moments. I am very proud of my daughter. I like her very much. I have a great love for her in my heart, but I also have a lot of respect for her. I respect her. And that is because I feel she is true to her work, she is true to life, she is true to her family and her friends. Her heart is in the right place.

Which is your earliest memory about Farhan that you can recollect for us?

There are many. Farhan was a very interesting child and so I remember many of his stories. I think he was four or five years old. I was lying on the bed and he was sitting beside me. He had both his hands on my chest and he was talking to me. I said to him, 'Farhan, tell me something: When I get old and I won't be able to do any work, will you look after me?' He said, 'Yes, yes, of course!' I asked, 'What will you do for me?' I used to smoke cigarettes at that time. So he said, 'I will get cigarettes for you.' I asked, 'How will you get the cigarettes? Where will you get the money for them?' He said, 'I will take the money from Mummy.' I said, 'But I give money to Mummy. When I am not working, Mummy won't have money too. What will you do then?' He thought for a moment and then he clung to me and said, 'Papa, don't get old!' Once, I had written this incident about Farhan and I had also written that when he asks me to write songs for films like *Rock On* and *Dil Chahta Hai*, actually, there is a great conspiracy behind it. By getting me to write such songs, he doesn't want me to get old, ever! Because if I get old, he will have an additional responsibility! And that is why he asks me to write youthful songs for his films.

That Farhan will carry forward the family legacy of creativity, the legacy that has been handed down for generations... when did you first realise this?

Look, our family tradition is that we consider our son to be worthless to begin with. My father was considered worthless by his father, and my father thought I was a no-good waster, and I thought Farhan was incompetent. For a long time, I was worried about Farhan. I used to wonder if this boy will ever do anything or not. But see how he has amazed me and proved me wrong... it's something that makes me very happy.

As a scriptwriter, as a poet, as a film-maker, how do you assess Farhan? What do you expect from him in the future?

Look, I am a very objective person. If I don't like the songs of my own film or any other film, I never listen to them again. If I don't like a script I have written, I will not watch that film again. But I will say this about Farhan that his very first film, *Dil Chahta Hai*, was a path-breaking film. It was in a class by itself. It influenced many films down the years. After this film, the style, the class, the feel of several films changed. One of his great achievements is that not only was he successful, but he was successful in making a film that was written about in the editorials of some of the greatest national newspapers. This is not an ordinary achievement. It is a very big thing. I rate Farhan very highly as an actor, too. I think he is a very good actor. He is a good dialogue writer.

You have given total freedom to your children and raised them as equals. When did you first realise that these children have now become your friends?

I have never adopted the traditional father's role towards my children from the very beginning. I have always spoken to them with love and informal ease, especially Farhan, who has a terrific sense of humour; he can keep regaling us with endless jokes, incidents and stories. I, too, try to keep pace so that he doesn't think he is the only one with a sense of humour. So, when

Zoya and Farhan Akhtar with their mother Honey Irani

we meet this is how we talk. And yet I respect my children's individuality, their opinions, their views and ideas. The manner in which these children have been raised and the way their own opinions have formed, forget communalism, not a trace of religion or religiosity has gone anywhere near them. They were never told or taught any such thing. They never saw any such thing around them or in their home. I remember that when Farhan was nine or ten years old and used to watch matches, the first thing he would do would be to affix the national flag on top of the television set and then watch the match holding the flag in his hand. A child who has been raised in this manner, when someone casts aspersions on him, I feel very sad. I tell him that such people are mad and that he should not take what such people say to heart and that, actually, this country is a country of very good people.

When you see Farhan and Zoya's continuous success, what do you, as a person who has a sense of the film industry, feel?

It is still too soon; such a decision cannot be made yet. They have just started. It is true that both have made several films, but as to what will be their influence in later years, or how long that influence will last, it would be hasty to come to any conclusion just yet. It is true that *Dil Chahta Hai* or Zoya's new film, *Gully Boy,* have presented a certain standard for other young film-makers. There are many talented people around today. Young boys and girls are doing exceedingly good work. These two are not alone. All I can say is that *Dil Chahta Hai* has influenced many people and as a consequence, young film-makers have changed their approach, technique, production style and presentation.

Farhan had shot for his film, *Lakshya*, at the IMA (Indian Military Academy) in Dehradun. Two or three years ago, he was invited to deliver the annual keynote address there. There were approximately 900 young men in the hall there who will be officers in our armed forces in the years ahead. When they were asked how many of them had decided to join the army after watching *Lakshya*, almost 75 per cent of them raised their hands. Farhan told me that when he saw this, tears came into his eyes.

Dil chahta hai
Kabhi naa beete chamkeele din
Hum na rahein kabhi yaaron ke bin
Din-din bhar hon pyaari baatein
Jhoomein shaamein gaayein raatein
Masti mein rahe dooba-dooba hamesha sama
Humko raahon mein milti rahein yun hiin khushiyan
Dil chahta hai
Jagmagate hain jhilmilaate hain apne raastey
Ye khushi rahey ye roshni rahey apne waastey
Dil chahta hai

SINGER Shankar Mahadevan **MUSIC** Shankar Ehsan Loy

FILM *Dil Chahta Hai*

DIRECTOR *Farhan Akhtar*

2001

'Saahab, banaane wale ne to eik dharti banaayi thii... par insaan ke laalach ne iss par lohey aur barood ki lakeerein kheench diin.'

OM PURI IN THE ROLE OF SUBEDAR MAJOR PRITAM SINGH

FILM *Lakshya*

DIRECTOR *Farhan Akhtar*

2004

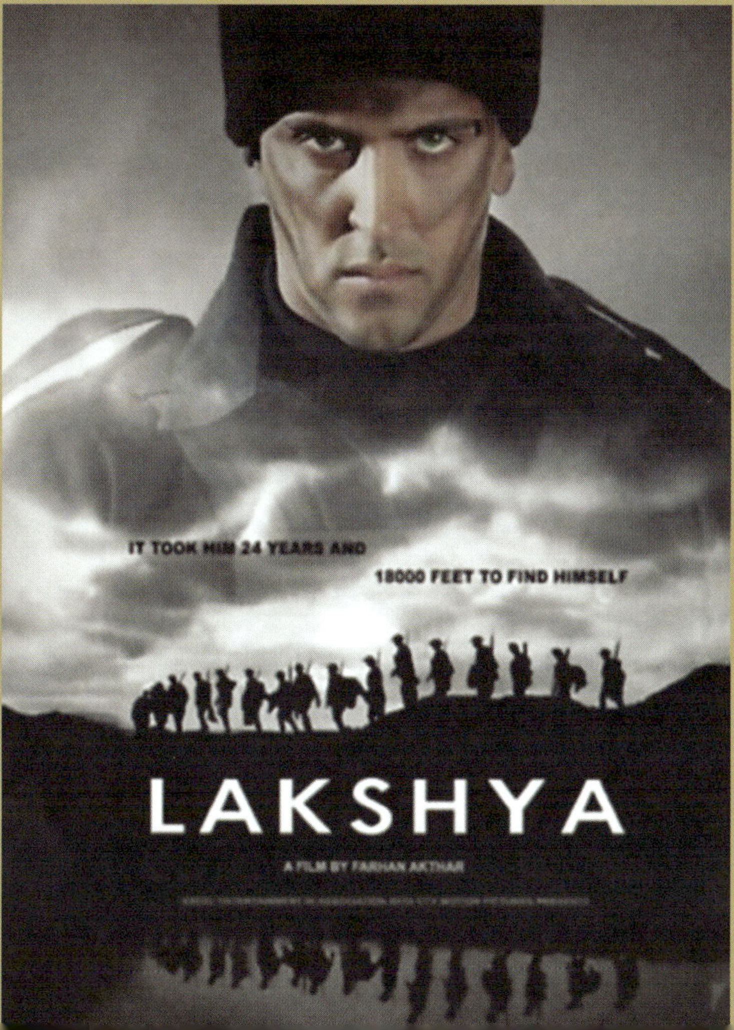

Uljhi huyii ye doriyaan suljha le
Dil ki tu suney agar
Dil sachha hai dilwale
Raahein nahi aisi to kahiin
Jahan kahiin koi morh nahii
Kehta hai ye dil ab jaane bhi de
Tootey shishon ko tu jorh nahii
Raahon mein do raahe aatey hain sau baar
Qadam-qadam iqraar hai
Qadam-qadam inkaar
Phir bhi ye zindagi
Pal bhar ko bhi kabhi rukti hii nahii...

SINGERS Farhan Akhtar, Vishal Dadlani, Divya Kumar

MUSIC Shankar Ehsan Loy

FILM *Dil Dhadakne Do*

DIRECTOR *Zoya Akhtar*

2015

Aasmaan hai neela kyun

Paani gila-gila kyun

Gol kyun hai zameen

Silk mein hai narmi kyun

Aag mein hai garmi kyun

Do aur do paanch kyun nahii

Perh ho gaye kum kyun

Teen hain ye mausam kyun

Chaand do kyun nahii

Duniya mein hai zang kyun

Hai bahta laal rang kyun

Sarhadein hain kyun har kahiin

Socha hai ye tumne kya kabhi

Socha hai ke ye kya sabhi

Socha nahi to socho abhi...

SINGER Farhan Akhtar **MUSIC** Shankar Ehsan Loy

FILM *Rock On*

DIRECTOR *Abhishek Kapoor*

2008

GUFTAGU

In conversation with Zoya Akhtar

Arvind Mandloi

My father has never looked at me as though I am a girl and so I should stay like this or like that

What are those qualities that you think make Javed sahab who he is?

I think primarily his sense of fairness and his views on equality. When Farhan and I were growing up (Farhan is a year younger), we were like twins. I never sensed any difference. I didn't know that my mother's family were Parsis who are supposed to be very liberal. Even in college, I had more freedom than Farhan. When I made new friends and found out that girls were not allowed to go out, it was like a shock to me. My father never looked at me as though I am a girl and so I should stay like this or like that...

When you were growing up, did your father notice any changes in you?

One tends to be very rebellious during teenage, so I used to fight a lot with him because I wanted to do this or that, and I wanted to leave college. I didn't want to study. Only once he said to me, 'Do whatever you want in life, I won't interfere, but it is my responsibility that you should be educated.' Afterwards, I went to America to study film-making. Now when I look back, I say, 'Thank you very much,' because all that I studied has come in great use in my writing and in my work as a film-maker. Later, when I began to work, I got a lot of guidance from him when it came to choosing a career. Now I feel we are friends; we are not a parent-child. Now we can say anything to each other.

Is there any 'proud moment' with Javed sahab that you can remember?

He helped me a lot when he watched the rough cut of my film *Zindagi Na Milegi Dobara*. He watched it six times; he liked it so much. When he saw the rough cut of *Dil Dhadakne Do* for the first time, he liked it very much as well.

Is there anything about Javed sahab's life that none of us know, possibly not even his friends, that you know as his daughter?

Yes, he is very scared of dogs, but not of my dogs. My dogs recognise him. My mother used to have two Doberman when we were young. Once, when he came from somewhere, he could not enter the house because of the dogs. Then Farhan and I had to go and catch the dogs so he could come inside.

Any other remarkable quality?

Yes, he has great skin. Even at the age of seventy-five, his skin is healthy and taut. Farhan and I hope that we have inherited it from him and we won't get any wrinkles either. Farhan and I are proud of being his children. We hope that he remains healthy and continues to write.

As a film-maker, how do you see Javed Akhtar's work?

I want to make a documentary on Salim–Javed because never before, or since, has it happened that writers should suddenly appear and work together for eleven years, writing twenty-four films out of which twenty-two are blockbusters. Their price was a little more than that of the lead actor and this was unheard of in the film industry. The names of writers began to appear on posters because of them. HMV used to make records of their dialogues. They were a very special combination. The character they created out of the socio-political turmoil in the country, the mood of the nation, the mood of the common man, became a larger-than-life Bollywood character, one that was a mix of reality and imagination.

All the film-makers of my generation have grown up watching his films. So, he has certainly left an impression. His films were very secular. The other thing I find very unique in Salim–Javed films are the dialogues which we still see in films and advertisements. The impression they left on pop culture, it has not faded with time. And not just the dialogue of *Sholay,* but *Deewaar* too... *'Mere paas Maa hai.'* Memes are still being made on it in our digital world. I find this fascinating because I do not see it with any other writer.

The relationship between your parents, and their subsequent separation, how did it affect you, first as a child and then as an adult and a mentally mature person?

Look, the effect is there. My parents were very young. When they got married my mother was eighteen and my father was twenty-five years old. So ten years later, or whatever be the length of time, when the relationship was not working, they took a very mature decision. But in the 70s, divorces in the film industry were seen a bit weirdly in schools. People would say that only kids from the film industry have broken homes. But divorce is very common now. It was very healthy that my mother never said anything bad about him, nor did he ... never, not a thing!

DORAHA:

Apni Beti Zoya ke Naam

Ye jeevan eik raah nahi
Eik doraha hai

Pehla raasta
Bahut sahal hai
Isme koi morh nahi hai
Ye raasta
Iss duniya se bejorh nahi hai
Iss raaste par milte hain
Reeton ke aangan
Iss raaste par milte hain
Rishton ke bandhan
Iss raaste par chalne wale
Kehne ko sab sukh paate hain
Lekin

Tukde-tukde hokar
Sab rishton mein bant jaate hain
Apne palle kuchh nahiin bachta
Bachti hai
Benaami sii uljhan
Bachta hai
Saanson ka indhan
Jismein unkii apni har pehchaan

Aur unke saare sapne
Jal bujhte hain
Iss raaste par chalne wale
Khud ko kho kar jag paate hain
Upar-upar toh jeete hain
Andar-andar mar jaate hai.

Doosra raasta
Bahut kathin hai
Iss raaste mein
Koi kisi ke saath nahii hai
Koi sahara dene wala haath nahii hai
Iss raaste mein
Dhoop hai
Koi chhanv nahii hai
Jahan tassalli bheek mein de de koi kisi ko
Iss raaste mein

Aisa koi gaanv nahi hai
Ye unn logon ka raasta hai
Jo khud apne tak jaate hain
Apne aapko jo paate hain
Tum iss raaste par hii chalna.

Mujhe pata hai
Ye raasta aasan nahi hai
Lekin mujhko ye gham bhi hai
Tumko ab tak
Kyun apni pehchaan nahii hai.

Dilon mein tum apni betaabiyaan leke chal rahe ho
To zinda ho tum
Nazron mein khwabon ki bijliyan le ke chal rahe ho
To zinda ho tum
Hawa ke jhonkon ke jaisa azaad rehna seekho
Tum eik dariya ke jaise lehron mein behna seekho
Har eik lamhe se tum milo khole apni baahein
Har eik pal eik naya sama dekhein ye nigahein
Jo apni aankhon mein hairaniyan le ke chal rahe ho
To zinda ho tum
Dilon mein tum apni betaabiyaan le ke chal rahe ho
To zinda ho tum

SINGER Farhan Akhtar **MUSIC** Shankar Ehsan Loy

FILM *Zindagi Na Milegi Dobara*

DIRECTOR *Zoya Akhtar*

2011

Eik hi raasta jis pe
Chupchap sar ko jhukaye huye
Band aankhein kiye
Log chalte hain saare janam
Jaante bhi nahi
Sochte bhi nahi
Puchte bhi nahi
Unko ye raasta
Lekar kahin jayega?
Ya kahin bhi nahi?
Chalte chalte kahin
Eik morh aata hai
Seedhe raaste se bilkul alag
Koi deewana hi hota hai
Jo udhar jata hai
Warna baaqi to
Sab seedhe raaste pe hii
Apne saare janam chalte hai
Sir jhukaye huye
Band aankhein kiye
Aur ye dukh liye
Morh jo dekha tha
Uss pe murh jaate hum
To na jaane kahan tak
Pahunch paate hum

SINGER Ranveer Singh **MUSIC** Rishi Rich

FILM *Gully Boy*

DIRECTOR *Zoya Akhtar*

2019

Farhan and Javed Akhtar

GUFTAGU

In conversation with Farhan Akhtar

Arvind Mandloi

Everyone I meet says to me, 'Yaar, I have never seen a person as witty as your dad'

Javed Akhtar sahab has left a mark on Indian cinema. As a director, how do you see his contribution?

When you see his films, be it *Deewaar* or *Haathi Mere Saathi*, you feel very clearly that he has left melodrama far behind. The relationships that existed in Hindi cinema till that point became very realistic with the coming of Salim–Javed. They were very modern, modern in their thinking. They wrote realistic characters. Their sense of dialogue was such that everything they wrote had a huge impact, yet it did not seem like rhetoric or bombastic wordplay. It was a painstakingly created craft and extremely intelligent writing. The way they used dialogues, how they began their scenes, where they ended them, this craft was very impactful. It has left its mark all these years later, on present-day writers.

The two of you worked on *Lakshya*, with him as scriptwriter and you as director. How did this combination of father-son and scriptwriter-director work?

First of all, there is the happiness and displeasure between each that you can understand without saying anything; that, in itself, solves problems. Because sometimes when you work with a much older or a very experienced person, it is very difficult to say, 'Sir, this line that you have written... how do I say it, how do I find the courage to say that it...' Whereas with him, he looks at my face and he can tell from my expression that I don't like it and he will say, 'Okay, okay, so you don't like this line.' He told me the story of *Lakshya*. Then we both worked on developing the screenplay. By then, he had understood my sensibility in making a film which, incidentally, is very important for a writer to grasp. I must give him the credit, 100 per cent credit, for adapting to my sensibility. You must understand that as writer, he has to adapt to the director's sensibility, which he did. And I learnt a great deal from his experience.

What effect did your parents' separation have on you as a child and, later, as an adult?

I think Zoya would recall its 'conscious impact' better than me. I haven't fully understood those years yet. I have talked to him, and I have talked to my mom to try and understand what had happened. When you are an adult, you understand. But as a child I didn't. At the same time, my mom never ever let either Zoya or me feel that we had been abandoned by him. This was very important. They made us feel that their separation had nothing to do with the children. The children will come to meet you whenever you want to meet them, she told him. She made us feel that his home was our second home where we could go whenever we wanted. I never had the feeling of discomfort that so much has changed that I cannot meet him now. And then there was the effort he made and so did Shabana ji. They never let us feel that our father has left us and gone away. That never happened.

There are many sides to Javed sahab's personality. He is a good poet; he is a concerned citizen. He has his own political vision. Of all these facets, what impresses you the most?

All these combine to make him unique. How can I say that this is better and this is not? He is Javed Akhtar because he is the sum of his parts. He doesn't consider his different responsibilities—be it creative, social, humanitarian— separate from each other.

What do you like the most about Javed sahab... something that makes him who he is?

His language, his prodigious memory for poetry, his understanding of writing, and his passion, his zeal to constantly improve himself, to forever re-invent himself.

When he was working with Yash ji, he was simultaneously working with me and with Karan Johar. So the man who can write songs for *Jodha Akbar* and *Rock On*... that in itself tells you a lot about him.

People say he is full of fun. He is the life and soul of any party.

Everyone loves his wit. Everyone I meet says to me, 'Yaar, I have never seen a person as witty as your dad.'

He used to call me 'naujawan', not Javed

Actually, my relationship with Sahir sahab is a very intense and very old one. My father was a poet, my uncle was a poet and all these writers, be it Bedi sahab, Krishan Chandar, Ismat Chughtai, Sahir sahab, Majrooh sahab... I have known all these people since my childhood. It was a clan, a tribe of writers who met each other all the time.

I can't remember when I first met Sahir sahab. I have seen him and all the others since my childhood. When I came to Mumbai, I was estranged from my father. I was twenty or twenty-one years old. Perhaps Sahir sahab saw his youth in me. I had nowhere to stay, nothing to eat. Every month or so, I would go to meet Sahir sahab. I never asked him for anything. He would give me food to eat and liquor to drink and talk to me as an equal. He knew that even though I was barely twenty or twenty-one years old, I had an understanding of poetry. I knew thousands of sher at that age, I still do, and I can recite them for hours. He would read aloud for me whatever he had written in the past month or so and he would take my reactions to his new songs and poems. He called me 'Naujawan', not Javed. He would say, 'Tell me, naujawan, how are things?' Once, when I didn't have any work and I was completely unemployed with no money in my pocket either, I went to him. Usually, I used to go to his house in the evening. I would eat dinner and sleep there. The next day I would go back. But this time, I went in the morning. I reached there and said in clear, unequivocal words, 'Sahir sahab, the thing is that I have no work at all. If you put in a word, I might get a job somewhere. If possible, please get me a job as an assistant director or dialogue writer.' He said, 'Yes, yes, naujawan, why do you worry? It happens sometimes in life. I have also been through this stage.' He said all this and went to his room which was adjacent to the drawing room.

He called me from there, 'Naujawan!' I went in. Sahir sahab had a very strange habit. He would begin to comb his hair whenever he was nervous or in some tension. He used to keep a small comb in his pocket. If he was combing his hair, it was safe to assume that he was a bit anxious. As he was combing his hair, he said to me, 'Look, I too have experienced such circumstances. *(Gesturing towards a table)* Keep this for now; you can return it to me later.' I looked at the table; there was some money kept on it. I said, 'I had not come to ask you for money. Let this be. Please, just put in a word for me somewhere. I want to work. If they like my work, they can employ me.' But he insisted that I keep it and eventually put the money in my pocket.

Anyhow, I came out. I took out the money from my pocket; there were ₹200. This was in the year 1966–67. Sahir gave me ₹200 and that was a big amount at the time. It was enough to keep me going for the next two months. Anyhow, times changed and I began to get work. And I began to make a name for myself. Then a time came when Sahir sahab and I would be working together in a film, such as *Deewaar, Trishul, Kaala Patthar.* He would be writing songs while the script would be by Salim–Javed. We would often meet at sittings and parties where some of the biggest stars, directors and others would be present. I would always tell him in front of everyone, 'I have ₹200 of Sahir sahab's and I am not returning them.' He would get a little embarrassed, laugh a little and say, 'No, no, I will take them... there's nothing to it.' And I would say, 'But I have no intention of returning them; they are going to stay with me.'

Time passed and one day I got a phone call informing me that he had passed away. I went to his house. There was no one there. There was only his friend Sabir Dutt and me. The two of us went to sleep in that house. By the next morning, some people arrived, like Yash Chopra and a few others. Then, his body was taken to the graveyard. After he was buried, as I was coming out of the graveyard, a man came running. I remember who he was. He asked, 'Do you have ₹200?' I said, '₹200? Why? What happened?' He said, 'The man who has dug the grave has to be paid. There is no one else here I can ask. I left my house in such a hurry when I heard about Sahir sahab's death. I don't have my wallet with me.' I took out ₹200 from my pocket and gave it to him and came away. As I was sitting in my car and coming home, I suddenly realised: It was a debt which was paid today. Anyhow, he is no longer amidst us, but his songs are with us. As long as they are with us, Sahir will remain with us.

Javed Akhtar with Nusrat Fateh Ali Khan

A sea of melodies

Nusrat came to India to give music for Rahul Rawail's film *Aur Pyar Ho Gaya* on the condition that he wanted Lata Mangeshkar to sing and Javed Akhtar to write the songs. It was his greatness that he took my name, that too alongside an artist of the calibre of Lata Mangeshkar. When we were working on the film, the people at HMV hit upon the idea of getting us to work on an album. I had received such proposals earlier, but I always thought I was writing for films and that was enough. But when the idea of an album called *Sangam*, featuring Pakistani artist Nusrat Fateh Ali Khan and Indian writer Javed Akhtar, was broached, I felt that it would be an honour to represent my country. So, I began work on this album. We were working in a bungalow beside the sea. He would be immersed in his music all the time. Sometimes, I used to think there are two seas in front of me: one was the Arabian Sea and the other was the man sitting before me. There was a sea of music and melodies inside him. To achieve that simplicity of melody that Nusrat had, one needs a great deal of knowledge and intricacy. This simplicity doesn't come easily. Nusrat's personality left a deep impression on me, which I still carry within me.

I met him several times during that time and I got the opportunity to see him at close quarters. He was totally focused on his work. I have never heard Nusrat speak ill of anyone. He would either listen to my poetry or be lost in his own music.

Husn-e-janaa ki tareef mumkin nahiin
Afreen afreen afreen afreen
Tu bhi dekhe agar to kahe hum-nasheen
Afreen afreen afreen afreen
Chehra ik phool ki tarah shaadaab hai
Chehra uss ka hai ya koyi mahtaab hai
Chehra jaise ghazal, chehra jaan-i ghazal
Chehra jaise kali, chehra jaise kanwal
Chehra jaise tasawwur bhi tasweer bhi
Chehra ik khaab bhi chehra taabeer bhi
Chehra koyi alif lailawi daastaan
Chehra ik pal yaqeen, chehra eik pal gumaan
Chehra jaisa ke chehra kaheen bhi nahi
Maah-ru maah-ru mah-jabeen mah-jabeen
Afreen afreen afreen afreen

SINGER Nusrat Fateh Ali Khan

ALBUM: *Sangam*

1996

Mujhko yakeen hai sach kahti thiin
Jo bhi ammi kahti thiin
Jab mere bachpan ke din the
Chaand mein pariyan rahti thiin

ALBUM *Silsiley*

1998

SINGER Jagjit Singh

Jagjit Singh
A magical voice

Jagjit Singh was one of the great personalities of India. In our country, music is normally seen in association with the film industry. Those who sing for films usually get greater attention, but Jagjit Singh was different. He made a place for himself with the ghazal, something that is not an easy task. Times changed, the styles and genres of music changed, but Jagjit Singh's style and glory remained undimmed. He had risen like a star with his magical voice in the 70s. And he held sway for the next forty years.

Koi jo mila to mujhe
Aisa lagta tha jaise
Meri saari duniya mein
Geeton ki rut aur rangon ki barkha hai
Khushbu ki aandhi hai
Mehki hui si ab saari fizaayein hain
Behki hui si ab saari hawaayein hain
Khoyi hui si ab saari dishaayein hain
Badli hui si ab saari adaayein hain
Jaagi ummangein hain, dhadak raha hai dil
Sanson main toofaan hain,
hoton pe naghme hain
Aakhon main sapne hain...

SINGER Shankar Mahadevan

A talented singer

Shankar Mahadevan is a talented singer and musician. Breathless *was his first album. I have great respect for his talent.*

ALBUM: *Breathless*
1998

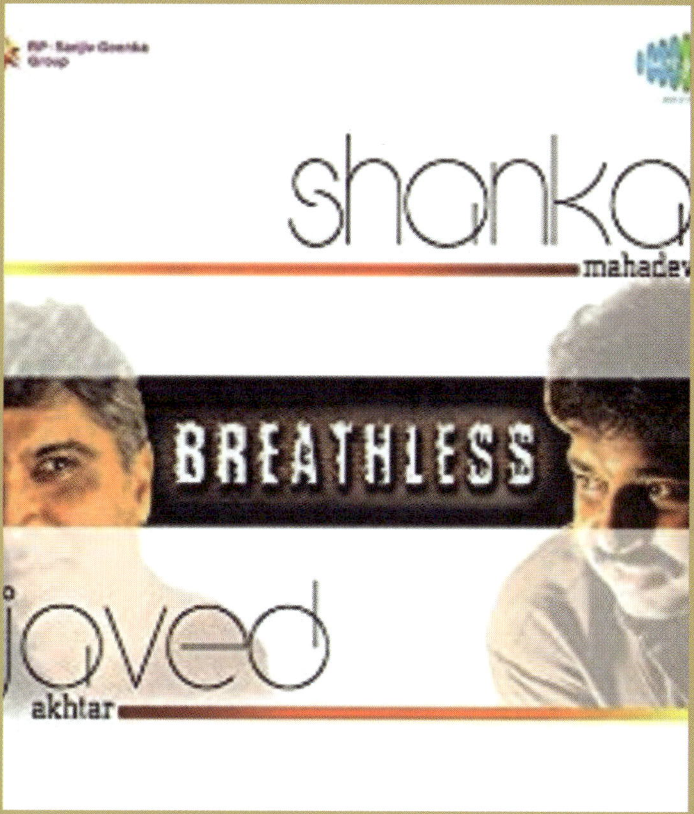

Shankar Mahadevan, Javed Akhtar and Shabana Azmi

GUFTAGU

In conversation with Shankar Mahadevan

Javed sahab is a father figure for me and a person with vast knowledge

What was special about the album, *Breathless*, that you did with Javed sahab?

We, that is, the people from HMV and I, met him in his office. We were talking about working on an album. Javed sahab said, 'Shankar sahab, an idea has been going around in my head for a long time and I have discussed it with many classical artists, film singers and composers. Everyone gets excited, but they don't know how to go further with it. They can't go beyond a certain point.' And he elaborated, 'When I listen to classical music, there are different tunes, there is the *sargam* and then there is the improvisation. It has no form, no fixed direction. But when you sing a song, it has a structured *mukhra*, then some music, then the *antara*. That makes it seem as though you are tied down because there are these set parameters. So these patterns of the *taan* and the sargam, can't we bring this parabola into a song where we do something with words but without a pattern?' I said, 'Sir, let's begin the album with this and let us keep the entire song in one breath. It should seem as though a river is flowing, it has no direction... it can go left-right, backwards-forwards, up-down like you would in a taan. But it should have words. And it should have a starting point. I will give you a half second metre. You go forward with that metre.' And so I sang just this much for him: *'Tannn nnnn nnnn nnnn.'* He said, 'Oh, I will write on this. No problem.'

He called me ten days later. I went to his house in 'Saagar Samrat', Juhu. He came with four foolscap sheets of paper and said, 'Here, take this.' From top to bottom, there were words, just words, only words. I asked, 'What is this, Javed sahab?' He replied, 'This is your "Breathless".' I said, 'Okay, so let's do one thing, sir, please recite this entire thing for me in one particular style.' He read the whole thing out for me. I left carrying those foolscap sheets. I sat in the taxi in Juhu and began to compose on my Dictaphone. By the time I had composed and analysed each word, I had reached Vashi where I live in Navi Mumbai... And *"Breathless"* had been composed. Once I had gained enough confidence, I said, 'Javed ji, come and hear your *"Breathless"*.' He came and heard it. Then he said, 'I have never in my entire life heard anything like this... the way you have executed it...' He gave me a lot of love and blessings. And the connection we formed then, that is still intact to this day.

By now you have done many films with Javed sahab. What is special about the songs he writes for you?

As an artist, Javed sahab is considered a senior because he has been in the industry for a very long time, but senior does not mean that he has become old and dated. He is an artist who moves with the times. He doesn't dwell on past glories; instead, he moves on. He has a child-like enthusiasm in him. He will call me ten times and say, 'Arre yaar, what is happening? Tell me, what are you doing? When are we meeting?' And the songs!... The number of songs we have written over the telephone! We had written *'Kal Ho Naa Ho'* on the telephone. When he has an idea, he calls me... it can be seven or eight in the morning and he will write the song right then. He has written in the Emirates lounge, in the car, he can write anywhere. He has such an amazing enthusiasm. He will write a line or two and then change or tweak it till it is perfect, like an artist who adds finishing touches after completing a painting. The remarkable thing about him is that he can say something big, something profound in very simple language, in words that even a common man can understand. For instance, the song *'Kal Ho Naa Ho'* has such depth of feeling that it touches anyone who lives anywhere on this earth. The words are so simple, yet they touch you so deeply. I share a very special relationship with him. I don't have even a distant relative in the film industry. I come from a very different background. He is my constant support. He says to me, 'You do it, yaar, I am with you.' He has seen this industry from inside out. He knows everyone. He also knows exactly how to deal with them. He is like an elder brother to me. He is a father figure. He is a strong personality and a person with vast knowledge.

When you work with a genius like him and then you work with some other lyricist, do you ever feel that Javed Akhtar should be in this place?

Many times... many times. Let me explain it to you with a technical point. A word must fit in a particular place, but it must fit in that place like a block of Lego. Holds true for words in a song as well. You should get the feeling that, yaar, there could have been no other word in this place. Sometimes a song is in metre, yet you feel that there should have been something here, something that has been made for this place. At such times, one often feels that if Javed sahab had been here he would have written something that was exactly what was needed, that too in the right words.

Old songs should be left alone, exactly as they were

This trend of re-creating old songs according to new needs should be stopped. I don't like it, but because this is a democratic society, everyone has the right to do exactly what they want. Old things should be left exactly as they are and new things should be created. What is the need to turn old things into new? Today, Anand Bakshi sahab (who had written '*Tip tip barsa paani...*') is no longer in our midst so he can't oppose it. Some tinkering was done with my song '*Ghar se nikalte hi, kuchh duur chalte hi...*' The same thing was attempted with the great poet Neeraj's song '*Ai bhai, zara dekh ke chalo...*'

I don't know why people make re-mixes of old songs. It is an acceptance by music directors of their inability to make songs of this standard. They should have the belief in themselves that they can give superhits. Why must they take loans? What is the need for that? Moreover, the songs of Lata Mangeshkar, Mohammed Rafi, Kishore Kumar are part of our cultural legacy, just as the caves of Ajanta–Ellora are part of our heritage. These days, nude models are dancing on the songs of Mukesh and Mohammed Rafi. Only the ordinary public can stem this growing danger.

At the retro theme party on the occasion of his seventy-fifth birthday, Javed Akhtar with Shabana Azmi, Janki Kutir (2020)

No strong villain has appeared in cinema in recent years

When you take your children to the zoo, the first thing they do is run to the cage that houses the tiger. They look at the pretty, multi-coloured birds later. This is because we all first want to see powerful, dangerous animals, those who create fear in us. It is the same with cinema. The way a tiger attracts you, so does a villain—be it Teja from *Zanjeer* or Gabbar in *Sholay* or Shakaal in *Shaan* or Mogambo in *Mr India*. They had their own distinct style yet they all share a common link. They are not crude, lewd types and none of them have tried to molest women. In *Sholay*, Gabbar makes this comment about Basanti, *'Arre O Sambha, ye Ramgarhwale apni betiyon ko kaun si chakki ka pisa atta khilate hai re? Jara daari ke haath-paanv dekh, bahut karare hain, saale.* (Arre O Sambha, what do these Ramgarhwallahs feed their daughters? Look at her limbs; how strong they are)'. This is a comment not on her sexuality but her strength. He could have said the same thing about the horse. In the film *Shaan*, Shakaal abducts Rakhee and says, *'Tum paneer ka eik tukda ho aur tumhara pati tumhare peechhe eik choohe ki tarah daudta hua jaal mein aayega* (You are like a piece of cheese and your husband will come running after you like a mouse in a trap)'. Rakhee doesn't weaken but Shaakal says, 'Don't worry; no harm will come to you because I don't have the time for such useless things. You only have to stay here till your husband arrives.' This dialogue was praised by people. If a villain has his inherent dignity, then he will be praised, not hated. The sort of roles essayed by Jeevan, Kanhaiyalal, Ranjeet or Prem Chopra will not be praised by viewers. There has been no strong villain in cinema for some time now. Ronit Roy is good but he is not seen in a lot of films.

(Based on a conversation between Javed Akhtar and the photojournalist Pradeep Chandra)

Some of the famous villains of Hindi cinema: Ajit and Amjad Khan (top), Kulbhushan Kharbanda and Amrish Puri (bottom)

Indian music unites Indians

Old songs are not mere songs; they also inform you about the values of those times. How was life lived back then, what were people's beliefs, how did they behave with each other, what were their values... you come to know all this from the tune, the voice and words. When we hear songs from the 50s and 60s, we see certain values, a basic decency. It is there in the songs, in the tune, in the words. Whatever is being said or sung is with utmost decency. The tune is moving forward in a dignified manner. You don't see that anymore.

The people in the middle, those who convey our products to the public, say that this is what the public wants, and this is what the young generation wants. If the young generation wants this then why do young girls sing Lata Mangeshkar's songs in all the musical contests that are telecast on TV? You will find only those old songs being sung there by the contestants—by Rafi, Kishore and Mukesh ji. No one sings present-day songs. It is evident that a false allegation has been made against the young generation. The truth is that this is the taste of those who rule the market; it is their thinking, their opinion that is moulding modern song-writing. Indian film music is such a remarkable thing that you can go anywhere—America, England, Poland, Singapore, or anywhere else—whenever there is a reception or party in the evening, someone starts playing or singing a Hindi film song and it is invariably a song from the 1950s, or 60s or 70s. Indian film music unites Indians.

This is the biggest contribution of our Hindi film songs. Look at the amazing songs written by our lyricists, be it Shailendra or Sahir. They haven't just written on a particular situation in a film; their songs have become a part of our life. When Lata ji sings a song, it becomes a part of our life. A song becomes our reference point for a special feeling or emotion. We remember that song when we are in a certain 'mood'. These songs have given us so much! They were once repositories of the common man's philosophy.

Javed Akhtar with musician Laxmikant Pyarelal and producer-director Yash Chopra

Hindi film songs and music: *The Golden Years 1950–1975*

Every single episode of Javed Akhtar's popular show *The Golden Years (1950–1975)*, on the channel Zee Classic in 2016, was greatly appreciated by viewers and cine-music lovers. Many told and untold stories related to not just film songs but Hindi cinema and the film industry were narrated in this musical journey in the company of Javed Akhtar.

Classic Legends: A discovery of the lives of Hindi cinema's great actors

Classic Legends is a Hindi entertainment show on Indian television in which Javed Akhtar talks about some of the most notable and brilliant people from the Hindi film industry in a very interesting and meaningful manner. The first four seasons of the show were telecast on Zee Classic and the fifth was broadcast on Zee Anmol Cinema, Zee Bollywood, and Zee Cinema HD. In this show Javed Akhtar has cast light on the lives of some of Hindi cinema's great artists who have brought laurels to the silver screen with their impressive performance. The first season was premiered on 11 December 2011. Every episode focuses on one actor and the series goes on to feature some of the most popular heroes, heroines, musicians, directors, singers and music composers.

Javed Akhtar presenting the Tata Sky programme

TATA SKY JAVED AKHTAR ACTIVE:

Everyday life, classic poetry and Hindi *dohe*

Tata Sky presents a special programme in which film writer, lyricist, poet Javed Akhtar recites a piece of classic poetry or a *doha* and analyses them in the context of ordinary, everyday life. This helps to inculcate life-affirming values among the viewing public.

Sher

Kuchh to hote hain muhabbat mein junoon ke aasaar
Aur kuchh log bhi diwana bana detey hain
–Zaheer Dehlvi

Indeed, that is how it happens. When a person focuses on something, when he loves something so much that all other things seem unimportant, people look at him or her with incredulity. This is possibly because, normally, one is so scattered, one's mind is divided into so many compartments, that one is seldom complete, whole. Some people are so in love with their work or with a person, a goal, a purpose or a thing and they are so consumed by a passion that others consider them 'crazy'. I think there can be two reasons for this. One, people might consider such a person mad because how can any one thing become so all-consumingly important? Such an obsession borders on madness. The other reason can be that this strength, this focus, this concentration of one's energy on a particular point scares people and, in order to rid themselves of their fear, people call such a person mad or crazy. 'He is mad because he is not like us. And because he is not like us, he is wrong,' that is a popular assumption. Those who love passionately are also considered crazy. A person so in love that he or she forsakes everything else in the world instils fear in the heart of people. Considering such a person mad and treating such a person as crazy seems the better bet.

Love creates its own passions and frenzies; but then there is also love's madness. There is no doubt about this because, indeed, you need a touch of madness to sacrifice many things, to break down walls and to accept many challenges. You need a head that you can keep butting against a wall and the wall breaks. So, truly, a certain passion is needed if you really want something in life. To find true love, one strives to possess, to reach the final destination. Such a love can be for anything or anyone; it can be for a person but it can also, equally, be for an aim, a goal, an ideology. Passion will give rise to frenzy, zeal, ardour. I will recite a sher for you; it's from my ghazal which was sung by Nusrat Fateh Ali Khan in the album *Sangam*:

Ishq be-ghar karey ishq be-dar karey,
ishq ka sach hai koi thikana nahi
Hum jo kal tak thikane ke thhe aadmi,
dekhiye aaj kaise thikane lagey

After all, there is a certain comfort in slavery. As a slave you get some things but when a person breaks bonds, ties and says 'No' to slavery, then you lose all those other things that come with it. Here is a sher by Mir, the king of poetry; he is the poet of emotions for in his poetry you see a surfeit of emotions, a passion that borders on frenzy:

Hoga kisi deewaar ke saaye mein pada Mir
Kya rabt muhabbat se uss aaram-talab ko

Mir makes this accusation about himself that he must be lying somewhere in the shade of a wall. Why in the shade of a wall? Why not in his own home? Because he is a lover, he has lost everything, he is lying in the shade of a wall. What lies beyond this? There's the fact that love makes you homeless, *ishq be-ghar karey, ishq be-dar karey*. But those who love or those who have true respect for love cannot bear the fact that one is lolling about at ease in the shade of a wall; instead, you should have been out and about, offering full display of your passion, your frenzy, your willingness to forsake your life for your love. So hard is the test of love that no laxity is to be tolerated!

Jamiluddin Aali is one of our finest Urdu poets. He used to live in Delhi but now he doesn't live in India. There is an excellent sher by him:

Kuchh na tha yaad ba-juz kaar-e mohabbat eik umr
Woh jo bigda hai to ab kaam kai yaad aaye
(*bajuz* means *siwaye* or except; *kaar-e mohabbat* means the act of love)

For an age, an era, I remembered nothing except love.

It was only when I was disenchanted with love, or when love broke my heart, or I lost my faith in it or my belief diminished or I was disillusioned that I realised all that I had lost, all the things still left incomplete. Having said that, the world will never be empty of people who love. I am reminded of a fine sher by Faiz:

Hum sahel-talab kaun se Farhad the lekin
Ab shahr mein tere koi hum sa bhi kahan hai

The epic tale of Shirin–Farhad is well known. Farhad was instructed to dig through a mountain for a stream of milk to pass through and only then would he be allowed to marry Shirin. Alone, he chipped away at the mountain with a chisel till he finally cut through the rock. Whereas we are easy-going people who want to do trouble-free things. Life has become materialistic. Where are the Farhads who would cut through a mountain for a Shirin? It is true we can't love like a Farhad, but the love that we have, the way in which we love, that too is rare in the world we live in. So we should be thankful for the love, howsoever little compared to the legendary lovers of yore it might be, should remain safe in our hearts. The fact is there are still Farhads and Majnuns. It is true that they don't go around calling out Laila's name in jungles and wastelands because it is hard to find jungles anymore! They live in cities—the Lailas, Majnus and the Sohnis who cross the swollen Chenab river on an unbaked clay pot. There is a Chenab now too; you will find it in every home, in every city, which a Sohni finds the courage to cross, because:

Kuchh to hotey hain mohabbat ke junoon ke aasaar
Aur kuchh log bhi diwana bana detey hain
(There are some signs of love and the madness of love
And then there are people who deem you mad)

Doha

Rahiman dhaga prem ka, mat torho chatkaye
Jorhe se phir naa jurhey, jurhey gaanth parh jaye

Abdul Rahim Khan-e Khana was Akbar's Poet Laureate and a very close friend of the great poet Tulsidas. Given above is one of his most famous dohas (two-line couplet). It might seem like a very simple thought but, as often happens in a doha, there is a depth in it, a nuance and layers of meaning. If you go looking, you can see far into its depths, and see a great deal. Put simply, Rahim is saying: Don't snap the thread of love! Because it doesn't join, or when joined there is always a knot in it. But I feel that there's something else hidden in its two lines. Rahim could also have simply said don't break this thread of love. Why has he used the word 'chatkaye'? The word carries a connotation of breaking with a tug, a sharp pull, a use of force, a snap. The second line, too, has two remarkable qualities. He says, for one it (the thread) will not join, and two, if it does, it will have a knot. Now, let's go back to the very beginning. First of all, the basic premise of the doha itself is a noble one: Don't break the thread of love. And the truth is that relationships, these bonds and ties of love, should not break. As far as possible, one should remain true to them and ensure they remain intact. Such relationships are our true wealth, our reason to rejoice in the beauty of life. But, sometimes, it happens to all of us and we feel that these bonds of love must be broken, or they will break on their own. Because life is very complicated and there is too much going on in it. It can never be that the thread won't break; sometimes, you have to break it. Break it, if you must, but Rahim gives you one proviso. Don't snap it. Don't break it with cruelty and heartlessness. I think this is important. I believe that you are tested on three occasions. The popular adage is about two occasions but I will add a third. If you stay with a person for fourteen years, or travel with them, you know what he/she is like. There is a third occasion: when you see a person in anger. Every person displays anger in a different way; he shows his true character, his 'level, as it were, in moments of extreme anger. A decent person's anger, too, will have a decency and so when he breaks off a relationship it will not be with a jerk, nor will he do anything distasteful. This is possibly what Rahim is saying to you. If it was simply a question of not breaking off a relationship he would never have said *'Jorhe se phir naa jurhey, jurhey gaanth parh jaye'*. Why would he, after all? Don't break a relationship; that's all there would be to it. But Rahim is wise enough to know that sometimes ties, relationships break. This thread of love... it breaks sometimes. So, at the very least, it should be such that it can be re-tied. In the worst of times, one should not say things that, were the relationship to be revived someday, should not stand like a wall between friends. Sometimes, the reason due to which friendships end, ceases to be a reason but the quarrel remains. That shouldn't be. Sometimes we can be careless. Words can be dangerous. They can be keener than a sword and sharper than an arrow. Sometimes we speak without thinking, especially with those we consider our own. Those we consider the 'other' or not close to us, to them we speak with great care. But we can get careless with those we consider our own, those with whom we are bound by the thread of love. I will say that first and foremost that thread of love that ties human beings should not be allowed to break; and if break it must, then it should not be snapped abruptly so that it can be joined again at some point. It must be kept in mind that human nature is very strange; sometimes one is willing to forget something that is as large as a mountain whereas sometimes a twig or a straw can pierce one's heart. And so, it is necessary for all of us that we should not take for granted those with whom we are tied by the thread of love; instead, we should speak with kindness, gentleness, softness and the utmost care. If this plant of love is not watered daily with the water of softness, kindness, care, it begins to wilt. The thread begins to fray and we are surprised when it breaks. So remember:

Rahiman dhaga prem ka, mat torho chatkaye
Jorhe se phir naa jurhey, jurhey gaanth parh jaaye

Friends, Majaz Lakhnawi has been called the Keats and Shelley of Urdu poetry. When we take the name of Majaz, the very first poem of his that comes to mind is the one entitled 'Awara':

Nazm

Raaste mein ruk ke dum le loon, meri aadat nahiin
Laut kar waapas chala jaaoon meri fitrat nahiin
Aur koi hum-nawaa mil jaaye yeh qismat nahiin
Ai gham-e dil kya karoon
Ai wahshat-e dil kya karoon

It's a long poem. It's about a person who is roaming around like a vagabond. Actually, the word *awara* is not a bad word in Urdu poetry. Awara doesn't mean loiterer or who stands by the roadside and whistles at passers-by or teases girls. In Urdu poetry, an awara is a person who leaves the straight and narrow path though he himself doesn't know where he will go. All he knows is that he doesn't want to take the conventional route. There was a famous writer, Albert Camus. In one of his stories he has written a beautiful sentence. A master is telling his servant: 'I am going away from here.' The servant asks, 'But, master, where are you going?' The master replies, 'Can't you understand, I am going away from here. That is where I am going.' I am going away from here; that is the only reason for my going. The awara in Urdu poetry has left the secure, regular life, the everyday and the known paths and set off on a search. Sometimes, he knows what he is searching for and sometimes he doesn't know why he is wandering around. Nevertheless, he is roaming and wandering about and certainly there are moments, when one is far away from home, that one remembers all that one has left behind. Look at this beautiful sher that is brimming with a strange pathos, a strange helplessness, a strange emotion:

Yeh sard raat, yeh awargi, yeh neend ka bojh
Hum apne shehr mein hotey to ghar chaley jaatey
(This cold night, this vagrancy, this burden of sleep
Had I been in my own city I would have gone home)

Why? What is he in search of? I don't know. But perhaps you can guess one of the reasons, and I might think of some other. That is how you make a sher your own. Now, you form your own opinion about this awara and I will make my own. Kaif Bhopali was a fine poet from Bhopal. He, too, has created a beautiful picture:

So gayiin shehr ki saari sadkein
Eik awara magar baqui hai
(All the roads in the city are asleep
Except one vagabond that remains)

Then, there are some vagabonds who take great pride in their vagrancy. Here is a fine sher by Habib Jalib:

Yeh aijaz hai apni awargi ka
Jahan bhi gaye daastan chhorh gaye
(Such is the marvel of my vagrancy
Wherever I went I left behind a story)

Such is the marvel, miracle, magic of my *awargi*! The vagabond has his own story, one that is different from others because the path he has chosen is different.

Hamare har shaoor-e zindagi ka raaz thheregi
Yahi i awargi kal bais-e aijaz thheregi
(The secrets of the consciousness of life
This vagrancy of mine with be a cause to marvel)

Tomorrow, if I find my path and reach my destination, this vagrancy will be regarded as a virtue, a good trait that is worthy of praise. Articles and books are written on it; it becomes the subject of biographies. Look at this beautiful sher by Shahryar:

Justuju jis ki thi usko to na paaya humney
Iss bahane magar dekh lii duniya humney
(I didn't find what I yearned for
But I managed to see the world)

I saw the world and fulfilled my yearning. So your life is made! Had you not wandered through cities and alleys, had you not been a vagrant, you wouldn't have had this understanding of the world and its ways. You have been successful only because of this. You left the road that everyone else was taking. You set off somewhere else in the true spirit of the wanderer:

Jidhar jaatey hain sab, jaana udhar achha nahii lagta
Mujhe paamaal raaston ka safar achcha nahiin lagta
(I don't like to go where everyone else is going
I don't like to travel on trodden paths)

The vagabond forsakes the known and trodden paths. In his journey he faces cold dark nights, loneliness, sadness, the burden of sleep. But if perchance he were to find his true destination, then all this vagrancy becomes a thing of beauty and the reason for his success.

Pearls lie hidden in closed oysters in the seas; they cannot be reached from the shores. He who dives deep into the waters can retrieve those pearls. It needs a certain passion, a certain awargi. Certainly, this awargi can destroy a person, too. But it is also true that this awargi can reach you to a place where those who walk on the simple and straightforward paths look at you with amazement and respect. Once I had written using the radeef (rhyme) of awargi:

Phirte hain kab se darbadar
Ab iss nagar, ab uss nagar
Eik doosre ke humsafar
Main aur meri awargi
(We have been wandering
Now in this city, now in another
Companions of each other
I and my awargi)

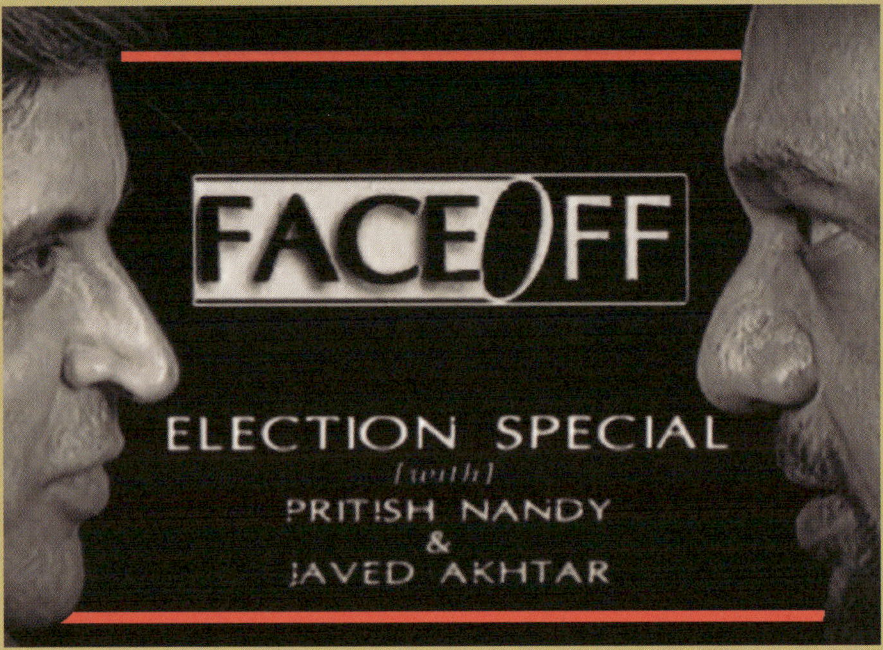

FACE OFF:

The most-watched chat show on Doordarshan

The well-known journalist and poet, Pritish Nandy and Javed Akhtar had hosted an election special chat show, named *Face Off* on Doordarshan in 1998. It was directed by the film-maker Pankaj Parashar. The show had included interviews with great national leaders such as Manmohan Singh, Atal Bihari Vajpayee, George Fernandes, Mulayam Singh Yadav, Jyoti Basu and others. *Face Off* was the most-watched election-related chat show on Doordarshan. Given below are excerpts from the interviews of two former Indian prime ministers.

When we had formed the Jan Sangh and today when we are working under the banner of the Bharatiya Janata Party, we had kept our doors open to all. We have not done so with the intention of having an open door through which no one enters. In all truthfulness, we want the Muslims to come with us and that is why we have opened the doors of not merely our Party, we have also kept the doors of our heart open. The Party has a very clear view on the minorities: they are citizens of this country. Minorities are equal stakeholders in this country. They have equal rights. They have equal responsibilities. No difference has ever been made on the basis of religion in this country, nor will it ever happen in the future. The entire Party agrees that India was a secular state, and it will remain so.

–Atal Bihari Vajpayee, Former Prime Minister

No country can refuse to accept the importance of individualism. We need programmes and policies, but we also need people to run all those programmes. And so we cannot rid ourselves of the importance of the individual in human history. Only some very special people have made a place for themselves in history who have emerged as motivators of change. This happens everywhere in the world.

–Manmohan Singh, Former Prime Minister

Yeh khel kya hai

Mire muhalif ne chaal chal di hai
Aur ab
Meri chaal ke intezar mein hai
Magar main kab se
Safed khanon
Siyah khanon mein rakkhe
Kaale safed mohron ko dekhta huun
Main sochta huun
Yeh mohre kya hain

Agar main samjhun
Ke yeh jo mohre hain
Sirf lakdi ke hain khilaune
To jeetna kya hai haarna kya
Na yeh zaruri

Na woh aham hai
Agar khushi hai na jeetne ki
Na haarne ka hi koi gham hai
To khel kya hai
Main sochta huun
Jo khelna hai
To apne dil mein yaqin kar luun

Yeh mohre sach-much ke badshah-o wazir
Sach-much ke hain payade
Aur in ke aage hai
Dushmanon ki woh fauj
Rakhti hai jo ki mujh ko tabah karne ke
Saare mansube
Sab irade
Magar aisa jo maan bhi luun
To sochta huun
Yeh khel kab hai
Yeh jang hai jis ko jeetna hai

Yeh jang hai jis mein sab hai jaaez
Koi yeh kahta hai jaise mujh se
Yeh jang bhi hai
Yeh khel bhi hai
Yeh jang hai par khiladiyon ki
Yeh khel hai jang ki tarah ka

Main sochta huun
Jo khel hai
Iss men iss tarah ka usuul kyuun hai
Kii koi mohra rahe ki jaaye

Magar jo badshah hai
Uss par kabhi koi aanch bhi na aaye
Wazir hii ko hai bas ijazat
Ki jis taraf bhi woh chahe jaaye
Main sochta huun
Jo khel hai
Iss men iss tarah usuul kyuun hai
Piyada jo apne ghar se nikle
Palat ke wapas na jaane paaye

Main sochta huun
Agar yahi hai usuul
To phir usuul kya hai
Agar yahi hai yeh khel
To phir yeh khel kya hai
Main in sawaalon se jaane kab se ulajh raha huun
Mire mukhalif ne chaal chal di hai
Aur ab meri chaal ke intezar mein hai

Desh ke hum hain rakshak
Jaan bhi dengey beshak

Desh ki raksha mein
Veer jiyale hum hain
Shastr sambhale hum hain
Desh ki raksha mein
Desh ka kan-kan yeh jaane
Drohi bhi, dushman bhi maane
Aantrik suraksha hai humse
Hum raat din hain yeh jaane
Jai Jai Bharat
Jai CRPF
Baadal jo hinsa ke chhaye
Khatre ka dar sar uthhaye
Himmat ka jwala jagaye
Hum yeh andhere mitaayein

– CRPF ANTHEM

I have a special bond with the CRPF. I have written an anthem for them. I met several officers from the CRPF before I wrote the anthem. My respect, admiration and love for these brave men have only increased after meeting them.

Active on the micro-blogging site, Twitter, since 2010, Javed Akhtar tweets on a range of topics from across the world and within the country.

Bharat Mata teri qasam, tere rakshak rahenge hum
Vande mataram, vande mataram
Ma humne tan man, jeevan tujhse hii paaye hain
Teri dharti se janme hain tere phal khaaye hain
Hum par teri mamta, teri karuna ke saaye hain
Teri baahon mein hain pale, Maa hum tere
hain ladley
Deewaarein hum baneingey Maa, talwarein
hum baneingey Maa
Choo le tujhko hai kisme dum
Bharat Mata teri qasam...
Humko pyara hai tera har zarra Bharat Maa
Humko pyare hain tere parvat, jungal, nadiyan
Humko pyare tere gaanv, nagar, tere raaste, galiyan
Koi dushman kabhi agar bhoole se dekh le idhar
Bharat Mata...

– INDIAN MILITARY ACADEMY (IMA) ANTHEM

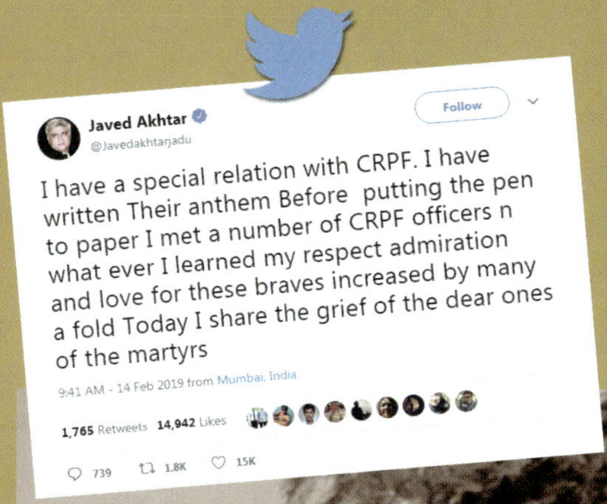

Javed Akhtar
@Javedakhtarjadu
Follow

I have a special relation with CRPF. I have written Their anthem Before putting the pen to paper I met a number of CRPF officers n what ever I learned my respect admiration and love for these braves increased by many a fold Today I share the grief of the dear ones of the martyrs

9:41 AM - 14 Feb 2019 from Mumbai, India

1,765 Retweets 14,942 Likes

739 1.8K 15K

Protest against the Bombay blasts, Mumbai (2012–13)

Purushottam Agrawal and Javed Akhtar at the book launch of Mr Agarwal's book Kaun Hai Bharat Mata? at Jawahar Bhavan, New Delhi (2021)

You kept improving higher education while primary and basic education kept disappearing

My life's achievement is that I have taken his (Jawaharlal Nehru's) autograph. When I was fourteen or fifteen years old, I had three heroes—Pandit Jawaharlal Nehru, Krishan Chandar and Dilip Kumar—in exactly this order. I remember that day in 1964 when Pandit Jawaharlal Nehru passed away. I consider myself very fortunate that when his last birthday was celebrated in 1963 there was a Youth Festival in Delhi. I was there, too, to take part in a debate. Those were such amazing days! All the students lined up to go to Teen Murti House. They took a side road and reached the back lawn. There was no metal detector, no guard, and no body searches. Naturally, now when one looks back, one sees a lot of beauty in those days. But one thing surprises me greatly and this is a question I want to pose for you first and foremost. Nehru left this world in 1964. How much the world has changed since then—economically, socially, morally, politically!

It is true that we need a mixed economy. Be it economy or health, the government cannot completely forego its responsibility. And what about the reality of what we once dubbed the 'Permit Raj'? I am not giving a statement here; I am asking a question: isn't it true that life had become difficult for the private sector? That sector could have been more productive. I remember the days when, if you wanted to buy a Fiat car, you had to wait for eleven years. There were enough buyers who had the money and could afford to buy the car but production was so low that you had a waiting period of eleven years. When I had first gone to Mumbai, it took eight to ten years to get a telephone connection. There were many 'curbs' on the private sector. The public sector is important for any country. We in India could not have reached where we have today if it were not for the public sector. The kind of heavy industry we have had in this country could not have been set up by any single individual. But it is also true that the middle class did not flourish as much as it could have. In my childhood, three things were considered very expensive in my home—an electric iron, a Murphy radio and an Usha fan. I cannot comment on what has happened in the villages but in the urban areas clearly the middle class has made a huge, exponential jump. Could they not have made this jump earlier?

The laws, values, principles and ideals formed during that time were all good to see, hear and read about. Those ideals and values are still valid. Nothing has gone awry in them or in the value system they mirrored. What we see is their misinterpretation and misuse. Take, for instance, the case of education. We are here today because of the IIMs, the IITs and the other institutions of higher learning. It is true. But I sometimes feel that a 100-storey high building was built; a lift was also installed in it. But the lift was from the eightieth floor. Only if you can climb till that floor will you get a lift to take you to the top floor. You will have a smooth ride all the way up to the top. All possible amenities have been given to you to facilitate your ride. But how does one reach the eightieth floor? I am unable to see any serious attempt to build the basic and primary educational system. Had the poor too got a good education, he too could have reached the hundredth floor. But this basic and primary education kept disappearing gradually as you were intent on improving higher education. As a result, it becomes accessible only to the privileged class.

Let me tell you a true incident. A few days ago, some people went to a channel—which has an R&D wing to vet what sort of programmes or serials should be made—with the proposal for a short story series. They said we have thirteen short stories and we want to make films on them. The lady from the R&D wing asked who the author was. She was told the stories were by Premchand. She said: 'But he should have come himself!' Now, this is the state of the world we live in.

I find it very strange that our films are still censored. And they are censored in the strangest of ways. Let me narrate a few incidents which happen to be true. Once, there used to be comedian called Maruti who was also a director. He made a film titled *Yeh Bambai Hai*. It was a funny sort of film. A man was going along Marine Drive flying his umbrella. The Censor Board objected saying this is not Marine Drive because no one can fly an umbrella there. So Maruti said, 'All right, I will change the title.' And he changed the film's title to *Kya Yeh Bambai Hai?* and the film was duly released. So, these sorts of stupidities don't happen too often but the Censor is still very much there; we call it 'Certification' now. You can give it any fancy name you like but the fact remains that there is a check. Now the OTT is being scrutinised so that it too can be controlled, or cut, or curtailed. The strange thing, however, is that there is no censor for education. The most impressionable years for a child are from six or seven till twelve to fourteen years. There is no one to ask what is being taught in these schools where children from different communities, religions, language groups, etc., study. Anything can be taught. There are ten or twelve versions of history. You will find one version when you go to the south, another in the north. Some history is a legacy of the English. There is a historian, whose name I can't recall right now, who is considered a 'great' historian but he had never ever come to India.

He sat in London and wrote the history of India which is considered a very 'valid' history.

What is the conception of history? Are there truly so many versions of history? You are poisoning a child's mind and then you ask why he behaves the way he does. Has anyone ever censored such textbooks? Has anyone seen what is being taught in schools?

Tarkash: The First Collection of Poetry

Freshness, depth and diversity, a fidelity of emotions and a search for new emotions—these are the special qualities of Javed Akhtar's poetry. A delicacy of feelings and an eloquence of expression has come to him by way of legacy. Tarkash (meaning 'Quiver') is full of the arrows of *gham-e jaana* (the sorrows of love) and *gham-e dauraan* (the sorrows of the world). He is a realistic, down-to-earth, cosmopolitan person. He has no emotional or intellectual ties with the feudal and mystical lineages of his parents' families. In fact, his father and mother themselves had rejected these values in their own lifetime. My personal opinion, however, is that Javed has, perhaps unconsciously, accepted and assimilated some of the unique qualities of Sufism via Urdu culture, such as secularism and humanism. *Tarkash* is a valuable addition to modern Urdu poetry. *–Qurratulain Hyder, Novelist*

'...What have you done with your life?' Have you ever loved someone deeply and truthfully? Have you given good counsel to a friend? Have you looked at a foe's son with love in your eyes? Did you ever take a ray of light to a dark place? For as long as you lived, was there any meaning to your life? *–Krishan Chandar in the Dedication Note of* Tarkash

Lava: The Second Collection of Poetry

Javed has his own genre, his own unique style, a style to which the keen watchfulness of his intellect has added greater allure making him unmatched. The vocabulary that Javed has at his command to make his ideas touch our heart is immense. You can never consider the folly of re-arranging even a single word from here to there in anything that he writes. Every word is complete and perfect in its place. This ability to choose the right word comes after great practice. He has a magnificent treasure trove of words. He knows exactly which words to use where and how. He has never walked on trodden paths; he has the confidence and morale. He is bent on causing new suns to rise.
–Pushpa Bharti, Writer

Ordinarily, when you open a book of prose writings, there is a sher on the opening page. When you open the first book of poetry I published, *Tarkash*, on the very first page you will find a piece of prose. It is by Krishan Chandar. His writings have influenced me a great deal.
–Khwaab Ke Gaon Mein, 2015

Talking Films and Songs, 2018

Talking Films and Songs showcases both aspects of Javed Akhtar's versatile genius through freewheeling conversations with Nasreen Munni Kabir. Originally published as *Talking Films* (1999) and *Talking Songs* (2005), these extremely popular books have delighted readers, researchers and scholars of Indian film. Full of wit and wisdom, this edition is a must-read for Hindi cinema enthusiasts.
–From the Blurb of the Book

It is a pleasurable experience to talk about Javed Akhtar and Nasreen Munni Kabir's book *Talking Films and Songs*. The book is useful for all those who are curious about a comprehensive phenomenon that comprises Hindi film songs. *Talking Films and Songs* is an important text for all those who wish to understand the art and craft of writing film lyrics. The book talks of all those elements that come together to create film songs. And Javed Akhtar is known for the most notable changes in the vocabulary and diction of film songs.
–Prasoon Joshi, Lyricist

The truth is that I have never ever met another person whose views about Hindi cinema are so lucid, and who is a master at moving from simple, straightforward things to deep matters within a matter of minutes.
–Nasreen Munni Kabir, Writer

Khwaab Ke Gaon Mein: Chosen as Amazon's Bestseller

It is for the first time that a book published in the city of Indore in Madhya Pradesh has been chosen as a bestseller by Amazon. The book is *Khwaab Ke Gaon Mein*; it contains Javed Akhtar's poetry and his views on films and society. The book was published four years ago by Manjul Prakashan (Bhopal). So far, three editions of this book have been published. The book is the result of the efforts of two cultural activists from the city, Arvind Mandloi and Ashok Dube. This is the second book in India that has been written by hand. Earlier, the biography of MF Hussain was written by hand.
–Dainik Bhaskar, 6 April 2020

Khwaab Ke Gaon Mein: A Calligraphic Collection of Poetry and Thoughts

This collection of poetry by Javed Akhtar is unique; it is a little experimental too. The reading pleasure is enhanced by the images that run alongside the poetry. The images are evocative of poetry posters.
–Rachnakar, *an e-magazine*

The music maestro Pandit Jasraj and Javed Akhtar in the programme Tiranga

It would not be an exaggeration to call Javed sahab today's Ghalib

Pandit Jasraj

Truly, I fell in love with him the first time I met him. He has such positive vibrations that you will always remember him even if you meet him just once. Javed sahab is one of those personalities that we in India really need today. His writings show us how even simple things written in Hindi and Urdu can convey such deep thoughts. It would not be an exaggeration to call him today's Ghalib. His poem written for the concert *Tiranga*, which I had sung, is outstanding; it brings a whole ambience come to life. When he writes on 'kesaria' it seems as though the entire universe has become saffron coloured. When he writes on the colour white it seems there is peace all around and when he talks of the colour green it appears as though the entire earth has become green.

In the years past, we have had several great lyricists such as Sahir, Shakeel Badayuni and Majrooh Sultanpuri. I am mindful of the fact that today we have a great lyricist such as Javed Akhtar in our midst.

– ASHA BHOSLE

How I Wish I Had Written That Song: Javed Akhtar

Although Gulzar and I do not have any facial or physical resemblance, people often tend to confuse us for each other. I believe that an average person's mind is like a scrapyard, into which he tends to toss all thoughts and images that he encounters – randomly, without any chronological order to them. Then names and faces are then pulled out from this scrapyard, as and when required: 'Oh, isn't this by so-and-so, the eminent *shaayar*?'

I have an anecdote that proves this. Once, Shabana and I were flying back from somewhere on a Jet Airways flight. The airline's stewardesses kindly offered to collects our bags for us while we waited at a bench. As we sat there, a stranger approached us and addressing me, said enthusiastically, 'Aadab, Gulzar sahab!'

To which I replied, 'Ji, aadab!'

'Gulzar sahab, how come you're here at the airport today?'

I replied, 'Oh, I'm here to receive Javed Akhtar sahab, who'll be arriving shortly.'

He appeared a bit confused, probably thinking – how come such an eminent personality has come to receive Javed Akhtar – and asked, 'You've come to receive Javed Akhtar?'

Continuing with the spoof, I replied, 'I always come to receive Javed Akhtar sahab, whenever he comes from anywhere.'

Disappointment writ large on his face – he was probably shocked at the idea that his idol, Gulzar, came to receive Javed Akhtar at the airport every time the latter flew into the city! Flabbergasted, he decided to flee, managing to murmur to me, 'Okay, Gulzar sahab, I'll take your leave.'

The thing probably is that names and work of all *shaayars* and poets get dumped into a common scrapyard in the minds of people, and the name that is grabbed and pulled out first when needed, then sticks.

It has happened many a time that while listening to a song written probably many years ago by Gulzar sahab but which I've somehow missed hearing, just the 'antara' has been enough for me identify it distinctly as a Gulzar song. I've then often called him to ask as to when he had penned it, but never whether he had penned it.

I am totally woebegone that the song '*Beedi jalai le jigar se piya…*' has been written by Gulzar sahab. How I wish I had written this one. It is an exceptional song. Can anyone make out that it was written for a film? Every single line of the song seems like something that people have been singing for hundreds of years, imparting it the feel of a timeless folk song.

Something New Blossoms Every Two Minutes While Talking To Him

I read and write only in the Urdu script, even today. Javed sahab has learnt the language formally. And therefore, whenever I get stuck at the correct articulation of an Urdu word, I call him.

While talking to him, something new blossoms every two minutes. I have seen him excited but never angry. This is because when he argues in his excited state about something that angers him, he utilises the intrinsic but sarcastic humour that a word or two he has used in his argument, impart. And it is with this weapon that he keeps needling you – never getting angry or letting the situation translate into a full-blown fight.

Javed sahab's memory is phenomenal. He must know at least a hundred and fifty thousand *shers* by heart. He can retell Krishan Chandar's novels verbatim at any time. Sahir sahab had once given me a copy of *Parchaiyaan*. Later, when Nasreen Munni Kabeer planned to collate a diary on Sahir sahab, she called me to ask if I would have a copy of the book. I promised her I'd look for it. When I asked Javed sahab during a casual phone call if he, by any chance, had a copy, pat came the reply, 'No, but I could recite it in its entirety, if you'd like.'

The relationship that Javed sahab and Sahir sahab shared was extraordinary. Sahir sahab did something remarkable. Those days, Vividh Bharati did not announce lyricists' names for the songs it broadcast. Only the singer and music composer were mentioned. Sahir sahab protested this, demanding all songs to be broadcast should first be passed by the Writer's Association. This turned the tide, and lyricists' names started being announced. Years later, when Javed sahab became a Rajya Sabha member, he accomplished an even more important task – that of getting the Copyright (Amendment) Bill passed. With this, he managed to free all lyric writers from the shackles of an archaic and oppressive law that had been passed down from the British period.

This is a gigantic achievement of yours, Javed sahab.

Ek ladki ko mai bhi mila tha
Bada accha laga mil kar
Meri muddah thi
Eik fan thi meri
Woh meri shayari ki khoobiyan pehchanti thi
Mere misre meri tashbeehein uske dil ko chooti theein
Mujhe mil kar achanak baukhlane lag gayi thi
Badi nervous hansi hans kar kaha
Mujhe dar hai mai apna naam hi na bhool jaoon
Bagalgeer hoke mobile pe selfie bhi le li
Gayi toh mera naam lekar shukriya keh kar gayi woh
Woh mera naam na tha

Hamesha se yahi dar tha ki
Woh kambkht mujhse accha likhta hai

(A nazm penned by Gulzar for Javed Aktar)

Awards and

FOR BEST LYRICIST

- Five times National Award
- Fifteen times Filmfare Award
- Five times Screen Award
- Six times AIIFA Award (a record for winning it the maximum number of times by a lyricist)
- Three times Mirchi Music Award

FOR BEST SCREENPLAY

- Three times Best Screenplay Filmfare Award (with Salim Khan)
- Twice Best Story Filmfare Award (with Salim Khan)

Filmfare Lifetime Achievement Award – 2007
Seventh Royal Stag Mirchi Music Award – 2015

Lifetime Achievement Award
Hridyanath Mangeshkar Award – 2017

Padma Shri – 1999
Awadh Samman Uttar Pradesh – 2001
Indira Gandhi Rashtriya Ekta Puruskar – 2005
Padma Bhushan – 2007

Member, Rajya Sabha – 2010
Sahitya Akademi Award – Urdu 2013 (for *Lava*)
Delhi Government's Hindi Akademi's Shalaka Samman – 2017–2018

Shanti Doot Award, Sankat Mochan Mandir, Varanasi – 2018

Tata Literature Live Poet Laureate Award – 2020
Richard Dawkins Award – 2020

2020 Richard Dawkins Award
to
Javed Akhtar

Certificate of Registration

Be it known from this point forward that the National Star Association will hereby designate the star located at RA 21h24m26.70s D -23°39'57.57" epoch 2000 in the constellation Capricornus, to the name

JAVED AKHTAR

Be it further known that this star, along with name, is permanently recorded in the official National Star Association Catalog which is protected under the copyright laws of the United States of America.

Signed and sealed for the 17th day of January, 2006

Julie Steeper - Secretary

Greg Thomson - Record Keeper

The first Indian to be honoured with the Richard Dawkins Award

In 2020, Javed Akhtar became the first Indian to be awarded the Richard Dawkins Award. He was given this award for his atheism, rationalism, critical thinking, holding religious dogma upto scrutiny, advancing human progress and humanist values. Every year the award is given to a distinguished individual from the fields of science, scholarship, education, or entertainment. Javed Akhtar was chosen by the Board of the Centre for Inquiry in America which is associated with the Richard Dawkins Foundation.

A society that does not permit asking questions cannot be healthy

It is a strange thing about this word; people say it is a tradition, a way of leading our life according to age-old customs. Who are you to change it? How can you say this is not correct? There are many countries where worst excesses happen and we are gradually inching our way towards a similar situation. If we allow what is happening to continue, or what had been happening all along had continued, then Man would still be living in caves or sitting on trees. Every new generation, every age has thought of something new, understood something new, something that no one before them had thought of. And that is how the world moved forward. That is how the world has improved. Slavery existed in the world for thousands of years. People were bought and sold and so it continued for thousands of years. How did it become all right? Today, if someone asks to put an end to slavery, will he be considered wrong?

A space that does not allow you to ask questions—be it any philosophy, any system, any pathway—is a dangerous space. That system will be faulty and so will that government and that society, that village, that habitation that does not permit the asking of questions. Wherever Man has reached today, whatever knots he has untied, it is by only one means... by asking questions.

If there is such a thing as fate, if whatever is happening is because it is destined or written down, then how can there be sin and virtue? It was written in someone's fate that he would be murdered by another man and so it happened. Why are you now calling him a killing? What is his fault? It was written in my fate that I would steal his money then why are you calling me a thief? After all, it was predestined for me that I would steal his money. So there can be no sin and no virtue.

If you look at religions carefully, you will find that there are a lot of contradictions among them and within them. Now, either there is a God, a Khuda, or Ishwar who has total control. If he has total control, there can be no sin and no virtue. And if sin and virtue exist, there can be no total control. Now, it is for you to decide what is correct.

The communal Muslims we have in our country hate the secular Hindus and the communal Hindus hate the secular Muslims because they are bent on proving the other wrong. If you were to go back in time you will recall that the communal Muslims did not respect even Gandhi ji. The interesting thing is that neither did the communal Hindus! Communal Hindus send me messages telling me to go to Pakistan saying: 'You are a jihadi.' And the communal Muslims tell me to change my name to a Hindu one because: 'You have sold yourself.' For as long as both are abusing me, I am absolutely fine!

Jidhar jaate hain sab, jaana udhar achchha nahin lagta
Mujhe paamal raston ka safar achchha nahin lagta

Ghalat baton ko khamoshi se sunna, haami bhar lena
Bahut hain fayede iss mein magar achchha nahin lagta

Mujhe dushman se bhi khuddari ki ummeed rahti hai
Kisi ka bhi ho sar, qadmon mein sar achchha nahin lagta

Kabhi to insaan zindagi ki karega izzat
Yeh eik ummeed aaj bhi dil mein pal rahi hai

NAYA HUKMANAMA

Kisi ka hukm hai
Iss gulistan mein
Bas ik rang ke hii phuul honge
Kuchh afsar honge jo ye tai karenge
Gulistan kis tarah banana hai kal ka
Yaqinan phuul to yak-rangin honge
Magar ye rang hoga kitna gahra kitna halka
Ye afsar tai karenge
Kisi ko ye koi kaise bataye
Gulistan mein kahin bhi phuul yak-rangin
nahin hotey

Kabhi ho hii nahin sakte
Ki har ik rang mein chhup kar
Bahut se rang rahte hain
Jinhonne bagh-e-yak-rangin banana chahe the
Unko zara dekho
Ki jab ik rang mein
Sau rang zahir ho gaye hain to
Kitne pareshan hain
Kitne tang rahte hain
Kisi ko ye koi kaise bataye
Hawaain aur lahrein

Kab kisi ka hukm sunti hain
Hawain hakimon ki mutthiyon mein hathkadi mein
Qaid-khanon mein nahin ruktin
Ye lahrein roki jaati hain
To dariya kitna bhi ho
Pur-sukun betab hota hai
Aur iss betabi ka
Agla qadam sailab hota hai

Jo baat kehte darte hain sab, tu woh baat likh
Itni andheri thhi na kabhi pehle raat likh

Jin se qaseede likkhey the, woh phenk de qalam
Phir khoon-e-dil se sachche qalam ki sifaat likh

Jo roznamon mein kahin paati nahin jagah
Jo roz har jagah ki hai, woh waardaat likh

Jo waqeyaat ho chuke hain unka to zikr hai
Lekin jo hone chaahiye woh waqeyaat likh

Javed Akhtar outside Parliament House

Creativity gets muffled when marketing is strong

The speech given by Javed Akhtar in support of the Copyright Bill in the Rajya Sabha in 2012

Indian artists had been experiencing many difficulties for a long time but they possibly felt no one will hear if they speak up. But times are changing, things are different now.

I am hopeful that the law too will change and the destiny of Indian artists will change with it. I am speaking here today with the certain belief and the people in this House, from this end to the other, are listening with the utmost care and concentration. And rightly so because I am talking about the musicians and songwriters of India and this country is a land of musicians and singers. I am not saying this because it sounds nice; I am saying it because it is the truth.

There is no other country which can boast of two traditions of classical music forms that date back to thousands of years, namely Hindustani and Carnatic music. There is no other country that has as many colours as its rainbow of folk music. You can see from Kashmir to Kanyakumari, Maharashtra to Manipur. There is such an amazing variety in the music.

There is no other country where even the sacred texts are replete with poetry. There is no other country where from birth till death there is not a moment that is not filled with scores of songs. Be it any state of emotions, any season of feelings, any colour of thoughts—you can find a song to describe it. Take the case of our film songs—when they are released they are film songs but soon afterwards they become folk songs. Everything is filtered out in the sieve of Time—the actor's face and the name of the film. All that remains is the immortal song that one day becomes a part of your past and your memories. Today, when you hear an old song, you feel as though a friend from your youth has placed his hand on your shoulder and is saying, 'Sit down; where are you going? Talk to me.' A flood of memories swells up: Where did I first hear this song? When? With whom? And sometimes one can even remember who one had heard it for? One is amazed but more than amazement there is sorrow that in a country where so many lamps of music and poetry burn bright, why is there darkness beneath these lamps? Our musicians and writers have been spending their last days in abject darkness. Nevertheless, there is a hope in one's heart that a day will come when our voices will be heard, when we will get the justice that is our due, when we will gain our rights. Sir, *'Aayega aane wala'* was a very famous song. It is more than sixty years old. The song was composed by Pandit Khemchand Prakash, a great music scholar of his time. Something strange happened recently. What happens is, when a song is recorded, two royalties are generated for it: one is a sound recording royalty, which is for the owner of the sound recording—who is the producer or music company. The other is a performing royalty, which is meant for the writer and musician. This is not a new law; it has been in existence for some time. It exists in other countries too except that there it extends to paying the writer and musician! So, about ₹13,000–14,000 had collected in the account of Khemchand Prakash overseas. This money was sent to him here. Khemchand Prakash is no longer alive but when a search was made, his wife was found begging at the Malad station. This should not surprise anyone. There are many such stories. A film had been made when I was very young; it was called *Mujrim* and it featured Shammi Kapoor and Padmini as hero and heroine. Its poster did not feature the hero and heroine; instead, OP Nayyar stood holding his harmonium—'The Magician of Music—OP Nayyar'. Till his dying day, this very OP Nayyar lived in a tiny room in a settlement named Nala Sopara outside Mumbai in a fan's house. All he could afford was homeopathic medicine for his treatment whereas his songs continued to be heard and music companies continued to rake in his royalties. And after this there were Majrooh, Shailendra, Ghulam Muhammad. How many names shall I list of all those who have contributed so much? Will a lyricist like Shailendra be born again? Why is it so? When we in India too have the provision of royalty and the laws for it, why do we have such a sorry state of affairs for our artists?

The Beatles broke up in 1969–70. Last year Paul McCartney, who has written only 27 songs in his life, received a royalty of 16 million dollars. Elton John, who has not made any record in the past five years, received 22 million dollars as royalty last year. Here, in our country, the Indian Performing Right Society (IPRS) collects royalties from all over the world. But where does the money go? If you permit, I want to read out a short paragraph.

(This is a compulsory move that all contracts contain—be it for Bharat Ratna Pandit Ravi Shankar or the twice Oscar-winning AR Rahman or an ordinary person such as me or Gulzar, or anyone else.)

'The rights assigned, included but not restricted to the rights of mechanical, digital reproduction, in any manner or format or media, will existing, or feature publication, broadcasting, reproducing, hiring, renting, translation, adaption, synchronisation, making a use in cinematographic film, performing in publishing in any other way, whole or the part of the literary work, the rights to grant the mechanical and reproduction, publication, sound, television broadcasting, transmission over the airways, electronically, or through satellite, or literary works.' And now hear the proethicals:

'Including all forms of communication, transmission, reproduction, an exploitation of the literary work, that may be discovered or invented in the future, the said work has been assigned by me, for good and valuable concentration.' What is this if not bonded labour? Just because it is written in English it is not bonded labour? Who complained against this? If Pandit Ravi Shankar and AR Rahman have a complaint you can well imagine the state of all the others? What is even more shameful is that it isn't just desi or Indian companies that make you sign such a contract. Companies from Japan, Germany and America also make you sign such a contract though they will not dare to ask an artist in Japan or Germany or America to sign it. What is the difference between them and the East India Company? And what is the difference between the Indian companies and Mir Jafar for working in cahoots with them? This is not just a problem of the film industry; it is everybody's problem. And it isn't just about money either; it is about being humiliated. When marketing becomes so strong it muffles creativity, and begins to give the commands.

Recently, a highly esteemed artist such as Shiv Kumar Sharma ji was called by a music company and told, 'Look here, you begin very slowly. The crescendo that comes in the end should come in the beginning and then it will work very well.' Imagine, this is what the music company person is telling Shiv Kumar Sharma ji. He said, 'Sir, there is a band in my mohalla. It goes for wedding processions. You call them and please excuse me.' Something similar happened to me once. I was in a music sitting when the owner of the music company showed up. I thought perhaps he might be my fan and had come to hear what I had written. He heard me and then said, 'Remove the word *roothna* from your first line.' I asked, 'Why?' He said, 'It doesn't work anymore.' I asked, 'Where does it not work?' I gave the example of several songs that had the word *roothna*. He said, 'That is all very well but remove it from here.' I said, 'If that is the way you want to work, I can't do it. You get someone else to write for you.' The man had great respect for me. He immediately agreed. The very next day he got someone else and fired me.What do those who are opposed to this Bill have to say? Some say, 'You wrote the song, others composed the music. A producer spent his money to record the song. Too bad! But, again, it has nothing to do with us. The same producer then went to the most unique locations and picturised it on some of the biggest stars. He put in great shots and stunning visuals. And why did he do all this? For the film, naturally! He is a film producer, not a music producer. He records the song for the film.' Whereas we say, 'We are not asking anything for your film. If your film is a superhit, good for you! If it flops, again, we have nothing to do with it. No matter how big a hit the film is, you will still not give us an extra paisa.'

I have written many superhit films but no producer has ever come to me to say, 'Sir, you wrote *Sholay, Deewaar, Trishul,* so here I have brought something for you.' No, that never happens. We write our films and the rest is your fate and what sort of film you make. We are not responsible for it. You get the credit for it if it is a hit and the brickbats if it is a flop. The law says 50 per cent should go to the artists and 50 per cent should come to us. We said, 'No, if it is done suddenly, it won't look appropriate. Let them take 75 per cent.' The change was made at our behest. It was our decency. And their decency is such that they are not content with even 99 per cent; they want all 100 per cent. If this is indeed their due, then let's consider this: A man makes a film with Shah Rukh Khan as a hero. It doesn't matter if the film works or doesn't work. The man takes out four shots—he is after all the owner of the print—and uses it in an advertisement for beedi. The man will say, 'It is my right; I can do what I want with it.' Shah Rukh Khan will say, 'But I gave this shot for the film. How can you use it in an advertisement for *beedi*?' And that is precisely my question here today. We had given this song for a film. We are making no claim there. When you take it out of the film and use it elsewhere, even then we say: Take 75 per cent. And you still have an objection to giving 12.5 per cent—12.5 per cent to us! This is plain and simple greed.

Actually, this limitation is not for directors, nor is it for music companies. It is only for us—on artists and writers—and yet they are the ones who are affronted. All the artists in India are pleading with the Indian government and the Opposition and, with folded hands, saying: 'Please make it 25 per cent non-assign.' You are getting 75 per cent; what more do you want? They say it poses a hindrance in the contract. Well, then, 'minimum wages registration' is also a hindrance to the contract. Today, where we are standing in Delhi, a minimum wage of ₹328 has been fixed for skilled labour in the agriculture sector and ₹270 for unskilled labour; you can't employ people on anything less than this. Suppose someone is saying, 'Sir, I am ready to work for ₹150; why are you stopping me?' What is Dowry Prevention? It's a Prohibitory Act. A man is ready to give dowry for his daughter. His daughter is ready to accept it, the groom is ready to accept it and the groom's family is happy too. What's the government's objection? The government's objection is based on the fact that this is not a decision among equals. One party is unequally placed and so this practice has to be stopped. What is the problem with child labour? What is the Child Labour Prohibition Act all about? The parents are ready to have their child work, the child is ready, the factory is ready but we know the reason behind their readiness.

The Standing Committee on the Copyright Act said, 'Bring us any contract which shows that the writer did not give you his/her publishing rights.' They couldn't bring them because there are no such contracts.

This is bonded labour. And on top of all that you have tied both his hands; the poor writer and artist is helpless.

With the permission of MK Singh sahab, I want to quote Shakespeare because I think at least here, in this House, he has the copyright for Shakespeare:

'Tis time to fear when tyrants seem to kiss.'

When the music company is saying: What will happen to the writer if he doesn't have the rights? And who are the people opposed to this? Those who are saying, with folded hands, 'Please do not do this.' I can't give all the names but I can mention some names: Pandit Ravi Shankar, Pandit Shiv Kumar Sharma, Pandit Hariprasad Chaurasia, Shobha Mudgal, Vishal Bhardwaj, Gulzar, Prasoon Joshi, Jagjit Singh, Amjad Ali Khan, Aman Ali Khan, Ayan Ali Khan.

Ravi ji passed away while he waited, so did Jagjit. Their signatures are with us. Vishal–Shekhar, Zakir, so many artists from the South, so many other names of artists from the film industry, musicians and singers from Bengal—they are all asking for this Bill to be passed. After all, why? And, they don't want the Bill to include old songs. This is right to some extent, and not right in some ways, too. Tomorrow you can say, 'This Bill has been passed now. My song was released in 1919; you give me an account for it.' This is wrong. No law can be applied retrospectively. But henceforth when that song is played, its royalty will start accruing according to the law. Whatever was done was done, forget about it, we too have forgotten about it.

Sir, this is the only way forward. All the writers, all the musicians cannot be wrong. They are on one side and arrayed against them on the opposite side are all the big music producers and multinationals pretending that the producers will suffer immense losses whereas the truth is that the upfront money is only given to ten or twelve producers; the rest don't get a single paisa. When this Bill is introduced, the small producers will also get money for the first time because publishing will be in our hands and they will be the publishers. Till now, the music companies were raking it in. With this Bill, 90 per cent of the producers will benefit and the remaining 10 per cent, who think they will suffer losses, they too will still benefit because they have hitherto been selling at low prices. Till this Bill is passed, injustice, cruelty, exploitation and looting will continue. For far too long we have been walking amidst darkness. I am reminded of the sher:

Siyaah raat nahi leti naam dhalne ka
Yahi to waqt hai suraj tere nikalne ka

This Bill should be passed today, right now. Thank you.

Javed Akhtar in conversation with musician Shankar Mahadevan, Loy Mendosa, Sulaiman Merchant, Lalit Pandit, and others

If Javed sahab had not been a writer, poet and songwriter, he would have been an excellent lawyer

Amit Datta

It is very difficult for me to summarise in two or three pages Javed sahab's long and tumultuous journey to have radical changes made in the copyright law and eventually succeed in pushing through the revolutionary Copyright (Amendment) Act in 2012. In much the same way that he re-imagined the process of screenplay writing in Indian cinema and took the art of writing songs for films to new heights, he has succeeded in making ground-breaking changes in the field of copyright laws in India.

I am sure we can all agree that no one can better understand the struggle of writers and poets to claim their lawful rights in the Indian film industry in a historical manner and the pain when they are denied these rights by producers than these artists themselves.

It would be correct to say that had the Indian film companies not stopped Javed sahab from entering the Board of the Indian Performing Rights Society Ltd (IPRS) in 2004, the fortunes of the Indian creative artists would possibly never have changed. The fact is that permission was sought from Javed sahab to join the Board of the IPRS. The said board is a copyright institution meant to gather royalties from composers, musicians, and music companies from hotels, radio, TV and other platforms. On the day of the election, when the results were announced, Javed sahab was handed an injunction obtained from the District Court of remotely located Zilla Barasat in West Bengal, whereby he and other directors were removed from the Board even before they had assumed office.

As Javed sahab himself says, till then he used to think music publishing is about publishing songs in books. What he has done is something only a visionary and leader can do. He raised a question on an old and extremely strong practice. The entire music industry had this completely wrong assumption that the creative group of writers and musicians are worthy of no more than the meagre amounts they received from music companies. Javed sahab had the courage to not merely question this practice but to work collectively and proactively for the betterment of every person associated with the music and film industry. The incident of the IPRS stirred his curiosity about copyright laws. The more he dug into the subject of the rights of ordinary writers and musicians, the more shocked and amazed he was! Here was a group of artists who had contributed to the making of the cultural legacy of India and yet they had gained nothing except empty, hollow words of praise whereas the earnings accruing from their works went entirely to the film and music industry. Javed sahab understood that this was not merely a problem of the attitude and tradition of the industry; in fact, at the very root of this problem was a piece of legislation which had, from its very inception in 1957, very heartlessly disregarded the rights and shares of artists.

I met Javed sahab for the first time in mid-2009 and from then on began my training in legal redressal and improvement. I can say with complete certainty that if Javed sahab had not been a writer, poet and film lyricist he would have made an excellent lawyer. For the next three years, he literally lived, breathed and spoke about copyright laws. He sought one-to-one meetings with ministers, leaders of opposition parties, politicians and parliamentarians of various big and small parties. He told them about the piteous, exploited condition of Indian musicians and artists and advocated the need for legal redressal and change in laws. Seeing his boundless enthusiasm and passionate zeal for the improvement of his fellow artists, politicians from across the political spectrum such as Arun Jaitley, Sushma Swaraj, Sonia Gandhi, Kapil Sibal, the then-Speaker of the Rajya Sabha Meira Kumar and Prakash Javdekar lent him strong support in his bid to introduce a radical change. Despite the political unrest and constant parliamentary delays and stalemates, the political support enjoyed by Javed sahab was unmatched and unheard-of. As Javed sahab himself says, it was because of this support from across party lines that a vast group of artists gathered around him. The efforts being made to propel Javed sahab to lead this change was accepted and appreciated by his fellow artists causing all of them to speak in one, unequivocal voice.

Javed sahab paid a heavy professional price for this tireless commitment; this took the form of a cruel and entirely spiteful, though informal, boycott by the music industry. And I feel this continues, in some way or the other, even to this day. I feel the Indian copyright laws needed a person such as Javed Akhtar who could bring about radical changes in the unfair, exploitative and heartless way Indian artists had hitherto been treated.

In April and May 2012, after being passed nearly unopposed in both Houses of Parliament and after being duly notified by the Government in June 2012, the Copyright (Amendment) Act came into effect from 2012 itself.

But life is seldom easy. When this law that would be troublesome for the industry came into effect, there were many who opposed it. It took another five years for the law to be respected and implemented and for all the arguments to be resolved, under Javed sahab's leadership, among the artists who had rallied around him in support. This compromise among all the concerned parties was a historic one. It brought together the two warring groups, namely music companies and artists, in a bid to safeguard

At the house of the famous writer Victor Hugo in Paris

the rights of lyricists and musicians so that the music industry as a whole—that had been floundering for decades—could be encouraged to stand on its own feet. As was expected, in this face-off with some stubborn people within the industry, the IPRS—comprising a substantially large number of artists under the leadership of Javed sahab—emerged from this battle as one of the fastest growing copyright bodies in the world. As of now, royalties are being duly paid to artists and every day that dawns is a better day for Indian artists.

If you were to ask me to describe in the briefest possible words exactly what Javed sahab has achieved for Indian artists then I will unhesitatingly say: Laws are made by Parliaments and governments, not by one individual person. But which Parliament or government would have made these amendments if there had not been a person such as Javed sahab who took this story of injustice and misbehaviour to the highest quarters—at great personal cost.

Victor Hugo played a huge role in the fight to make changes in copyright laws. Inspired by him, Javed Akhtar launched the crusade to fight for the rights of Indian artists which resulted in significant amendments by the Government of India in the existing copyright laws in February 2012.

Amit Datta and Gulzar sahab with Javed Akhtar at the IPRS function

It is for the first time that a bill has been unanimously passed in both Lok Sabha and Rajya Sabha

Javed Akhtar's statement at a function organised by the IPRS for the passing of the Copyright (Amendment) Bill

Friends! I am extremely grateful. Some very great things have been said about me today. Yes, it's true I made many efforts and met many people. Believe me, and I say this with utter sincerity, this is not my victory; this is your victory. The names I had gone with, the people who accompanied me time and again, their power and prestige are immense. You, the artists of India, yourselves don't know your own strength. You have no idea of the power of your name and your goodwill. People know you by your name, by your voice, by your tunes, by your words. Arrayed against us was everything that is considered powerful in a worldly sense. But what happened? What happened was that for the first time we realised what our strength is. The strength is not one person's strength just as this was not one person's problem. The piece of paper I had carried with me contained the signature of Bharat Ratna Pandit Ravi Shankar and two-time Oscar winner AR Rahman, along with all the rest of us. We went before the Standing Committee and showed them our contents, over 200–300 contents, of writers, music directors, singers. 'Tell us, what is the difference between this and bonded labour?' we asked. And when the representatives of the music industry came before the committee, they claimed that all the writers and musicians had given this content of their own free will. To which we countered: 'If all these writers and musicians have willingly given their rights to you and you have been paying them fairly, show us one contract since the past 20 years.' But they could not show any such contract. This victory, then, is a victory of justice. We look at our politicians very cynically, and rightly so on most occasions. What can musicians, lyricists and singers give to any political party? It is after ages that a Bill has been passed unanimously in both the Rajya Sabha and the Lok Sabha. This is not my victory; this is the victory of Truth and it is proof of the fact that, no matter whatever might happen in our Parliament, people still have a beating heart in their breast. We have to understand our strength but, at the same time, we must not use it unlawfully. Not for a second should we feel that we have defeated our producers and that we have emerged victorious. They are the products of a system, just as we are. The truth is that the system emerged from the world we live in, it carried on without changes. It was not good for the producers, either; they too suffered losses because of the existing system. They are gradually beginning to understand that. With time, they will understand this better as the practice begins to settle in. I want to assure you that this Bill will be of immense benefit to producers as well. Till now, 95 per cent producers did not get a single paisa from the music they produced; in fact, they often ended up paying from their own pockets. It caused them much trouble and hardship. Similarly, there was anguish and humiliation among writers, script writers, composers and singers. Everyone felt that they were being denied the recognition, honour, money and credit that were their due. Even the producers were caught up in this wheel of injustice without realising that they too were a victim of the injustice. But the incident of 2005 finally broke the dam of patience. We felt enough was enough; now no more! I used to go for the meeting of the IPRS once a year; I didn't even know its full form. I used to go there, have tea and I would be handed an envelope containing a cheque for ₹ 1 or 1.2 lakh. I used to think I have got the money for free! I would take the money and come home. Then, one day some writers and music directors came home and said they want me to contest in the forthcoming elections because there is a lot of confusion and mismanagement here. I said, 'I have never stood for an election in my entire life; why do you want me to get into needless trouble? And after all, what is the IPRS; I don't even know anything about it.' Nevertheless, at the insistence of my friends I stood for the election, and I won. But when I went for the first board meeting, I was handed a court notice even before the meeting began. The notice said that the meeting could not take place as the election was legally invalid.

And so our struggle began. We went to meet many people. Ultimately, we understood that nothing could be gained like this. The only hope was if something happened in Delhi with a change in the law. We had only just begun to understand what royalty meant; understanding the law was a distant dream. We were told about a big law firm called 'Luthra & Luthra' in Delhi that had some of the best corporate lawyers in the country. But they were a huge law firm; their lawyers charged lakhs of rupees per day. Still, we said, 'Let's talk to them. We can't pay their full fees but let us see how much we can manage.' I remember that afternoon. There were 4–5 of us. It had never happened before that we would go to meet someone and Jagjit Singh would not be with us. I can't describe the pain I felt at his absence. Anyhow, we went for the meeting. We met Rajiv Luthra, the owner of the law firm. He introduced us to Amit Datta, the expert in copyright law. We explained the entire matter to him. He said he will tell us what our demand should be with the government and how we should frame it. I wish to thank Amit Datta sahab just as much as I wish to thank the government, the chairman of the UPI, the prime minister, Kapil Sibal sahab, Arun Jaitley sahab, Sushma Swaraj ji and Meira Kumar ji, the Speaker of the Lok Sabha.

When Sonia Gandhi ji saw our contracts personally and understood our situation, she wrote a letter to Kapil Sibal saying that the best rights for writers–composers anywhere in the world should be there in our country, too. Prime Minister Manmohan Singh too wrote a letter. And it was our good fortune that Kapil Sibal sahab was already sympathetic to our cause; he was further encouraged by these letters. Sometimes, there would be some confusion in my mind: Is this Bill being moved by the government or the Opposition? I can't begin to describe the manner in which Arun Jaitley sahab supported this Bill. It could not have been passed from the Rajya Sabha without him. When the debate on the Bill was going on, he stayed till the very end. Usually, the proceedings of the Parliament end by 6 pm. He ensured that they continued till 8 pm.

We read about the 'corridor of power'. Every time I walked down the Parliament House, I feel this is the 'corridor of power'. I am narrating to you the story of a single day whereas our issue spanned three years with many obstacles and only some 'passes'. Our achievement today would not have been possible if we did not get good suggestions: who to meet, what to say, what demands to make. Every single letter that we submitted, every single appeal that we made was drafted by Amit Datta sahab. Without him, our goodwill may have been acknowledged and respected but our job would not have got done.

ANAND BHAI

It was a very difficult task. Sometimes, it seemed it would come through, sometimes it wouldn't. But Javed sahab remained resolute and he has shown who an artist truly is. He has re-awakened our self-respect that had been put to sleep. He has done a great service. For this he will get the blessings of his elders and those younger than him. He has shown the way to future generations.

GULZAR

There are many who talk but few who actually do things. We were all among those who talked but it was Javed sahab who did it. His nickname is 'Jadu' and indeed he has done magic! There are few people who can show the way with complete faith. I followed him as best as I could. I knew that the path he had taken must surely be the right one. And so I walked along beside him.

PANDIT SHIVKUMAR SHARMA

This is a historic moment for us. We would see a man who has left everything and is completely engrossed in this crusade. Often it happens that when things are running smoothly for me, I tell myself: It's all good for me; let others fend for themselves. Javed sahab's name will be inscribed in golden letters for stepping outside the circle and thinking of the common people.

To chant 'Bharat Mata Ki Jai' is not my duty, it is my right

Javed Akhtar's farewell speech in the Rajya Sabha in 2016

Good times, bad times, they pass as Time must necessarily pass. These six years too have passed as though I have blinked my eyes six times. So fast has been the passage of Time. But whatever I have witnessed during these swiftly flowing years I shall always keep safe in my mind and heart because they are very precious. I have heard the speeches of Shri Arun Jaitley as 'Leader of the Opposition' and as 'Leader of the House'. I have also heard the debates of Chidambaram sahab and Kapil Sibal sahab. I have heard the logical arguments of Brinda Karat and Sitaram Yechury. I have seen the wit of Ravi Shankar Prasad. I have heard Ramgopal Yadav who has the ability to say the harshest things in the softest tone and tenor. I could have heard more but I am reminded of an incident. Majaz was one of the major Urdu poets and his sense of humour was equally well known. He went to Kashmir for the first time for a mushaira. Someone asked him, 'Majaz sahab, you have come here for the first time; have you seen the natural sights? What did you think of them?' he answered, 'They are very nice but the mountains came in the way or else I could have seen them better.' So, I can only say that I would have heard more speeches were it not for the many adjournments that came in the way. Be that as it may, whatever I heard was enough. I had come here with a special purpose, a clear intention. The composers and musicians of this country had a problem regarding copyright; I had come here bearing their sorrow. I met Sonia ji along with my fellow artists. She sent us to Manmohan ji. He heard us and he too was as affected as Sonia ji had been. Manmohan ji said, 'We will certainly support you but you should talk to the opposition, especially the BJP. You will not be able to pull this through without them.' And so we went to Arun Jaitley ji. I was a bit surprised and pleased that, to a great extent, he was aware of our problem. But we gave

Javed Akhtar in the Rajya Sabha

him some more details. The way he reacted that day I knew our job would be done. I liked what Manmohan ji said to me. He said I should talk to the opposition for the task I was trying to accomplish cannot be accomplished without them. And that is the way it should be.

Even countries with dictatorship have governments. So do countries with monarchies. So what is the difference between democracies and these other countries? There, there is only a government; here, there is both a government and an opposition. A poet has said it well:

Chaman mein ikhtilat-e rang-o boo
se baat bannti hai
Hum hii hum hain to kya hum hain,
tum hii tum ho to kya tum ho

(It is the diversity of colours and fragrances
that make a garden
If there's only us there's no us,
if there's only you there's no you)

The thing is, we are exceedingly fortunate people and yet we complain all the time against our governments, our country and our society. We are never sufficiently thankful for what we have. We are never as grateful as we should be for one singular thing that we have... and that is our Constitution!

Look around you. If you set off westward, the next democracy you will see will be on the Mediterranean coast. What is that quality, that strength that we find here? It is this Constitution that gives us democracy. But, remember, there can be no democracy without secularism. So those countries that do not have secularism do not have democracy.

Democracy means that only that thing will be followed that is agreed upon by the majority. But democracy also functions on the basic premise that majority and minority are not permanent; they change on every issue. If a certain definition is made for minority and majority that is permanent, then democracy will end that very day. If we talk of secularism or saving secularism, then we are not doing any favours to any one group at the cost of the other. We will have to save secularism simply because without it there can be no democracy. I believe this is the greatest achievement of our country. At the time of our independence, we were not capable of manufacturing a needle. Today, we are an industrialised nation. We are a great country, a powerful one with many achievements; yes, our achievements could have been greater, still. But whatever we have achieved so far is definitely good. But our greatest achievement, by far, is that we allowed democracy to penetrate our country. Today, its roots go down so deep that it cannot be uprooted. It is the greatest gift that our elders have given us. On the one hand, there is democracy and, on the other, this incredible Constitution. Then there is our country: in which over 75 per cent people are under the age of twenty-seven years, where 35 crore people are young (between 10–25 years). This is a young country. It has so much energy, an incredible set of laws, as well as education, talent and calibre. I say this not because I am an Indian, but because I believe it to be so. The IQ of an average Indian is quite high. Even if he is not educated and lives in a village, speaks in a rough, broken dialect, he has an understanding; he is not ignorant. When everything is in our favour, why then do we have the largest number of unemployed persons in our country? Why do we have the largest number of TB patients in our country? Why is every fifth child, who dies before the age of five years, an Indian? Why is it that, in any calendar year, 50,000 women die of minor, pregnancy-related complications? We will have to think about this. All this power, these laws, this system—we have everything. We want to progress but this progress will be for whom? Whose development and at what cost? Development is not GDP; development is Human Development Index.

Let me tell you, there is a country called Brazil which has the world's third largest fleet of private planes while one-third of its population lives below the poverty line. We don't want this in our country, sir! I would like to believe that any party would want its country to do well. I look around me and see that there are huge problems of unemployment, dearth of hospitals and lack of medical care, fewer schools, colleges and poor infrastructure, yet what are we expending our energy on? Why is our energy going waste? Every day we hear of something that is unfortunate. Just a few days ago, a certain gentleman suffered from the illusion that he is a national leader whereas the truth is that he is the leader of a *mohalla* in the city of Hyderabad in the state of Andhra Pradesh. He declared that he does not wish to say 'Bharat Mata ki Jai' because the Constitution doesn't ask him to do so. The Constitution doesn't ask him to wear a sherwani and a topi. I am not interested in knowing if my duty is to chant 'Bharat Mata ki Jai'. I don't wish to know this because it is not my duty, it is my right. And I say it: 'Bharat Mata ki Jai!', 'Bharat Mata ki Jai!', 'Bharat Mata ki Jai!' Who are these people? I condemn their words in the strongest possible terms. I condemn another slogan in equally strong words, a slogan that is often repeated in many Indian cities, namely: *'Musalman ke do sthhan: Kabristan ya Pakistan!* (There are only two places for Muslims: A graveyard or Pakistan!)' I condemn it too.

We cannot stop still because time does not stop. We can either go forward or backward. We have to decide. We are at a crossroad. In other countries and societies those people are considered intelligent who learn from experience, but more intelligent are those who learn from the experience of others. Look at the countries that gave the greatest importance to religion, or those that believe that their past was great and glorious, or those that are convinced that what they are saying is correct.

Sab tere siwa kafir aakhir iss ka matlab kya
Sar phira de insaan ka aisa khabt-e mazhab kya

(What does it mean that everyone except you is a kafir
What is this obsession with religion that turns even the head of a person)

What has happened to the countries that had this obsession? Should those countries be our exemplar where your tongue is cut off, where you can be hanged for speaking one word against religion, or those countries where every manner of freedom is granted, where a film such as *The Last Temptation of Jesus Christ* can also be made? Which country is right? Where are citizens at ease? Where is life better? We are at a crossroad. Today, what we call 'fringe' is increasingly getting bigger. There is no need for it. I truly believe that there are some very

Javed Akhtar acting in the film Manto *produced by film actor and director Nandita Das*

capable people in this government who are doing some good work and can do even better work.

I do believe that the Opposition too has its own role to play. Both the government and the Opposition must believe that much work has to be done here. These adjournments will not take us forward, nor will this polarisation. Let us all work to create an India, and indeed it can be done for it is not very difficult, where everyone has a roof over their head, clothes to cover their body, food in their belly, where everyone has access to medicines, schools, roads, electricity, bridges, etc. This can be done. If only people were to forget the next election, all of this can be achieved.

Are we living with our 'ground reality' or are we trying to make a *Pather Panchali*?

Javed Akhtar delivered the First Address in the Satyajit Ray Memorial Lecture Series, 'Ray Today', organised by the Satyajit Ray Society in Kolkata in 2009. Given below is an abridged version of his speech.

Javed Akhtar speaking in the Satyajit Ray Memorial Lecture Series, Kolkata (2009)

I think for an average Indian cinegoer, in any part of India, when we read or hear the name Satyajit Ray, a collage of images rises in front of us. *Pather Panchali, Aparajito, Apur Sansar, Charulata, Pratidwandi, Jan-Aranya, Jalsaghar*—and you get totally overwhelmed. And you realise that it is human nature. It is perhaps a compulsion with us that we have to rationalise everything, try to understand the process, try to understand the phenomenon, but sometimes we fail because life is not linear, particularly in art. Human progress, in many fields, is logical, organic, and rational; you can understand it. But occasionally, this logic, this rationality gets stuck in a bad place. Sometimes, a person comes along who doesn't seem to be part of this organic growth. It can be a Shakespeare, a Beethoven, a Michelangelo, a Satyajit Ray. And we try to rationalise and understand them, but genius is an element that we have never been able to solve or understand or lexicalise.

So what do we do except show our devotion, our respect and thankfulness that he was there, he did something, he left something for us. When the Satyajit Ray Society called me to invite me, certain memories were revived in my mind. I was reminded about when and how I had heard this name for the first time in my life. When did I first see his film? I was in Bhopal, in pre-university. I met a boy; he was very special. He had started a film society. His name was Anil. I don't remember his surname. Maybe it was Gupta or Agarwal. At that age, surnames were not very important. He used to write letters to Mr Ray. I saw *Pather Panchali* for the first time in that film society. Till then, I had not seen any film like it. After some time, I got the opportunity to see *Apur Sansar*. It was much later that I saw *Aparajito*.

After college, I joined the film industry. I had written films like *Sholay* and *Deewaar*. One day a film festival was organised in Mumbai and I entered the foyer of the theatre and, lo and behold, I saw Satyajit Ray standing there. I was looking at him with awe. Our eyes met and I felt that he had recognised me. Somehow, I gathered the courage to go near him. He offered me his hand. And I shook his hand. That was my first meeting. Before I could say something, other people came and that was the end. Then, after ten or fifteen years when I was in Kolkata, I went to his place with my friend Ayan Rashid. It was a long meeting, and as a matter of fact, most of the time, he was asking me questions. I didn't have the courage to start a topic of my own. He talked about *Sholay* and other films. I was very thankful to him because sometime in 1976, an interview of his had been shown on Doordarshan; it had been taken by the journalist Amita Malik.

In this interview, she had mentioned *Sholay* but not in an especially complimentary way. But Mr Ray had contradicted her and said, 'You are wrong. I am proud that such films are now being made in India.' So this was my personal interaction with him.

Today, I find myself in a strange situation talking about Satyajit Ray, his intellect, his sensitivity. In all honesty, I find myself completely incapable of doing so, especially here in this city for it is like carrying coals to Kolkata. But yes, I will say that when I think of him, and when I think of his films, certain words come to my mind. That is how I describe his work, his art to myself. Those words are: dignity, understatement, compassion. Do we see any of these associated with today's cinema and society? Even commercial cinema doesn't survive in a void. It reflects society and society reflects commercial cinema.

Although Hindi mainstream cinema is not known for any pursuit for realism, to put it very mildly, but the fact is ultimately they are making films for a certain audience that is living in a particular society. And, wittingly or unwittingly, that cinema does reflect the society. Sometimes, I feel that if you make a list of villains from Indian commercial films, you can write the socio-political history of this country for the past sixty years. In the 1940s, the villain used to be the zamindar. In the 50s, the villain became the capitalist, the industrialist, the millionaire. In the 60s, the villain was the underworld don of urban society. In the 70s, that underworld person became the hero. In the 80s and the 90s, you see the politician become the villain. By the late 90s, the Pakistani intruder was the villain, the terrorist. Now, we are totally deprived of villains. We have exhausted all our villains. So, be it dignity, understatement, compassion, or sensitivity for others, all these qualities must be in our society for it to find reflection in our cinema.

I think Satyajit Ray's films stand for these great human values. Talking of dignity, I feel that by and large it has become an obsolete, outdated quality. If you have dignity, if any work of art has dignity, if any poem has dignity, if any painting has dignity, if any novel, any play has dignity, any film has dignity, it is rather dated. But why has a brash, aggressive, uncouth attitude replaced that quiet, silent, confident attitude in art and literature, and in life? When you look at the characters of *Pather Panchali*, *Jalsaghar*, *Aparajito*, they are dignified. They may be right; they may be wrong. Ray has empathy for everybody. But I remember that mother in *Pather Panchali*, that poor woman, and that old lady... the moment her ego is bruised she walks out, walks out to die but she does so with dignity. I remember that little child who seizes the necklace and throws it into the pond. It is dignity. And he saved the dignity of his sister. I don't see this sensitivity, this urge and desire for this virtue. Why? Perhaps dignity means allowing others to give a second look because dignity is a state; dignity has what you call *sthirta*. Somewhere, people have simply lost confidence. Somewhere, as a society, we have lost self-confidence.

In Satyajit Ray's cinema I see that his characters are rooted and so they are universal. There is a scene in *Aparajito*: the boy is going away and the mother is packing his bag. She puts the Gita, some home-made food, other things into the tin box that acts as a bag. She is telling him, explaining all the things she is packing in the small tin box. She asks him: 'What do you have in your other hand?' He says it is the Globe of the world. 'I am taking it with me.' Here is a boy who is going out of his house with one tin box containing the Gita, some home-made food in one hand, and the Globe of the world in the other. I think, the film-maker is telling us something with great understatement and subtlety. There is another scene in *Apur Sansar* where Apu has gone to the village with his friend. And suddenly he finds himself in a situation where he has to marry a girl. Under the circumstances, he doesn't say '*Dosti nibhani hi padegi* (Friendship will have to be honoured)'. Instead, he says, 'I don't have another shirt and I have to shave too'. This understatement is missing in today's cinema and that is why whether it is dignity or understatement or compassion, they are relevant. And Mr Ray's values, his cinema, his sensibility are relevant.

The market we have before us has no place for subtlety. I am sure that it would be very difficult to sell a Mona Lisa to an advertising company that is making advertisements for toothpaste. The company executives will say that maybe it is an enigmatic smile, but we can't see the teeth. That is how it is. Look at the music. When I write lyrics, sometimes I wonder how many people will be able to decipher what I have written in this tempo and cacophony. In *Jalsaghar*, if you remember, there is a scene where a character is listening to music and the sound of a generator starts disturbing him. You never see the generator. That is the understatement. But what is interesting is that be it the zamindar in the film *Jalsaghar* or the nawabs of Lucknow in *Shatranj Ke Khiladi*, Ray shows a similar compassion and understanding. These zamindars and nawabs were not right, but they were human. They were prisoners of their own values, and the director views them with tremendous humanity and compassion. But where has that compassion gone today? Is it in our society? Is it in our films? If films mirror society, then we are in deep trouble. And I do believe films are a mirror of society.

There was a time in the 50s and 60s, when an average protagonist in Hindi films used to be from the working class—a teacher, lawyer, mill worker, farmer, student, or clerk. That is no longer the case today. Our protagonist doesn't work anymore. He has not been from the working class for the last ten or twelve years. He lives in a very big house and is a very rich person. When he steps out of the house, he is not on Indian streets. He is in Switzerland or New Zealand. Why? We make ghost stories, we make mystery stories, we make love stories, we make every kind of film, but rarely is a film dealing with a social issue today. It was not so in the 50s and 60s but it is so today. Why? Where is the room for compassion? Clearly, we are not interested in almost 75 per cent of the population of India.

When I had gone to the film industry after my graduation, I was nine years old. Then, the pundits had told me that if you want to be a writer, you should write a script that will appeal to the small-towners because how many big cities do we have anyway and in big cities, the theatre rental is so high that you hardly get any money. The real profits are in the small cities. You should write films, stories, characters that depict the fantasies, aspirations, concerns of small-town India. Forty years later, this mantra is standing on its head. Now, young film-makers are very clear about the fact that it doesn't matter if their films don't release in Bihar and UP. It's all right as long as a film does well in big cities and among the diaspora. Obviously, these film-makers are no sociologists and economists, but unwittingly what are they saying to us? They are saying that 75 per cent of the people don't matter to them. They don't matter because they don't have money. And these 25 per cent people who live in 'Shining India' are the people who matter and we should make films for them because they can shell out money.

So, if I am not making film for 75 per cent people, why should I show 'Sarbjaya' (from *Pather Panchali*). All the Sarbjayas and Apus of the world are not going to buy the tickets to my film, so why should I make a film for them. It may be that *Pather Panchali* and other films made in the 50s and 60s were not watched by the Sarbjayas of the world, but at least those films had compassion, concern. But today that compassion is missing and it is not just from cinema but everywhere. We have become insular and selfish. And this new-found affluence has not made us philanthropic; it has made us greedy and insensitive. This is seen in a film such as the

Javed Akhtar Special show of Indian Idol on Sony Television

At that time, everything in the world, all the logic, all the worldly wisdom told him that he should not make such a film, but he did

Middleman. Some people find cynicism in this film. But I think it is not cynicism; it is a deep hurt. The director could see what was happening in society. And if he had resolved it, Somnath (if I remember his name correctly) would not have done what he eventually did and he could have emerged with a clear conscience. But he did what he did. And that girl whose name was Kona, gives her name as Jyotika when she is working as a prostitute. I have great respect for Kona and other people like her because Kona, by calling herself Jyotika, somewhere, somehow, to some degree, is trying to save Kona. She is trying to say: 'Kona is somebody else. At the moment, I am not Kona, I am Jyotika'. There is a desperate, tragic attempt to hold on to some purity, some dignity. But what about Somnath? He did not change his name, and nor have any of us.

So ladies and gentleman, I will end my talk by talking of the beginning. Here was a young person who, while still in his thirties, was married, was shortly going to be a father. And he decided to make a film, a film which was not commercially viable, a film that perhaps had no future. Nobody was willing to put a penny in it. All the reasons combined to create a situation where he should have stayed in his comfortable job, and not wasted his weekends. But he pursued his dream. And it may have taken more than two years but, ultimately, he made a film, a film which was totally against the ground reality. At that time, everything in the world, all the logic, all the worldly wisdom told that young film-maker that he should not make such a film but he did. And the rest is history. All of us are living lives, making compromises, living unhappily, doing things which even we ourselves don't condone. And we call it ground reality. The question is to each one of you and to myself too, whether we are doctors, engineers, painters, businessmen or bankers, or whatever we are: Are we living with our ground reality or are we trying to make a *Pather Panchali*?

Autographs given to Javed Akhtar during the age of 12-14 years

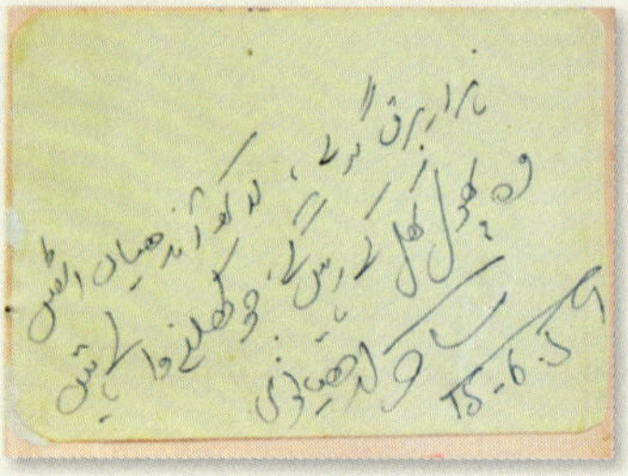

Hazaar barq girey
Lakh aandhiyan aayein
Woh phool khil ke rahenge
Jo khilne waale hain
Sahir Ludhianvi
15–6–59

CK Naidu

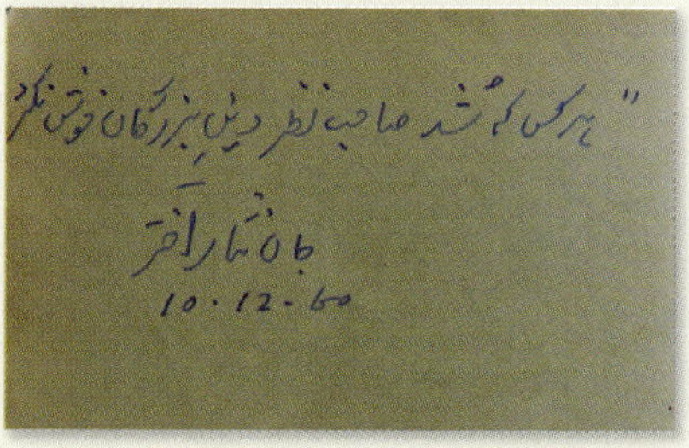

Har woh shakhs jo samjhdar ho gaya, usey buzurgon ke taur-tariqey pasand nahi aatey.
Jan Nisar Akhtar
10–12–62

Love!
Madhubala

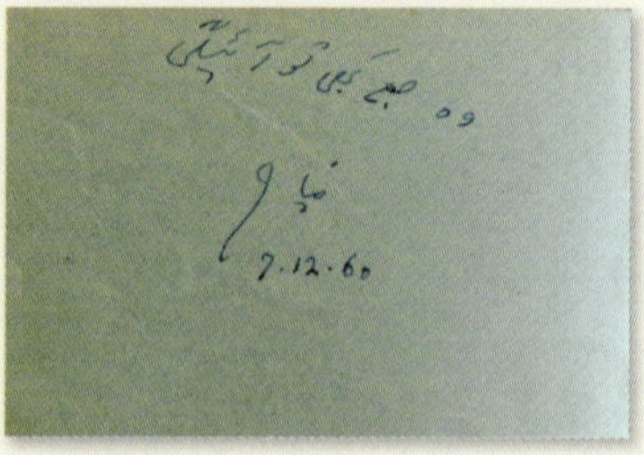

Woh subah kabhi to aayegi.
Khayyam
7–12–60

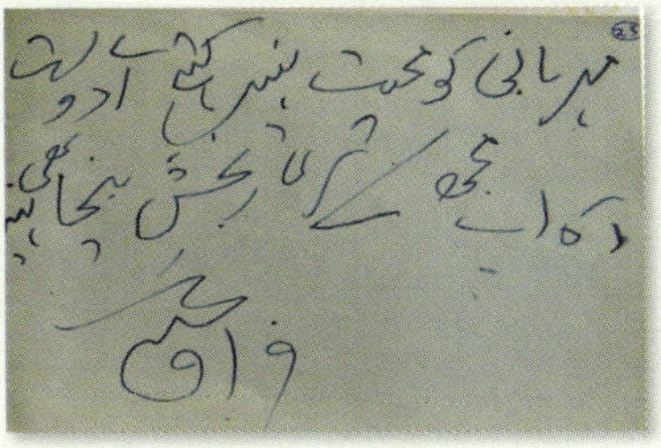

Meherbani ko mohabbat
nahi kehtey, ai dost
Aah ab mujhse teri
ranjish-e bejaan bhi nahi
Firaq Gorakhpuri

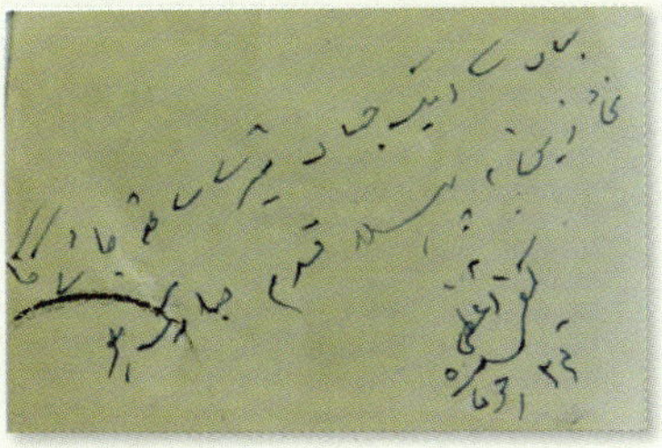

Yahan se eik jahan
tere saath jayega
Nayi zameen pe pehla
qadam mubarak ho
Kaifi Azmi

Jawaharlal Nehru

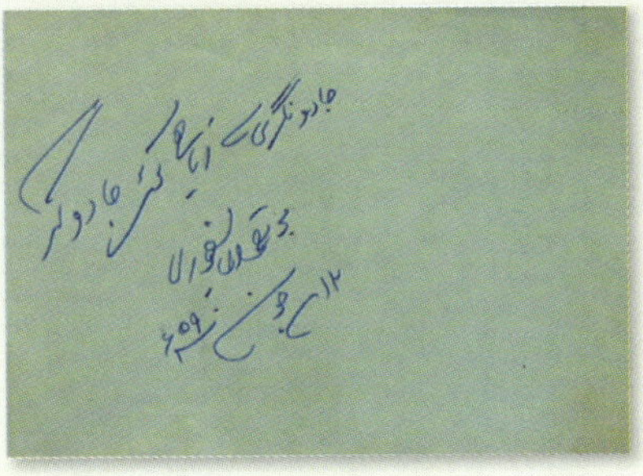

Jadu nagri se aaya hai koi jadugar
Majrooh Sultanpuri
12–06–59

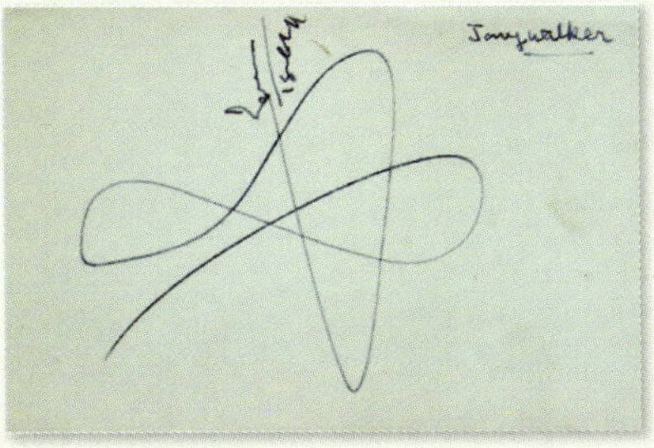

Johnny Walker

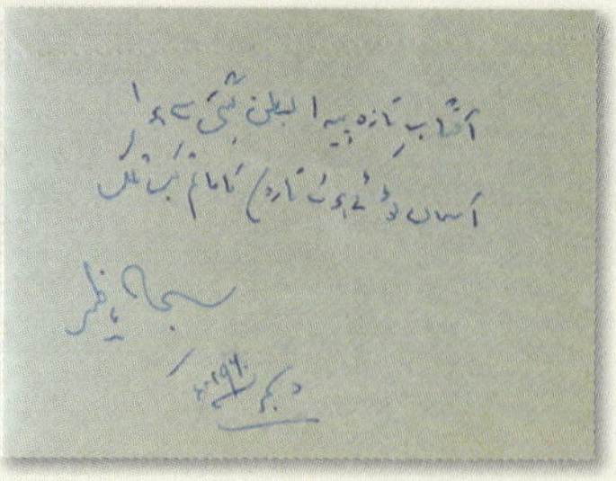

Aaftaab-e taaza paida
batan-e geeti se hua
Aasman doobey huye taaron
ka maatam kab talak
Sajjad Zaheer
December 60

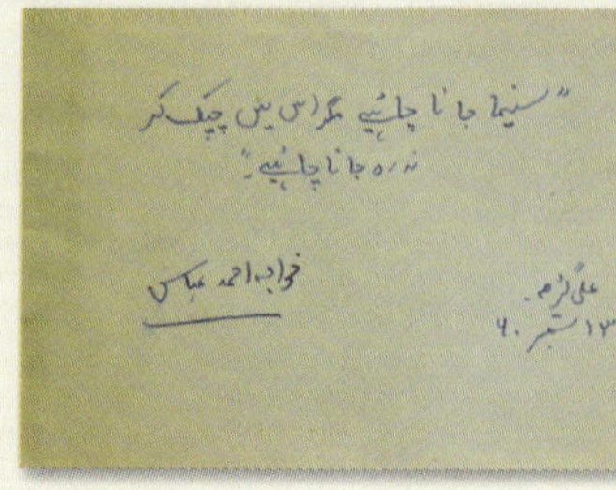

Cinema jaana
chahiye magar usmey
chipak kar na rah
jaana chahiye.
Khwaja Ahmad Abbas
Aligarh, 13–09–60

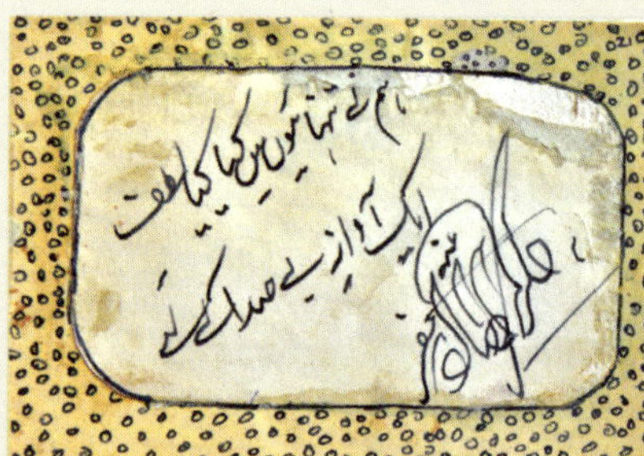

Humnein tanhaiyon
mein kya kya lutf
Eik awaaze be-sada
ke liye
Jigar Moradabadi

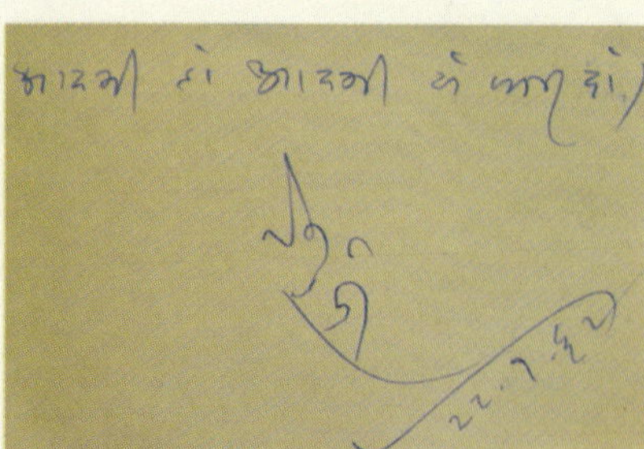

Aadmi ho aadmi
ko pyaar do!
Neeraj
22–1–62

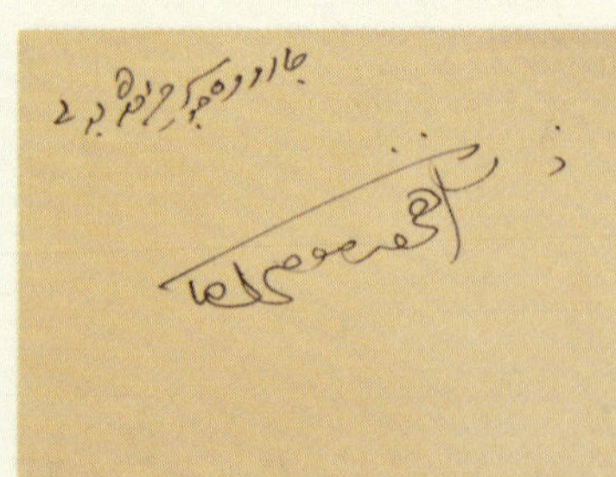

Jadu woh jo sar
charhh ke boley
Rahi Masoom Raza

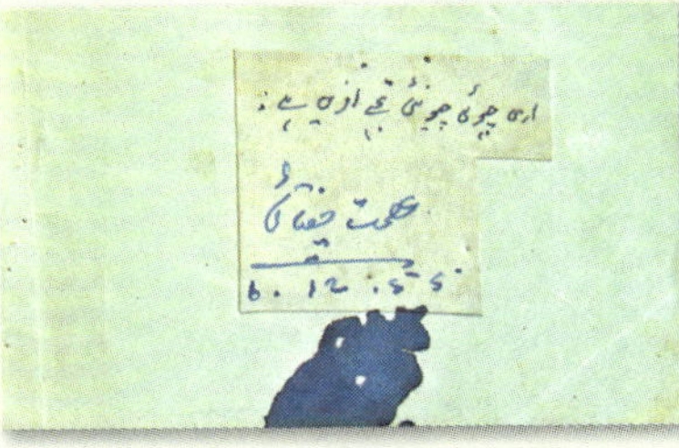

Ari chhoti cheenti tujhe aafreen hai
Ismat Chughtai
6–12–55

Pran

Dilip Kumar

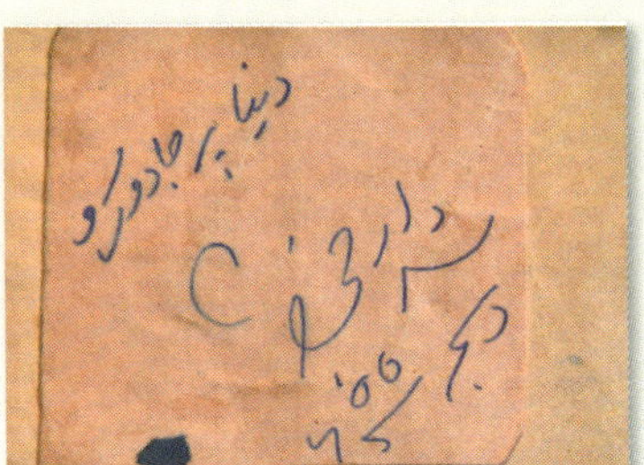

Duniya par jadu karo!
Sardar Jafri
December 55

EMS Nambudripad

Javed Akhtar receiving the Padma Shri from Dr APJ Abdul Kalam at Rashtrapati Bhawan, New Delhi (2007)

At the release of Prime Minister Atal Bihari Vajpayee's album of poetry, Samvedana *(2002)*

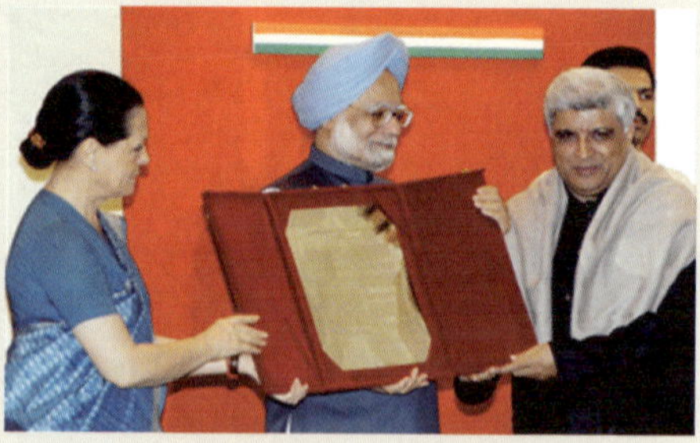

Receiving the Indira Gandhi Rashtriya Ekta Award from Prime Minister Manmohan Singh and UPA President Sonia Gandhi (2005)

At the dinner organised by Prime Minister Manmohan Singh in honour of the American President Barack Obama with Michelle Obama, Shabana Azmi and Salman Khurshid (2010)

With President Pranab Mukherji and Shabana Azmi at Rashtrapati Bhawan, New Delhi (2016)

Javed Akhtar receiving the National Film Award from President KR Narayanan at Vigyan Bhawan (2000)

With his favourite actor, Robert De Niro, and Shabana Azmi in New Delhi (2013)

With Rishi Kapoor and Neetu Kapoor, New York (2019)

With Mary Kom, the Indian boxer

With the IPTA artists in Mumbai

With students at the launch of the Italian translation of his poetry collection at the University of Rome

At the music release party of the film Duniya *with Rishi Kapoor, Ashok Kumar, Dilip Kumar, Pran, RD Burman, Amrish Puri, Amrita Singh and other artists (1984)*

Javed Akhtar with cricketer Kapil Dev and director Shyam Benegal

With Prime Minister Atal Bihari Vajpayee, Lata Mangeshkar and Sachin Tendulkar at the Padma Awards ceremony at Rashtrapati Bhawan (1999)

Javed Akhtar with the famous Hindi poet Shiv Mangal Singh 'Suman'

With the Nobel Prize-winning Bangladeshi economist, Muhammad Yunus, Mumbai (2018)

Javed Akhtar and Shabana Azmi with the evergreen actor Dev Anand

With the Nobel Prize-winning economist Amartya Sen

Javed Akhtar with the writer Arvind Mandloi (extreme left) and other eminent personalities at a function organised on his 75th birthday in Mumbai

Being awarded a doctorate by Jamia Hamdard University

Javed Akhtar with the famous tabla maestro Zakir Husain

Javed Akhtar, Alka Yagnik and AR Rahman with their Filmfare awards

Javed Akhtar at his home, 'Sukoon', in Khandala

MOMENTS OF LEISURE

Javed Akhtar with his grand-daughters Akira and Shakya

Javed Akhtar' with Faiz Ahmad Faiz

A most unusual meeting with Faiz sahab...

Javed Akhtar's very first meeting with the renowned Urdu poet, Faiz Ahmad Faiz, took place in a very unusual manner. As Javed sahab himself says, it is entirely possible that people would find it hard to believe. In fact, when Javed sahab narrated this incident to Faiz sahab's daughter, Salima, she asked her father to confirm its veracity. And Faiz sahab admitted that, yes, indeed such an incident took place.It was those days, when Javed sahab was looking to make a place for himself in Mumbai. Often, he wouldn't have a lot of money in his pocket. He must have been twenty-one or twenty-two years old then. One day he heard that Faiz sahab was visiting India after years to attend a mushaira in Mumbai. Javed sahab, who had always been an admirer of Faiz sahab, thought this would be a good opportunity to hear him. But when he found that he didn't even have the money to reach the venue of the mushaira, how would he buy the ticket to the mushaira? He was heartbroken: after all, Faiz sahab was visiting India after years and he couldn't even go to hear him. And so he drank a lot of alcohol, so much in fact that he became quite inebriated. In that state of intoxication, he got fixated on that one thought: he had to go and hear Faiz sahab! So, he got on a local train without a ticket and got off at the station closest to the mushaira venue. By then, it was quite late in the night and there were no guards at the station. He went inside the mushaira venue. He sat down next to a poet, adjusted the pillow behind him and, feeling drowsy, went to sleep.

When he woke up, he found that the mushaira was over. He was again heartbroken that he had not been able to hear Faiz sahab. He looked around and saw that Faiz sahab, accompanied by a few volunteers, was going towards his car. Suddenly, Javed sahab called out loudly, 'Let them go, Faiz sahab, you come with me.' And with these words he waved away the crowd, opened the door of the car, seated Faiz sahab, and then got in beside him! A volunteer was seated in the front but he seemed a bit intimidated by Javed sahab. Javed sahab told the volunteer, 'Start the car and proceed; what kind of arrangements are these?' Then he turned around and said to Faiz sahab, 'You have come after a long time, Faiz sahab.' He replied, 'Yes, it's been quite a while.' And as they talked, they reached Faiz sahab's hotel. The volunteer sitting in the front asked, 'Sir, will you keep the car or shall I let it go?' Javed sahab asked Faiz sahab and when he replied in the negative, he told the volunteer, 'You can let the car go.'

And then both of them entered the hotel. Javed sahab took the room key and entered the room. Then he lit one cigarette for himself and gave one to Faiz sahab. And then he began to talk of the Urdu language and script. After some time, Javed Akhtar went and lay down on the bed and went to sleep. When he woke up in the morning, he found that a press conference was going on right there in the room. And Kulsum Sayani, the mushaira organiser, was asking in the middle of the press conference, 'Faiz sahab, who is this person who is sleeping here?' Faiz sahab was doing his best to evade an answer because he himself didn't know who this person was. From under the bedcovers, Javed sahab could hear everything and was wondering how to get away. He figured it was best not to give a moment's respite. So, he got to his feet and said, 'Faiz sahab, I will take your leave.' Faiz sahab answered, 'Yes, indeed.' And Javed sahab came out of the room and went straight to his home.

Faiz Ahmad Faiz and Rajinder Singh Bedi at Javed Akhtar's Bandra flat (1979)

...and I chose life

I think there is glamour associated with drinking among young people

I was living my life thinking that I would live my life enjoying alcohol to the hilt. I was not drinking because I was sad or lonely or disappointed. I was drinking because I truly liked drinking very much. But then a point came when I had to choose between two things: alcohol or life. I chose life.

I drank for almost twenty-six or twenty-seven years. I had begun drinking from a very young age. When I had come to Mumbai after my graduation, I was nineteen years old. By then, I had begun drinking with my friends. At first, I was an apprentice in the film industry, then I became an assistant. In the early days, I had no money. But as I began to get work, I came into money and began to drink more.

There was a time, for about eleven or twelve years, when I would drink one bottle every day. What was the reason? Why do people drink? I think there is a glamour associated with drinking among young people. It seems as though we have become adults if we are drinking. In our youth we have seen the hero singing a song while he is drunk and the song is usually a good one. But drinking alcohol is not as was shown in the films, and still is shown even now. The hero speaks great dialogues when he is drunk and it seems grand but in real life that is not how drunks behave.

In my adult life I have never committed a mistake when I was not drunk. But from that day till now I have not touched alcohol. It has been twenty-five years. My advice to people would be: As far as possible, please don't drink.

Javed Akhtar at the India Today Conclave, New Delhi (2005)

Every Indian is proud of Krishna, Gautam, Kabir and Vivekananda, and their philosophy

The India Today Conclave is one of India's biggest platforms where ideas are exchanged. Professionals, leaders, politicians, thinkers and icons from different fields are invited. Javed Akhtar spoke about religion, spirituality, hypocrisy, science and rationality at the fifteenth edition of this conclave, held in New Delhi. Given below is the edited text of his entire speech.

I am quite sure, ladies and gentlemen, that in this august assembly nobody would envy my position at the moment. Speaking after a charismatic and formidable personality such as Sri Sri Ravi Shankar, is like coming out of the pavilion to play after Tendulkar has made a sparkling century. But, in a weak moment, I had committed myself. There are certain things which I would like to make clear at the very outset. Don't get carried away by my name—Javed Akhtar. I am not revealing a secret. I am saying something which I have said many times, in writing, on TV, in public. I am an atheist and I have no religious beliefs and obviously I don't believe in spirituality of some kind or another. Another thing, I am not standing here to criticise, analyse or attack this gentleman who is sitting here. We have very pleasant, civilised relations. I have always found him an extremely courteous person. One is talking about an idea, an attitude, a mindset, not any individual. I must tell you that when this session was opened, for a moment I felt I had come to the wrong place because if we are discussing the philosophy of Krishna, Gautam, Kabir, Vivekananda, then I have nothing to say. I can sit down right now. I am not here to discuss a glorious past of which, I suppose, every Indian is proud, and rightly so. I am here to discuss a dubious present. India Today has invited me and I have come here to talk of 'Spirituality Today'.

When I was invited to give this talk, I had thought, 'Yes, I am an atheist, I try to be a rationalist in any given situation, maybe that is why I have been called.' Then, I realised I have another quality which I share with the modern-age guru. I make films. We have other things in common. Both of us sell dreams. Both of us create illusions. Both of us create icons. But with a difference, after three hours we put a play card, 'The End' and go back to reality, but they don't. Plato, in his *Dialogues of Plato*, has said many wise things and one of them is: 'Before starting any discussion, decide the meaning of words.' Let us try to define what this word 'spirituality' means. Does it mean love for mankind that transcends all religions, caste, creed, and race? If that is so, I have no problem, except that I call it 'humanity'. Does it mean love of plants, trees, mountains, oceans, rivers, animals, and the entire non-human world? If that is so, again, I have no problem, except that I call it 'environmental consciousness'. Does it mean heartfelt regard for social institutions like marriage, parenthood, fine arts, judiciary, and freedom of expression? Again, I have no problem. Sir, what possible objection can I have, except that I will call it 'civil responsibility'?

Does spirituality mean going into your own world to understand the meaning of your own life? If that is so, who can possibly object to it, except that I will call it 'self-introspection' or 'self-assessment'?

Does spirituality mean yoga? Thanks to Patanjali who has given us the details of yoga. Yam. Yatan. Aasan. Yoga. Pranayam. We may do it under any name, but if we are doing 'Pranayam', wonderful. I call it 'health care', 'health fitness'.

Is it a matter of only semantics? If all this is spirituality, then what is the discussion? All these words that I have used are extremely respectable and totally acceptable words. There is nothing abstract or intangible about them. So, why stick to this word spirituality? What is there in the word spirituality that is not covered by all these other words? Is there something? If that is so, what is it?

Now somebody, in return, can ask me what my problem with this word is. I am asking to change it, leave it, drop it, make it obsolete, but why so? I will tell you what my reservation is. If spirituality means all of the above, there is no discussion. But there is something else which makes me uneasy. According to the dictionary, 'spirituality' is rooted in the word 'spirit'. When mankind did not know whether this earth was round or flat, he had decided that human beings are a combination of two things—body and spirit. Body is temporary, it dies, but the spirit is, (shall I say?) non-biodegradable. In your body, there is liver, heart, intestines, stomach and brain, but since brain is a part of the body, and the mind lies within the brain, it is inferior because ultimately the brain too shall die with the body. But don't worry, you are not going to die because you are your spirit and spirit has the supreme consciousness that will remain and whatever problems you have are because you listen to your mind. Stop listening to your mind, listen to your spirit, the supreme consciousness that knows the cosmic truth.

If you leave your mind behind, what do you do? You need the guru to find the next station of consciousness that lies somewhere in the spirit. He has reached that supreme consciousness, he knows the cosmic truth.

Javed Akhtar, Rajeev Mehrotra and Sri Sri Ravi Shankar, India Today Conclave (2005)

Can he tell you? No sir, he cannot tell you. Can you find out on your own? No sir, you need him but he cannot guarantee that you will know that ultimate truth. What is that ultimate truth? What is the Cosmic Truth relating to the cosmos? I have not been able to understand what it is and how I should relate to it. The moment we step out of our solar system, the first star is Alpha Centauri. It is just four light years away. How do I relate to that? What do I do?

One, who is rich, successful, doing well in his life, making money, acquiring property. Once he has everything, he wants a solution too. So, the guru tells him: 'Whatever you are doing is *nishkama karma*. You are playing a role; all this is maya. You are not emotionally involved in the money that you are making every day and the property that you are acquiring; you are just playing a role. You came to me because you are in search of eternal truth. Maybe your hands are dirty but your spirit and soul are pure.' And, this man starts feeling wonderful about himself. For seven days he is exploiting the world and at the end of the seventh day, he goes to the feet of the guru where he feels he is a good and sensitive person.

There is another category; that too comes from the affluent class. But he is not a winner like the first one. Winning or losing, being victorious or vanquished, that is also relative. A rickshaw wala, if he wins ₹100 at a roadside game of cards, will feel victorious. And, a man from the corporate world who earns only three million dollars, while his brother is a billionaire, will feel like a failure. Now, what does this rich failure do? He needs the guru to tell him: 'Yes, you have failed but you have another world, you have another vision, and you have another sensibility that your brother does not have. He thinks he is successful; he is wrong. The world is very cruel, you know. The world tells you honestly, "No sir, you got 3 out of 10, the other person got 7 out of 10." They will treat you that way and meet you that way.' Here, with the guru, the rich failure gets compassion and he gets invigorated to play another game.

There's another category. I will talk about this category not with contempt, nor any sense of superiority, or any bitterness but with all the compassion I have. This is a very big clientele of the guru. It is the unhappy rich wife. Here is a person who has sacrificed all her individuality, all her aspirations and dreams at the altar of marriage and, in return, she has got an indifferent husband who has given her a couple of children while he himself is busy all the time with his work or with other women. This woman needs a shoulder. She knows that she is an existential failure and that there is nothing to look out for. She has a vacuous, empty, comfortable, purposeless life. It's sad but true. Then, there are people who are suddenly traumatised. They lose their child, or their wife dies, or the husband dies, or they lose their property or they lose their business. They want to know: 'Why me?' So who do they ask? They go to the guru. The guru tells them this is karma but there is another world for you if you follow me where there is no pain, where there is no death, where there is immortality, where there is only bliss. He tells all the unhappy souls: 'Follow me and I will take you to heaven, to a paradise where there is no pain.' I am sorry, sir. This is disappointing but true: There is no such world. Life will always have a certain quota of pain, hurt and defeats.

I have great respect for people who are spiritual or religious and in spite of that they are good people and I have a reason for saying so because I believe that every emotion or feeling you have, has a limitation. You can see up to a point but you cannot see further. You can hear up to a point but not beyond. You can mourn up to a point and after that you will get over that mourning. You have a capacity for nobility also. You can be so noble and no more. Now, suppose we turn this capacity and nobility in an average man in ten units. Anybody who is going to pray in a mosque five times is consuming these five units. Anybody who goes to a temple or sits at the feet of their guru is consuming their quota of nobility there, in a totally non-productive way.

I don't go to offer namaz. I don't go to any guru or any mosque or any church. What do I do with my quota of nobility? I will have to help somebody, I will have to feed somebody, or I will have to shelter somebody. People use their quota in worshipping, adoring, praying to religious and spiritual figures and even then they have some nobility left, to them I say: Hats off!

You may ask me that if I have such a view about religious people why do I show such reverence for Krishna and Kabir and Gautam? I will tell you why I respect them. They were great contributors to human civilisation, they were born in different times in history in different situations but they had one thing in common, namely, they stood up against injustice, they fought for the downtrodden whether it was Ravana or Kansa or the pharaoh or the high priest and Pontios Pilatos or the British *Samrajya* in the case of Gandhi or the communal empire of Firoz Tuglaq in the times of Kabir. Today, none of these enlightened people who know the cosmic truth are standing up for the truth. None of them are raising their voice against the ruling classes, against the privileged classes. I want to know which guru has taken Dalits to those temples that are still closed to them.

The things you are fed in your infancy

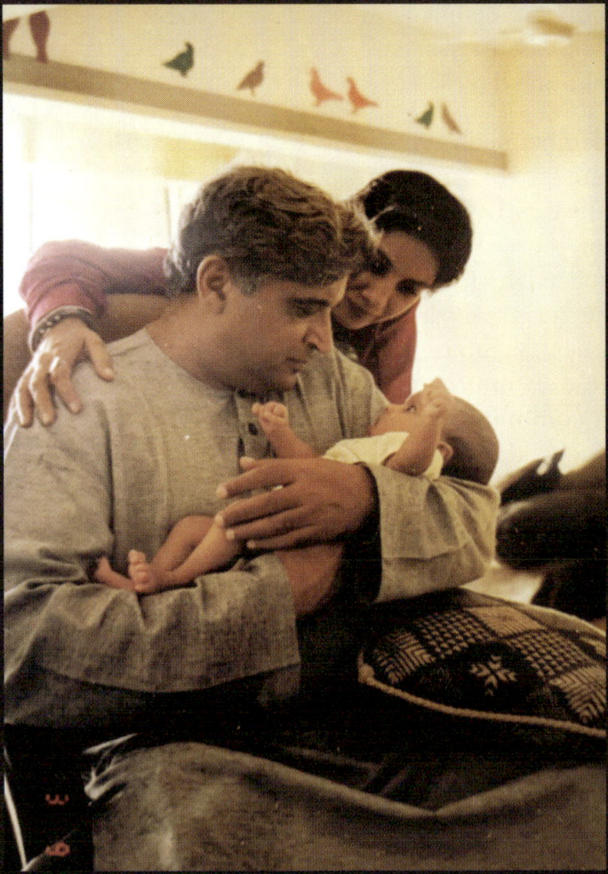

Javed and Shabana with Javed's granddaughter Shakya

I must have been three or four years old when the Communist Party was banned. In the heydays of the Telangana Movement, all the Communists were either sent to jail or they went underground. Majrooh and Jafri sahab were in jail; Kaifi sahab and my father were underground. My father lost his government job. My younger brother and I lived with our mother, Safiya. Our mother taught for a living and took care of us. She would tell us that the Revolution (inquilab) would come one day and that we too have to grow up and work for the Revolution. We were told that people go to jail for the sake of the Revolution. Sometimes, if I complained that the dal was not good, my mother would say: 'What if you get the same dal in jail?' And I would quietly eat that dal. Then, one day, I don't remember who told me that the food in jail has a lot of chillies. So, when I was still very young, I began trying to eat green chillies so that one day when I went to jail, I wouldn't have any problem.

When I remember such things, I am no longer amazed how can anyone remain religious when they grow up. That poor person is taught from his infancy just as I was taught in mine. Thank God, I have got out of it a little but a great many don't. They continue to believe what they have been fed in their infancy. And so it continues for the rest of their life. Anyhow, forget all that. Basic love for humanity, sense of equality, sense of fairness, sympathy for the weak and oppressed that seeps deep inside you and cannot be taken out—these are important. Anyone who is born in a communist or socialist home, no matter where he goes or how far he goes, the essentials of communism and socialism will never quite leave him.

I have had a great fondness for films since my childhood. When I was admitted in the first standard, I was asked: 'Now that you have got your admission, do you want to go to the zoo or to watch a film?' I said I want to go and see a film. The first film I remember seeing was *Aan*. I must have been six or seven years old then. So, I have been interested in films since my childhood. And my other great interest is literature.

I used to study in Saifia College where I never ever paid the fees. They had given me a room where I would stay free of charge. I had that room for a year or a year and a half. That room was close to a mosque. That is the closest I have ever been to a mosque.

Javed Akhtar, Farhan Akhtar, Zoya Akhtar and Shabana Azmi

Religion should not be foisted on children, nor should atheism

When a child is born, before it has any choice, its parents inject it with their religion. The child has no choice; he/she learns whatever is taught to him/her. If the parents are doctors, engineers, bankers, it is not as though they start making their child into a doctor, engineer or banker from its very infancy. Then why do you start making your child a Muslim or a Hindu from his/her birth? After all, you don't get your two-year-old started on an engineering course. In the same way, let your child be. I have not given any religious training to my children and nor have they ever seen any religious practice at home. If anyone has doubts about what I am saying, I would suggest one thing: Next time a baby is born in your family, do not give it any religion and when he/she is eighteen years old tell him/her, 'Adopt any religion you like.' He/she will not take any religion.

We should teach our children about our culture, instead of religion, but that should be fluid, changing. You may have seen children tie a small pebble to a thread and turn that thread over their head, slipping the thread gradually so that the stone keeps moving in an ever-widening circle. The pebble is like revolt; it wants to go further and further away. The thread is tradition; it stops the stone. If you break the thread, the pebble will fall. And if you remove the pebble, there is no way the thread can go so far. Both things are required. We should not break our tradition but we should gradually push it, widen it slowly, gently. Those things that are weak or wrong should go just as the leaves that have dried must fall from the branch so that new flowers and leaves can sprout and blossom. Both will be required; any one will not do in much the same way as a tree needs both its roots and its branches. A tree is not simply its roots nor can a tree merely be its branches no matter how high it grows or how wide it becomes; it will always need its roots to go deep down into the soil or else it will lose its balance and fall. Therefore, our biggest thing is tradition, and tradition comes with our language. A child should know his/her mother tongue but not at the cost of English. The child should also know English. Your own language will give you the roots but you also need English. If we are cut off from our language then we are cut off from our customs, traditions, history, our very identity. You must know your mother tongue whatever it might be. It is equally important to know English as without it you cannot grow and spread your wings in this world. The mistake we make is that we turn tradition, custom and culture into religion. We think that religion contains all these, but it is not so. I was not taught religion; does that mean I do not have tradition in me? Am I not rooted to my soil? I think it is a dangerous thing to make a child too religious. He becomes a frog in a well. All sorts of strange unnatural changes creep into him. There is nothing unnatural about culture, but there is in being religious.

My purpose in completing my graduation

When I was in college, I had decided that I wanted to join the film industry. But I had also decided that I would set foot in the industry only after graduation. The fact is my intention in completing my graduation was not to gain education. Those days there used to be some Hindi–Urdu magazines which carried a column about a film personality: where he was born, year of birth, hobbies, favourite colour, etc. There would be a column on education, too. More often than not, this column would say: 'Educated at home'. I didn't want that; when I joined the film industry it shouldn't say so in my column for education. I wanted it to say 'Graduate' at the very least.

Shabana and Javed, Spain (2016)

Poetry happens when language dreams

I believe that the tune is the body of a song and the words are its character.

People often ask me why songs are no longer memorable. A song is played for as long as a film runs and the day a film is taken off theatres, the song too fades. What is the reason then, for not just you or I, but even an eighteen-year-old to remember old songs? It is worth thinking: after all, what is so special in those old songs and what is lacking in these new songs. Here, I wouldn't blame the songwriter. If the dialogues are not good, I won't blame the dialogue writer. The truth is people don't really want good writing. They complain: 'What is this you are writing, brother?' When I had first begun to write songs, a distributor had said to my producer Boney Kapoor, 'Look, brother, you take the script from him but don't ask him to write songs. He puts poetry in the songs.' When I had first entered the industry, every producer–director talked of the 'public' as though they had a direct relationship with the public. Today, the public has become out of date; now no one takes the public's name. Now, youth has taken the place of public, now the youth is worshipped. Now a seventy-year-old producer or director says: 'This is what the youth will like.' How do they know what the youth will like?

Those days, it was difficult to become a Sahir because the great majority of song writers were very good at their job. At such a time Sahir was at the number 1 position and everyone agreed he was the best. Even today so many songs written by him are known by heart by countless people. Such is the power of his songs that often people sing his songs even without any accompanying music. This happened because Sahir respected his own work. It is important that we respect our own work. Surely in those days too there must have been song writers who would have said, 'This is what works, let it be.' But Sahir didn't do that. He said, 'If I write a song, I will write a good song, a correct song or else I won't write it.' He had many disagreements with the biggest music directors over this. As a result, many big music directors stopped working with him. He had disagreements with several singers, too, and those singers stopped singing for Sahir's songs. But Sahir survived. Gradually, the film industry accepted that a song needs very good words just as much as it needs a very good voice and a very good tune. It was Sahir who made the relationship between tune and words clear to people. I believe that the tune is the body of a song and the words are its character. If the words of a song are good, then such a relationship will be formed that will last for life. A song can't last for forty or fifty years without words. Today's lyricists must not just hear Sahir's songs but read them, too. They must learn the craft and technique of song writing from these songs.

It is said that poetry is the language of dreams. Poetry is not just about metre and rhyme, nor is it only about rhythm and rhyme; if it did then 71, 72, 73, 74, 75, 76 too would be poetry. Poetry flows from thoughts. I sometimes feel that poetry is the dream of language. When a language dreams, poetry happens. When a language is awake, there is fiction.

Our educational system, be it at the school and college or at home, does not give primacy to literature, language and poetry. This is not the fault of the younger generation; it is our fault. We want to teach our children only that through which he/she can earn money. Teach him/her only that which will fetch him/her a good job. Teach him/her that which will make him/her run a prosperous business. There is no doubt that these things, too, are important so that he/she can stand on his/her own two feet. But what will happen afterwards? What will he/she do later? Today, folk songs and folk music has almost disappeared from our homes and our villages. Earlier, folk songs would be sung during weddings but today film songs are sung. The folk traditions that came to us from our preceding generations, we failed to carry forward to the next generation.

Today's generation does not consider it important or worthwhile to read. It is these people who will make films and direct films in the years ahead. Today, directors give you the stepping stone of an English pop song and instruct you to get them something similar. They have had no exposure to Hindi music, forget folk songs. Their reference point is not Hindi music; it is American pop songs. In these circumstances, what sort of songs can you expect? Anywhere in the world, when the marketing people start telling the creative people what they want, then you can expect trouble. What should ideally happen is that creative people should do their work and then the marketing people should take on the onus of selling that work.

Ghalib could only have been in India

This country is rich in every way. We have more languages than any other country in the world, each with its own distinct history and literature. The writers and poets of our native languages are not just writers in their own language but they belong to the entire country—be it Ghalib, Tagore, Nazrul, Nirala, or Basheer, who wrote in Malayalam, or KR Narayan. They wrote in different languages; all were different Indian languages. Urdu, too, is an Indian language. There are many misconceptions that this language has come from somewhere else. The truth, however, is that Urdu is an Indian language and if there is anyone speaking it anywhere in the world then they are originally from here. Those speaking Urdu are not from New Zealand or Kenya; they are all Indians. Their citizenship may be something else but the blood flowing in their veins for centuries is Indian, and that is why they speak Urdu!

Ghalib and Urdu, Urdu and Ghalib... indeed this is a close relationship. There are many misconceptions about both. For instance, when the Two Nation Theory was first propounded, that caused our country to be partitioned, a version emerged for everything. There was a version of history, culture, and so on. Everything was separated. But this language, Urdu, was a living proof that the Two Nation Theory was wrong because it was truly the product of So, what was to be done with it? Now it couldn't be that the nouns would be given to Pakistan and the verbs kept by us; it was simply not possible. In order to prove the Two Nation Theory to be correct, this language had to be pushed to one side.

If you were to look at any of the languages of the world, you will find that the earliest poetry in any language is religious poetry. It is only later, with the passage of time that other topics come to be introduced.

Urdu has been a secular language from its earliest days. It has never produced any great poet who is a religious poet. It is true that Mir Anis wrote *marsiya* but his descriptions depict the culture of Awadh. Be that as it may, there has never been an Urdu poet who is a big propagandist of religion. All the major Urdu poets have been anti-fundamentalist, anti-regressive thoughts.

Ghalib was a major poet. When I was fifteen years old, I asked my father: 'Tell me, was Ghalib really as great a poet as people say?' He said, 'No, he's even greater.' The thing about classical poetry is that it never dates, it never gets old. Ghalib's *divan* (collection) is a slim one; he has only written a few thousand sher. In contrast, Mushafi, Mir, etc., wrote several divans. But Ghalib has only one divan, that too a slender one. Yet we will find an apt sher by Ghalib on anything that troubles us in life, when we find ourselves at a vexing turn in our life, in our thoughts, in our circumstances. Such is that man's range, such is his thinking! His language was considered difficult even in his own day. I can say with complete certainty that Ghalib could not have been born anywhere other than India. Ghalib is an unmatched synthesis of Indian philosophy and history with Persian and Mughal culture. The only other example to match this synthesis is the Taj Mahal.

Persian or Urdu alone could not have given birth to a Ghalib, nor could the Vedas alone have created him. Ghalib is born out of both. As he himself says:

Jala hai jism jahan dil bhii jal gaya hoga
Kuredte ho jo ab raakh, justuju kya hai

Where are bodies burnt? Where is ash scoured? In Arabia, Iran, or in India?

Then, there is another sher:

Na kuchh tha to Khuda tha, kuchh na hota to Khuda hota
Duboya mujh ko hone na, na hotaa mai to kya hota

This sher does not carry even the shadow of those religions whose gods sit far away counting your sins and virtues and, one day, will give you suitable punishment or blessing. Here, you see a philosophy where creator and creation are one. Where is this philosophy from? Where is it, if it's not from India? Ghalib could only have been from India.

Urdu is a very sophisticated language. It is an urban language. Much

Javed Akhtar with the great poet Neeraj

work has been done on its phonetics. By now Urdu is so evolved that it has a delicacy and deftness and can speak of anything with assurance and *tehzeeb*. Someone had once done an analysis whereby he had shown that ever since our Parliament has been formed and the work that has been done in it, among the poetry that was recited on various occasions, more than 90 per cent of it was Urdu poetry. This is in the Indian Parliament where people come from different parts of the country. This needs to be given some serious thought. While it is true that Urdu has some exemplary qualities, it is also true that no language can survive solely because of its aesthetic beauty; languages survive because of their economic utility. I will applaud Urdu because despite the dearth of economic utility in it, the language is so hardy that it refuses to die. It enters TV, it goes into cinema, it finds its way into the notebooks of youngsters, it stays alive. It even remains alive in everyday conversation of people.

Urdu poetry has performed a yeoman's service in the Indian Freedom Movement

There is no doubt that while Urdu is not yet dead, it is being killed. Those who know nothing about it, say, 'It's a beautiful language! The poetry is fabulous!' This way Urdu will shrink and become a language of entertainment. It is a beautiful, living language with an equally beautiful value system, but it has been treated very badly for the past 100 years.

People think Urdu poetry is only about wine or the beloved whereas if you look at the Indian freedom struggle, you will find that Urdu poetry has performed a yeoman's service at every stage of the nation's history. The Progressive Writers' Movement flowered in the 1930s; it brought together many writers from different Indian languages on one platform; a galaxy of stars was produced by Urdu literature during the heydays of the Movement. These included Krishan Chandar, Ismat Chughtai, Rajinder Singh Bedi, Majaz, Faiz, Sardar Jafri, Jan Nisar Akhtar, Kaifi Azmi, Majrooh, Sahir, among others. Their poetry was redolent with liberal and progressive values as were the stories of Krishan Chandar and Ismat Chughtai. So, Urdu has always been a progressive, liberal, secular and forward-looking language. The sad part is that few people know all this.

Once, someone asked me a very strange question: 'Why do Muslims have a sense of humour?' The fact is it isn't Muslims but Urdu speakers who have a sense of humour. Wherever you come across Urdu speakers, you will find they have a sense of humour!

The numbers of those who like to hear Urdu spoken, those who have an interest in Urdu, or those who love Urdu poetry are increasing exponentially day by day while the numbers of those who read the Urdu script are declining. There are many who can't read an Urdu book but they want to know what is written in it. So while there is a decline in the number of people who can read Urdu, what is on the rise is the number of people who want to hear Urdu. This has possibly never happened with any other language. And, while Urdu poetry is reaching more and more people, the prose writings of Krishan Chandar, Ismat Chughtai and Qurratulain Hyder are not. Many people may not even have heard their names. The fact is that many of those who talk of Urdu do so from having heard Urdu; they haven't read any Urdu. We can hear snatches of poetry here and there but who can read prose for us? That we have to read ourselves and, sadly, we haven't read Urdu.

Javed Akhtar with the singer Mehdi Hasan, Majrooh Sultanpuri and Kaifi Azmi, Mumbai (1978)

The concept of making the language 'pure' is a bit like peeling an onion

When we go to learn a new language, the thing that troubles us the most is the script, its grammar and, lastly, its vocabulary. Out of these, two things you don't need to learn in the case of Urdu: grammar, because you already know that, and its vocabulary, because you already know most of it and you can't possibly know the entire vocabulary of any language, in any case. All you have to learn is the script which will take you twelve or fifteen days at most. Therefore, anyone who can speak Hindustani can learn Urdu in 12–15 days. The thing is that when you and I are talking and for as long as I can understand you, I will say you are speaking in Hindi and when I find it difficult to understand you, I will say you must be speaking in Urdu.

The fact is that many of you don't realise it but most of you know Urdu. Till you can understand Urdu, you call it Hindi; when you stop understanding it, you say it is Urdu. Hindi and Urdu have the same syntax, grammar and 90 per cent words in common. Not a single sentence can be written in Urdu without using a Hindi word. A Hindi dictionary is not complete without at least 5000 Persian words. When you speak, you don't realise exactly how many Persian words you are using.

Dost, dushman, raasta, subah, sham, hawa, zameen, aasman—all these are Persian words. The concept of making a language pure is a bit like peeling an onion. You set out looking for the onion without realising that its skin is the onion. If you take off all the peel, there will be no onion left.

There have always been two types of languages in the world: one of the people and the other of the government. The *sarkari* language is not especially concerned whether or not you are able to understand what is being said; in fact, it is all the better if you don't understand what is being said as far as the sarkar is concerned. Consequently, *sarkari* languages are seldom understood and those who have sarkari protection pretend that they understand sarkari language as indeed they must. They think that you will be suitably impressed by them when you don't understand their language because if you understand what they are saying then you will definitely not be impressed by them! On the other hand, the people's language is the language of communication because we have to talk to each other, and we have to understand each other.

Be it Hindi or Urdu, when you make it so difficult that you cannot understand it then it defeats the purpose. That is why we take words from different languages so that communication improves. But the words we take are on our own terms. Take for example, *hawa*. Now, this is a Persian word. But the words we have made out it—*hawain, hawaon*, these are our own. There are no words such as hawain and hawaon in Persian. Similarly, *raasta* is a Persian word but raaste is ours. We take a word and make its plural, turn a noun into an adjective and vice versa. We can even change the pronunciation of a word. For instance, the original word was *faza*; we say *fiza*. When words enter a language, changes are inevitable according to the tone and tenor of our language.

Javed Akhtar with Farhan

If the Justice system and education are right, then everything else will fall into place

There are two or three important things in our country; if they are right the rest will fall into place. The first is education. The fact is that we have ignored primary and basic primary education in India for far too long. We have created excellent institutions of higher education, some being world-class institutions, but when you look at the lower rungs of education, i.e., basic and primary, it is lacking. Ideally, education should be the same all over the country.

The other thing is justice. If the justice system is efficient, correct, immediate and unbiased, then society will gradually settle into the right groove. If the education system and education are right, then everything else will fall into place.

I don't agree with the present education system. At present, you know only what you know. If you are an engineer, you will have no sense of history. If you are a doctor then you will know nothing about the folk art of India. If at all you know something then it is entirely due to your individual attempts; education has no role to play in it. Those who are becoming scientists, doctors, technicians today have nothing to do with the culture, mythology, folk art, folk music, or literature of this country. This is a dangerous trend. Are we preparing robots or human beings?

The distortion of history has become astonishing. And if you speak against it to say this history is wrong, not only are you regarded as ignorant but you are also branded as anti-national. All these are serious problems and they are acquiring alarming proportions by the day. I have stopped watching TV. There is no point in it. What is being talked about on TV has, actually, no bearing whatsoever on the country's future. Discussions rage on completely futile topics. People are shouting and screaming on irrelevant subjects. It is not such a difficult task to take this county upwards or forward. With a little discipline, some honesty, some sincerity we can go so far.

Respect words, love words

We think less about things that are near us. How many people wonder why the air is transparent or why water is wet? How many people wonder what is Time, or why did it come and why it has gone? Similarly, have we ever thought of the words we speak, or hear, from morning till night? Words are strange things. For instance, I look at an animal and I decide it is a cat whereas 'cat' is only a sound. 'Cat' has nothing whatsoever to do with that animal but I have decided it is so. That is, I have filled the meaning of that animal in that sound. Then I made a semi-circle, then a pyramid that I cut from the middle, then I drew a straight line and, below that, another straight line and called it a cat. I filled sound in these slanting lines and in the sound I filled meaning.

Regardless of whether we talk of love or anger, be it an idea or pain, joy or sorrow, or amazement—we gave a sound to everything. And to the sound we gave these slanting lines that we call script or writing. We connected three things that have no connection with each other and made words. And the great wonder is that we added sound, which is actually 'gibberish', to these and they became words.

I think, with time, words too become like human beings. For example, for a person it is said that 'A man is known by the company he keeps'. So is the case with words—which word has a word been close to, which words are used together? How many references can an average mind swiftly make with an average noun or an average verb? Where had we heard a word being used? What does the word evoke in us? What are its connections? What are my experiences with this word? Words evoke a swarm of memories. A good writer or a good orator is one who knows that when he uses this word this is the reference it will evoke in an average mind, what are the things they will be reminded of and how can he create the right atmosphere by choosing the right words. What is the power of words? Be it a mother's lullaby, a politician's speech, a lover's letter, a complaint or a revolutionary slogan, be it anger, happiness, sorrow, amazement, kinship, any thought, feeling, emotion, experience—till it is poured into words neither you nor anyone else can understand it. Words are not thoughts, just as bricks are not a house even though a house is built from bricks. If you have few bricks, you will only be able to make a small house. You can think as clearly as the words you have, and speak as lucidly too.

Speaking about 'Indian Film, Indian Society' at California University, Berkeley (2019)

I often hear young people say, 'You know what I mean?' I say to them, 'No, I don't know what you mean; you tell me.' Words end when you say, 'You know what I mean?' Everything has become fast, so has communication, but the sad part is that the use of words has been at the cost of depth and gravitas; and this is a bad bargain. The question here is: Are you able to communicate your thoughts, your feelings, your emotions in the right manner or not? If you cut a person off from certain words, he will be cut off from a certain culture and a certain history. That is what is happening to us. Language is a very powerful thing, so are words, but in themselves words are neither good nor bad. We should love words and know their power and strength because whatever has happened in the world has happened because of words, or else it wouldn't have happened. We can collect all our experiences, consciousness, thoughts, and experiences in words and pass them on from one generation to the other. How else will the experience and knowledge of centuries that has seeped into us gradually travel? How else except through words? And if there were no words, then we humans who are better than other life forms, will diminish. We have progressed so far because we had language. We wouldn't have been here if we didn't have language. We would have been right there from where our story started. And what is meant by language? Words! So, respect words, love words, make friends with words. Listen to them carefully and speak them carefully.

Javed Akhtar at a musical programme

The difference between lyrics and poetry

Film songs are different from poetry insofar as the poet can write exactly what he pleases in his poetry, in whatever style or metre or vocabulary

These days, songs are of two types: there are our folk songs, which used to develop with time as generations would keep improvising them and so they continued for years and years. No one knew who wrote them or when they were written. It is entirely possible they were never ever written; perhaps they took form and shape as they were sung. Film songs, on the other hand, are always written. First their tune is made and there is a given situation. If we were to talk of folk songs, we can say they grew out of the ground and changed gradually with the seasons and no one ever knows who wrote them or thought of them. They are a part of our history and culture. The thing about film songs is that they are different from poetry insofar as the poet can write exactly what he pleases in his poetry, in whatever style or metre or vocabulary. He chooses his own topics and decides the form and structure of his own nazm or ghazal. In contrast, film songs are part of a narrative. The script decides that at such and such point there will be a song and this is the situation for it. A director or scriptwriter describes the situation to the songwriter. Then there is the music director. In our films, we follow a somewhat strange procedure. Often, a tune is made first and then the poet is told that this is the situation and this is the tune, now you write the song.

As far as poetry is concerned, at any time, in any age, very good poetry has been written and, at the same time, very bad poetry has also been written. The same is true for film songs. Very good songs have been written and very bad ones too have been written. It is a bit sad that these days more bad songs are being written.

In the ghazal, you can occasionally falter and weaken. Certain meanings might emerge in symbolism that you had never imagined. But the nazm allows no such laxity. The nazm clearly demonstrates the poet's intellectual calibre. The ghazal too has endless possibilities. And so there is sometimes a fear that where there are such endless possibilities, how far can I go? Of course, the masters have written such incredible ghazals and such incredible experiments have been made in the genre of the ghazal.

What happened to Tulsidas happened to Shah Abdul Qadir too

It is completely irrational to say languages belong to religions; it can never be so. Punjabi is the language of Punjab, Bangla of Bengal, Gujarati of Gujarat, Sindhi of Sindh. Regions can have languages. For instance, the language of Italy is Italian. It is only now that we hear of language having a religion. There used to be a scholar in Delhi named Shah Abdul Qadir who translated the Quran into Urdu for the first time in 1798. This happened approximately 225 years ago. The Quran had been translated into Sindhi about 700 years before this. When Shah Abdul Qadir translated the Quran into Urdu, all the *imams* of that time gave *fatwas* of *kufr* against him declaring that this shameless man had had the temerity to translate such a holy, such a scared book into such a lowly language. Barely fifty years after this event in 1798, a *topi* was placed on this Urdu's head and a beard was pasted on its face. The same thing that happened to Shah Abdul Qadir happened with Tulsidas. About 200–250 years before Shah Abdul Qadir, Tulsidas wrote the *Ramcharitmanas* in Awadhi sometime during Akbar's reign. Many a great *mahant* and guru was perturbed by this act. How could a sacred text such as the Ramayana be re-written in a lowly dialect such as Awadhi! He too was banished and socially boycotted. There is an interesting *chaupai* about it.

Dhoot kaho, avdhoot kaho, Rajootu kaho, jolha kaho kouu
Kahuu ko beti son beta na byaahab, kahuu ki jaat bigaarb na souu
Tulsi sarnaam gulamu hai Ram ko, Jakai ruchai so kahe kachu Wouu
Maangi kai khaibo, maseet mein soibo, laibo ko eiku na daibo ko douu

The fundamentalist cannot tolerate it—be it Urdu or Awadhi. Ten crore Muslims in Bangladesh declared: 'We shall not study Urdu; we shall study Bangla'. My mother tongue is Urdu but I stand in solidarity with the Bangladeshis. They have every right to study in their mother tongue and no one can force them to study Urdu at the cost of their mother tongue. When ten crore Muslims said they don't want to study Urdu, they want to study Bangla instead, then how can anyone say that Urdu is the language of Muslims?

The decision to enter films was a well-thought-out strategy on the part of the Leftists

I think the Leftist writers, be they prose writers or poets, had thought it out carefully as a strategy to penetrate mass media such as cinema. Films allowed them to spread their message and their values to the maximum number of people. On the one hand poets such as Shailendra, Sahir, Majrooh, Kaifi, Jan Nisar Akhtar and on the other hand prose writers such as Krishan Chandar, Rajinder Singh Bedi, Ismat Chughtai all joined the film industry within a gap of five to six years. And it isn't as though they got the opportunity to speak about or spread their message and values right away. When you work in the commercial medium, often you have to write other kinds of songs or dialogues or stories. But when you carefully hear the songs of Sahir, Kaifi, Shailendra, Jan Nisar Akhtar, Majrooh, etc., you find they are seeding certain values in different ways in popular cinema. You will find countless dialogues and scenes written by Krishan Chandar, Bedi, Ismat Chughtai that are creating class consciousness, talking about exploitation, class struggles, etc. These people can be credited with bringing these Leftist ideas into mainstream cinema. I don't think it was an accident; if anything, it was an organised, well-thought strategy to take a certain message through popular mass media. Sahir's nazm '*Woh subah kabhi to aayegi...*' is almost like a manifesto of socialism. Similarly, Shailendra too has conveyed very powerful sentiments in simple words.

There is a scene in a film written by Inder Raj Anand where the hero is walking on the road. He is poor and hungry. He finds a wallet full of money that some rich man has dropped. He picks up the wallet, takes it to the rich man and says, 'Sir, you dropped your wallet.' The character of the rich man is played by Motilal. So, Motilal takes the wallet, looks at the hero (who happens to be Raj Kapoor) and says, 'Come with me.' A party is going on in a five-star hotel. Motilal takes him there. The poor man looks around him in amazement and says, 'Who are these people?' Motilal says, 'They are the people who found wallets full of money but they did not return them.' I am sad to say that this sensibility is gradually disappearing, both from songs and dialogues, in commercial cinema.

Speaking during a tour of the Council of European Nations (2019)

First of all, it was Krishan Chandar who impressed me

By a coincidence (since I do not believe in fate), the house I was born in was a house of writers. My mother was a writer, so was my father. Even my maternal uncle, the Urdu poet Majaz, was a famous writer. All their friends were writers. All the names of the major writers from the 1950s and 60s that you are likely to have heard of, I knew them all personally during my childhood. I met and interacted with them. Many magazines, books, novels would come to our house. By the age of thirteen I had read all those books, some of which I had understood partly and some I had not. By thirteen, I had read Pushkin and Gorky because that is what everyone in my house read. Children do not do what you ask them to; children do what you do. When children see their parents reading books and talking about books, there is a natural, instinctive respect for books in their heart too.

Anyhow, the writers who most influenced me during my teenage years were progressive writers.

First of all, it was Krishan Chandar who impressed me. Normally when you open a book of prose, there is a line of poetry on the first page. When my first collection of poetry, *Tarkash*, was published I used a fragment of prose from Krishan Chandar on its opening page. His writings have influenced me greatly. Sometimes when you are inspired by somebody you become their echo or copy. And when you are influenced by a lot of people, you are known as a research scholar. I have been impressed by several people. When I go to colleges and universities, I tell students, 'Read! It is important to read classical literature but it is also important to do light reading. Read the paperbacks and pulp fiction that is available on railway stations, too. Read thrillers, Mills & Boon romances, read all kinds of literature. If you read only heavy, "high" literature you might become a dry person.'

When children see their parents reading books and talking about books, there is a natural, instinctive respect for books in their heart too.

If you wish to write songs, remember that every voice has a visual effect

In order to make anything interesting, first and foremost you should be interested in it. If you yourself are not fully invested in your work, how can you expect others to be involved in it? And if you are fully engaged with your work, you will find others expressing interest towards it.

It is not as important to be a big poet as it is to be a Jack of all trades and to know how to write on a tune. If you are writing to a tune, you can't expect to write using the ordinary phrases and expressions; you will have to employ unusual and out-of-the-ordinary turns of phrases. You will have to write romantic songs, lullabies, bhajan, qawwali, songs about street children, cabaret songs, sorrowful dirges as well as ditties about village folk. You will have to write about every sort of character. Your vocabulary has to be very extensive so that you can find the correct words to suit a range of characters.

The meanings of words have great significance but their sound or the voice in which they are being sung is no less important. After all, songs are written in order to be sung. Therefore, it is vital that they are good to listen to. Words should have an inherent music of their own. If you have an interest in music, this happens automatically. You can instinctively sense that such and such word is not sounding good in such and such tune; it sounds like a conversation and is not as musical as it should be nor is it blending well with the melody. You might find it odd what I am about to say but every voice has some visual impact. If you take 'ज' (ja) it has a brightness that is very white whereas 'च' (cha) too has a brightness but I don't know how its lustre has turned yellowish, almost golden. With 'ठ' (thha) you feel you have thrown a ball on hard ground whereas if you throw a ball on wet ground, you will get the 'थ' (tha) sound. If you throw a ball against a hollow wooden wall, you will get the 'ध'(ddha) sound. Sounds create different images in your mind, for instance 'ढ' (dha) is a sticky sound, 'घ' (gha) is a dense sound and 'ग' (ga) is a clean sound.

We live in a use-and-throw culture and almost everything including music has the same disposable fate. As a result, we can't retain our interest in our present-day music for very long because the music itself does not have any staying power. It comes, gives you light entertainment (not mine at least) and disappears. It doesn't enter deep into your heart because it doesn't get the time to enter deep. The tempo of present-day songs is so fast that it is simply not possible. If the tune will not give enough space to the words, if the tune doesn't allow you to think and figure out what the song is actually saying, then that song will not stay with you for every long. That is reality.

I truly do not know how long I will enjoy writing songs as much as I do now. But I have learnt one lesson: the day I stop deriving pleasure from writing songs, I will find something else to do. I will write songs only as long as I find it challenging and feel that I have to do something and show it to the world. If you have to work in one field you must keep moving the goalposts further and further away. As soon as you feel that you have reached your destination, everything will be over.

Your vocabulary has to be extensive so that you can find the correct words to suit a range of characters.

Language is not vocabulary, it is grammar

It is a not a new or strange thing that words are being added to language. I think the day a language is formed, the work of adding new words begins. Mohammed Husain Azad sahab has extensively referred to this in his *Aab-e Hayat* explaining how words have entered our language from different sources. I will begin my talk from here. I will speak a few short sentences. They are in everyday Hindustani that you and I ordinarily speak. '*Eik makaan ke eik kamre mein eik gora-chitta aadmi aur eik nanha-munna bachha naashta karne ke liye baithe. Naashta karne se pehle naha liye eik balti paani se. Uske baad bawarchi naashta laaya. Naashte mein urad ki dal aur toast tha. Baad mein woh aadmi uttha, chik hatayi, sandook khola, usme se eik pistol nikala, deewaar par tangi bandook li aur chala gaya. Bachha vivash ho kar dekhta raha.*'

Now let us see: *makaan*, Arabic; *kamra*, Italian; *balti*, Portuguese; *chitta*, Punjabi; *nanha*, Gujarati; *bachha*, Persian; *urad*, Tamil; toast, English; *chik*, Turkish; *sandook*, Turkish; *pistol*, English; *diwar*, Parsi; *bandook*, Turkish; and *vivash*, Sanskrit.

I have also heard, '*Sallar-e jamaat misra-e uula ki naghmasanji mein masruuf hain, taawaqt-e deegar ashaab-e jamaat misra-e saani ke baquia arkaan ki adaaigi kar rahe hain.*' This means, 'The lead voice is singing the first line and the chorus is singing the second line.' I have also heard, '*Eik pake maati ke paatr mein dugdh-sharkara yukt zara kandra upjit ushan pe pradaan karo.*' It means, 'Give me a cup of tea.'

The attitude towards language is different among us Hindi and Urdu-speakers on the one hand and English-speakers on the other. The English speakers announce very proudly that our latest English dictionary has 60 lakh new words whereas we are proud of the fact that in the recent past we have deleted 200 words and are about to remove another 100 shortly. Now, tell me, what is the purpose of this purity? Purity of what?

What is language? Is language simply its script? If so, then all European languages are the same because they are all written in the Latin script. Punjabi is written in Gurmukhi, Devnagri and Farsi Rasm-ul-khat too but Punjabi remains Punjabi. Actually, a language is grammar; a language is neither its script nor its vocabulary. You can take the words from anywhere. The language will be formed by its grammar and syntax. Now look at the syntax of Urdu. The syntax of Urdu is Khari Boli. Khari Boli was written in the Sanskrit script but it was later changed to Devnagri. Therefore, actually, the syntax of both languages is the same. And, so there is no need to be scared of adding new words because vocabulary is not language. As long as our syntax is intact, all is well.

What has happened is that everywhere, in all societies, vocabulary is shrinking. We give very little importance to language. We do not understand that language is not simply a means of communication; language is our identity. No matter how religious you are, you spend at best 15 minutes out of the 24 hours in a day on your religion; the rest of the time you spend with language. I will go so far as to say that the importance people give to religion is wrong and those who do not give importance to language are being unfair. People should have love for their language and if they have a little less love for their religion, it might be better.

TIME

Art is your emotion, and craft your methodology

Any art form has two things: one is pure art and the other is craft. The two things are opposites, in a way. Art requires you to drown yourself, to lose yourself in your fantasy, emotions, dreams and expressions. Craft is all calculation, all mathematics. When 3000 years ago, Pythagoras had said, 'At one level music is pure mathematics', he was absolutely right. The same can be said for poetry and art; there is a perfect geometry behind poetry. There is a craft behind it, a foolproof craft. It is necessary to learn that craft. If you want to write poetry you must first read a lot of poetry and read all kinds of poetry. Read Meera and Kabir, Ghalib and Mir, read Neeraj and Sahir, read the young poets of the day, read the progressive writers and the classical poets too. It won't do if you begin writing poetry only after listening to film songs. Whichever art form you choose to enter, it is important to first have 'intake' before you show 'output' and the more 'intake' there is the better it will be.

Javed Akhtar in his study

Our civilisation is an ocean; the only way to cross it is to drown in it

Javed Akhtar was honoured with the Shanti Doot Award at the Sankat Mochan temple in Varanasi in 2018. Given below is an extract from the speech he delivered on the occasion.

It seldom happens, but today it is happening. I am a writer; my job is to work with words and all our activities centre around words. But sometimes it so happens that words fall short and it seems as though what is in my heart is not coming through in words. When I was on my way here, I tried a few times to think of what I would speak. Then it occurred to me that this is not something I should think about; this is something I should feel and I stopped thinking about what to say. I decided that once I reach here and stand up to speak to all of you, I will say exactly what comes in my heart. So I have not come with a prepared speech. When I was given the message that you want to honour me with the Shanti Doot Award, I felt I was completely not deserving of it. It is this temple that is a *shanti doot,* a messenger of peace. It is Vir Bhadr ji who is a shanti doot. There are some people who do not need to be told exactly how great they are. There is a certain luminosity all around them. I have seen that light all around *mahant* ji. There would be an aura around him when he walked. It seemed as though this great scholar had only nobility, compassion and love. If even a 100th part of what he had is to be found amongst us, then this world can become paradise on earth. There are very few people whose feet I have touched because that is something I very seldom do. But mahant ji was one such person whose feet I always touched. This *sangeet sammelan* today and the people who come here are the real people of India. This country of ours, this civilisation, this culture is like an ocean. You have to drown in it in order to cross it. These bonds with one another, this love for each other, neither language comes in between nor caste, creed and community, nor religion. There is nothing that can carry you through; only true devotion can.

When a small-time musician touches the feet of a senior or big musician, the big musician gives his blessings with compassion and love, saying may he live long and prosper and go far in his career. Our branches must indeed go up as we grow but our roots too must go deep into the soil, or else we will topple and fall. A big tree, a truly immense tree is one that stands tall and mighty but also goes deep into the earth. We must love our traditions, our culture, our history. History is of two kinds: one that teaches you to hate and the other that teaches love. We must learn that history contains lessons of love and unity where people have worked together harmoniously. Our true culture is found where the people have worked together in the field of music, art, dance, literature and architecture. That is the true India, that is called Hindustan. We have to safeguard that Hindustan and also protect that culture, that tradition that teaches us to love our soil and live in harmony and love. Nazir Banarasi was one of the great poets of your city. I was reading him when I was on the way here. He has written a beautiful poem entitled 'Ganga ke Teen Roop'. I was reminded of his lines the first time I visited Tulsi Ghat. He has said:

Yeh ghat Tulsi ke naam ka hai
Yahin woh karte the jaap dekho
Jahan par Ganga wahin par Tulsi
Pavitrta ka milaap dekho

This should happen at every level. Love is pure, hatred is impure. Friendship is pure, enmity is impure. I would want that the purity that is a part of our culture should be brought to the fore. That is what it means to be a true Indian, that you should love Indian traditions and arts, your cities and rivers, your mythology and cuisines. I feel very grateful that you have remembered me. It is a matter of great respect that I have been called a shanti doot here. I have received many awards before but this award that I have got here today is by far the greatest.

Receiving the Shanti Doot Award at the famous Sankat Mochan Temple, Varanasi (2018)

Photo by Javed Akhtar

GUFTAGU

In conversation with Javed Akhtar

Arvind Mandloi

The place you have reached cannot be your destination; the destination is a bit further and till it is a bit further away, you are alive

Javed sahab, tell us, what is life?

Look, life is a short interval between not being and again not being wherein a bubble (for that is all life is) gets the ability to hear, see, think, taste and touch. Then the bubble bursts and ends. But something strange happens during the gap in the middle: the moment you are born, you get the membership to a club. The membership is not permanent; it is temporary. The club is human society. Many other bubbles have formed and burst here before you. People have come and gone. But those who have contributed something in this club are the people who truly matter. Someone discovered electricity while someone else made motors, railways trains, aeroplanes, radios, televisions, telephone. Many different discoveries were made, cloth was woven, houses were constructed, and so on. We didn't do all this; it

Photo by Javed Akhtar

Photo by Javed Akhtar

was done by others before us. It is because of these other people before us that we get to hear music, eat food, travel on roads and so on and so forth. All the facilities we have today were made or discovered by people who came to this club before us. So it is our duty that we should not do anything to ruin or destroy this club, to which we have only temporary membership, and if possible, we should also contribute something new to the club, before our membership expires, so that future members might have an easier time. That is all there is to life.

Have you achieved what you wanted in the life you have lived so far? Were you able to do all that you wanted to do through your poetry, script writing and other activities, or does something remain?

The day there is nothing more left to do, life itself would not remain! I have a sher:

Sabka khushi se faasla eik qadam hai
Har ghar mein bas eik hii kamra kam hai

Don't just consider your house to be your home. Be it your poetry, painting or social service or any other thing that you like to do, there will always be one room short. You will feel if only there was one more room, then everything would be perfect. But when you get that room, you will need one more room. And this room is not just for yourself; it could be for your art, your social service, the work you do to make the world a better place. So, for as long as you feel the need for one more room and you want to make that room, you are alive. The day everything is complete, life is over; life is complete.

No, my question was: Do you feel that the journey you should have undertaken was the right one and it had to reach till this point?

That is exactly what I am saying to you: The day I feel that I have reached where I was supposed to have reached, my life will be over that day. Let me tell you another sher:

Hamarey shauq ki inteha thi
Qadam rakha kii manzil raasta thi

Till as long as the destination is the road, you are alive. Where you have reached cannot be your destination. The destination is always a little further ahead and as long as it is further ahead, you are alive, you are moving, you are moving ahead. But if you feel that you have arrived where you were meant to then you are over and done with.

Is there a memory that you would want to repeat?

Nothing is repeated in life, but there are some memories that I sincerely hope are never repeated. I must have been thirteen or fourteen years old when I travelled from Aligarh to Mumbai by train in a third-class compartment. I can never forget that journey because that journey lasted two and a half days. In the course of those two and a half days, I did not get a place to even sit; only I know the terrible state I was in. I remember that exhaustion even today. The third-class compartment was full. I was so sleepy that my body was aching, but there wasn't even a place to stand propped up against a wall. Sometimes when I am lying alone on a huge bed in a five-star hotel, I think if only I had got space on the sofa in front of me that day, forget this huge bed. I remember some nights when I went hungry for several days and I couldn't sleep at night because of the hunger. I remember one night in particular. I was so very hungry and I didn't know what to do, so I got up and started roaming on the street. It must have been 10 or 10.30 in the night. I don't know why, in the hope of what, I was roaming around on the street. I was wondering where I could find something to eat. I was roaming because I was hungry. Now, when I sit down to breakfast or lunch and see all the food laid out on the table, I am reminded of that night. I see the food on the table and I am so very grateful in my heart. Now, when I lie down in comfort, I am deeply grateful in my heart. Now when I eat breakfast, I remember how for years I did not know the concept of breakfast. I would get up and wonder what and where I would get to eat. If I managed to find some food by the afternoon, I was lucky. Now, in the morning when I see my breakfast on a tray, a fear enters my heart and, at the same time, I am struck by how fortunate I am. I don't think that I have any particular gifts and that is why I have got all these things today. Sometimes when I am sitting in my car as it is travelling down the road in heavy traffic, I see people coming out of their offices. There are people milling about on footpaths in Mumbai. I look at those people who will shortly go stand in long queues for the bus or sit in those local trains in which I, too, once used to travel. Then I wonder if I am more intelligent, more talented than them that I am sitting in an air-conditioned car while they are walking on the footpath? Are all of these people inferior to me? Do they not have as much intelligence as me, or as much talent as me? But no, it isn't so. Sometimes, the cards are dealt right and your game is played well. Of course, there is also the fact that you play well, or poorly but how will you play well if you have been given a bad hand of cards? You need good cards, too. There are countless people who can play well but they were not dealt the right cards. So, it is wrong to think that we are a better player than them.

Who are the people who you would like to remember, who you think are important characters in your life?

If you look at life closely, then you will realise that there is no character who has entered your life who is not important. The truth is that we turn our life into a screenplay with scenes from scene number 1 till scene number 100. Now, suppose, you decide that scene number 63 was not very important and there was nothing special about it, so let us remove scene number 63 from the story. You remove the scene that you think is least important but you later realise that it has caused scene number 75 to also go even though it was a very nice scene. Life is so tightly intertwined that today if you are happy, you don't have the right to be unhappy with what was in the past because even if there were fewer sorrows, griefs, failures and defeats, you would not be where you are today. Your life's story would have gone somewhere else. Every one's life has joys and sorrows, good people and bad people, people who help and people who inflict injury and all of them are equally important. Whatever be your story, it cannot be formed without all these characters.

To what extent were the characters sketched by you in your films drawn from your own personal life?

First of all, there are many scripts that were not written by me alone; since they were jointly written by Salim sahab and me, they must be influenced by both our lives. But obviously one writes what one knows or what seems right or wrong to you according to your value system. If you show someone or something as being bad it will be because, according to your value system, that person or thing is bad. So regardless of whether you make a story about a god and a fairy or about an upright man living in some present-day city, you are sure to be in the story. Incidents from your life, your mishaps, your understanding of right and wrong, your tastes, what you think is beautiful and what is ugly, what you like and what you dislike, your values, your thoughts, your beliefs, the way you look at life—all of it will come through even if you are telling a story about a god and a fairy. A story's writer is always present in a story.

Shabana Azmi and Javed Akhtar after casting their vote in the 2019 General Election

A virtue in us Indians is that we have tolerance

Sometimes people take an extreme stand on some issues, and an extreme stand is never correct. Nationalism is a natural quality; just as you love your city, *mohalla*, home, language so how can you not love the country you were born in. You may call it patriotism or nationalism or any other name but it is as natural as loving your city or your family.

There are many places in this country that I have never visited, yet when I see the success of their people, I feel very happy. Why do I feel happy? What is my relation with those people? My relation is that we belong to the same country. You cannot call this natural reaction obsolete or negative. I love my friends, my family and my city but that does not mean

I hate others. Love for our country is in our veins, in every fibre of our being, it can never leave us. We might tolerate someone; we might hear something that is amiss and it won't bother us too much. What we will not abide by is any insult to this country's traditions. At the same time, love for one's country does not simply mean sloganeering and not doing anything concrete.

No matter what anyone might say, I know only one thing: No Indian will destroy himself. He will only do that which is good for this country. A virtue among us Indians is that we have tolerance; we always give space to all kinds of thinking. This is the reason for the development of our 'intellectual muscle'. This is the reason why some great thinkers have been born in our country. This is why we have made progress. This is why we have democracy.

This country can never be destabilised; it is not possible. I can write it to you in my blood. High waves keep coming our way and sometimes our boat wobbles but it cannot drown. India has seen many ages but India has remained undaunted. As the poet Iqbal has said:

Kuchh baat hai ke hasti mita ti nahi hamari
Sadiyon raha hai dushman daur-e jahan hamara

The truth is that society is casting a bad influence on films

If you watch carefully, a film tells you everything. Films tell you what your moral values are, what changes have come within you, and what your ambitions are. For instance, in the films that were made in the 1940s, the villains were the zamindars. Then the villain became the mill owner. As cosmopolitanism and urbanism increased, the villain became the big daddy of the mohalla or the underworld don. When the era of terrorism began, we saw our neighbouring country as the villain. There was a time when our hero believed in destroying and dissipating himself like Devdas. Then other kinds of rebel stars began to appear who believed life was beautiful and that it should be loved and appreciated. Then, as society began to deteriorate, the angry young man appeared as a hero. Later, as greater comforts came into our life with liberalisation, and the urban middle class began to prosper, once again we began to see a phase when films showed grand houses, and the rich hero and heroine wearing very good clothes. The characters in these films didn't speak of poverty, hardship or discomfort because they didn't want to see any of this. They were happy like our middle class. Our middle class, too, might talk about certain issues, but it takes no real interest in our actual problems. But times have changed. Today, our middle class too is looking at the problems that beset our country. It is gradually coming into our cinema. But the OTT is far quicker to respond to social changes.

Often it is said that films cast a bad influence on society whereas the truth is society is casting a bad influence on films. I am deeply concerned by the effect of society on cinema. It is imperative to bring about positive changes in society or else films will not improve. It was this very film industry that gave us films such *as Sujata, Do Bigha Zameen* and *Mother India*. What has happened now? Are there no good film-makers now?

Look at who is the hero of our films. And by hero I don't means the male actor but the main lead, the protagonist. Who do we admire? Whose image do we have in mind? A hero is formed when you combine the ambitions, dreams and moral values of a society and create a character. When your ambitions and moral values change, the hero and heroine too will change. You don't draw your moral values from the hero and heroine; on the other hand, you create a hero and heroine like you who is drawn from your moral values and your ambitions. And so, as society undergoes changes with time, so do films and the hero and heroine. If you find any fault with films today, then films cannot correct them on their own. You correct society and those faults in films will be automatically corrected.

It cannot be that there is selfishness and self-centredness in society whereas films are being made about great causes. It is not possible. When people had a commitment, when people had the concept of 'Us' instead of 'Them', it came across in films, too.

There is a craft of living too

Life is strange. The thing is that when you are starting out in life you have more passion than good sense. With the passage of time, you grow in wisdom while your passion declines. The same is true for life and art. When you are first beginning to write poetry there are many things you have to be mindful of: Does your poetry have an impact? Are you making the correct use of words?, etc., etc. There must be many such things that you do not know when you are starting out; I didn't, either. But I had passion, zeal, enthusiasm. You are divided between technique and fantasy, between art and life whereas you need both. The strange thing is that both are opposed to each other and you need both at the same time. Where, on the one hand, you need emotions, fantasy, imagination, dreams, pain and memories to write poetry, on the other there is the craftsman who insists upon metre, rhyme, rhythm. The craftsman is warning you: This metre is correct, keep writing in it. You will find the right *kafiye* in this metre. There are fewer kafiye in that other rhyme scheme you are imagining; you will face a problem after four shers if you follow that. Stay with this rhyme scheme; don't go there. Don't write this poem as a *paband* nazm with a fixed rhyme scheme; write it in the free style because that will allow you greater scope.

The poet is drowning in emotions and writing what he is feeling and, at the same time, the other a voice is telling him: Don't go there, that path is closed, the road is narrow, do not enter it. Now, if someone is watching his work carefully—be it while making a painting, or writing a ghazal or nazm, or performing as an actor—while there is a certain element of self-forgetfulness, of drowning in the creative process, there is also someone sitting inside his head who is constantly showing him the correct path. Do this, don't do this, this is better. All of this is happening simultaneously.

The same happens in life too. But the sad part is that be it your poetry or painting or life, with time, the passion and emotion begins to fade somewhat. You are gaining something but you are also losing something which, regardless of whether anyone else knows, you know! So, there is a craft for life too: what sort of relationship to have, and with whom, what to say and to whom. If you don't know these, it isn't something to be proud of. You should know these things. But if you have this understanding and good sense, it doesn't mean that you become tough or hard, or start using and exploiting people, or begin looking at life as though it is a game of chess. That would not be good at all. If you don't love people, if you don't have the desire to make sacrifices, till you are not willing to be influenced by an emotion that can possibly even cause you harm, till then you are simply living. Or else you will gradually become a machine. If we were to sum it up in Ghalib's words, *'Saadgi-o purkaari, bekhudi-o hoshiyari'*, you need all four qualities together. If even one falls short, you are in for trouble. But if the choice is that a few should fall short then I will say let *purkaari* (skilfulness) fall short but not *saadgi* (simplicity), let *hoshiyari* (cleverness) fall short but not *bekhudi* (a state of not being in one's senses). Though, ideally, it would be best that neither falls short. Or else you will destroy yourself. Majaz and Jaun Elia did not develop this craft:

Ishq hii ishq hai duniya meri
Fitna-e-aql se bezaar hoon main

This is a sher by Majaz. But both *fitna-e-aql* and *ishq* are needed. Sometimes we feel that the dust that swirls over us because of time, circumstance, or our own doing, is settling over us. Years later when you see your face in the mirror of your conscience it feels as though your visage has become soiled. And that is not a good feeling. You need to wash your face somehow—it may be with the tears of repentance or some other means. Sometimes it feels as though good sense has come, or is gradually coming, but how much passion is actually there?

I consider festivals to be a part of my culture and tradition

I am not religious but I consider festivals to be a part of my culture and tradition, be it Holi, Diwali, Eid or Christmas. I celebrate all these festivals but there is something special about the *masti* of Holi. I have always believed that the festival of Holi comes simply to fill our life with colour. Ordinarily we get scared of even the smallest stain but on Holi we happily colour ourselves with so many colours. Such is my great fondness for Holi that even at this age I cover myself with myriad colours. I have done a lot of research on all the festivals celebrated in our country and I have found that, behind each one of our festivals, there is a lesson for society.

My childhood was spent in Lucknow which is why festivals such as Holi and Diwali are very dear to me. I was a child when I used to live in Lucknow, so I didn't get much opportunity to put colour on others as everyone would put colour on me. I went to Aligarh for my school education. There my love for Holi grew because everyone—from our professors to the entire faculty of our school—celebrated Holi. There was a new fervour for celebrating Holi in Aligarh. Lest I be left behind, I would make myself part of the group that was putting colours. The job of this group was to start filling the balloons and water pistols from early morning and collecting the coloured powders so that when the other group came to put colour on us, we would do the same to them. For as long as I lived in Lucknow and Aligarh, every Holi was memorable.

Shabana and Javed playing Holi,
Janki Kutir (2014)

Farhan and Javed Akhtar drenched in the colours of Holi

I remember that just one wish of mine was never fulfilled while I was there—something that still causes me regret. I had once seen a brass water pistol (*pichkari*) in someone's home and that pichkari made such a home in my childish heart that I still remember it on every Holi.

Years later, when I insisted I wanted one like that, I was handed a heavy steel pichkari, but it wasn't the same as the yellow brass one.

After Aligarh, I went to Bhopal. There, too, I celebrated Holi with great fervour. Then I came to Mumbai and here I was truly amazed by the Holi played in the film industry. It used to be said that you are not a member of the industry if you have not attended the fabled Holi parties hosted by Yashraj, RK Studios and Amitabh ji. Yash ji himself would put colour on everyone who attended his Holi party and welcome them. The same atmosphere prevailed at Amitabh ji's house and at RK Studio. So many artists found work at these parties. The Holi at RK Studios was no less than a Holi scene out of a movie.

Everything has changed now. With Yash ji gone, the colours of the Holi at Yashraj have faded and Amit ji too has stopped celebrating Holi due to health issues. Now Shabana, I, Shabana's brother and sister-in-law—Baba and Tanvi—celebrate Holi at Janki Kutir with about 200–300 people. It might be correct to say that this is the biggest Holi party today in the film industry.

From whatever I have seen of the world, I can say that we are living in the best of times. People do not associate festivals with caste and religion, nor do they tolerate the misdeeds that are done in their name. The youth of today knows that festivals are an occasion to celebrate happiness and that is why they give a stern response to those who spread hatred and enmity in the name of religion.

GUFTAGU

In conversation with Javed Akhtar

Arvind Mandloi

If you get the opportunity, would you like to direct a film?

I often have this dream but the job requires a lot of hard work. The thing is that I have got used to writing. You sit on a table and chair and you write. At best you have to deal with one or two people—a director, a music director and a producer. But when you are a director, you have to deal with so many people that they cannot be counted. A director handles not just people but their egos and complexes. He/she is not just directing a movie; he/she is simultaneously directing 100–150 people. So, the thought worries me a little but, at the same, time, it is one of my many hopes and dreams.

So, if this dream were to come true, what would be its star cast?

The star cast will depend upon the story. If I make a film, it will not be for a star cast. When I make a film, it will be a totally different sort of story with actors; if it has stars then it will only be because they are the best actors.

Have you written a story on which you might want to make a film?

Yes, I do have a story. But I don't want to tell you that story; instead, I want to show it to you.

Let's end with something that is both a message and your imagination.

I will say one thing only and especially since we have been talking in the context of films: people in our film industry are from different political parties, they subscribe to a variety of different ideologies and thinking. But when they make a film or when they work in a film then each one of them has the same ideology, the same thinking, that is, the film should be successful. If you were to see the titles of any film, the credits that come at the end of a film, you will find names of people from every state, every religion, every caste and creed of India present in the unit. They are working in some capacity or the other in the film. You will see a picture of complete national integration in the film's credits. Now, since all these different people work in the film, obviously they want it to succeed. They cannot afford to be communal or sectarian or hold on to different beliefs on caste and creed. They are all united in one purpose: their film should succeed, everything else is unnecessary. In much the same way if you were to decide that our country should become a superhit, then you cannot afford any sort of communalism and sectarianism, be it about region or language or religion or caste. Why? Because you have to make your country a superhit! But if you still want to get entangled in these things then it means that you are not interested in making your country a superhit.

Today, when I look back at my life after so many years, it seems, this river—coming down the mountains like a waterfall, dashing against rocks, finding its way through boulders, gurgling, twisting and turning, creating many a whirlpool along the way, running swiftly and sometimes cutting away at its own sides—has come into the plains and become deep and peaceful. Then, the thought occurs to me that I haven't done even one-fourth of what I could have done. And then the restlessness created by this thought refuses to leave me.

JAVED AKHTAR

Acknowledgments

Sharad Dosi, Indore
Praveen Aggarwal, Mhow
Vikas Rakheja, Manjul Publishing House
Carol D'Souza, Manager, Akhtar
& Azmi, Mumbai

Photo Credits

Baba Azmi, Mumbai
Pradeep Chandra, Mumbai

Portrait/Sketch

Safdar Shami, Mumbai

Editorial Assistance

Ashok Dube
Shree Prakash

Translation

Rakhshanda Jalil

Transcription

Aziz Irfan
Shree Prakash
Jaishree Purohit
Dinesh Dard
Raj Thakur

Graphics/Layout

Anuj Malhotra and Suryakant

Logistics/Support

Pinkal Hardiya and Team Roopankan